D0734736
(stamped in

Three American Frontiers

Three American Frontiers

WRITINGS OF THOMAS D. CLARK

Edited with an introduction by

HOLMAN HAMILTON

UNIVERSITY OF KENTUCKY PRESS
LEXINGTON 1968

Library of Congress Catalog Card No. 68-29637

Grateful acknowledgment is made for permission to reprint excerpts from the following works of Thomas D. Clark:

Selections from *Frontier America: The Story of the Westward Movement* by Thomas D. Clark are reprinted with the permission of Charles Scribner's Sons. Copyright © 1959 by Thomas D. Clark.

Selections from *The Rampaging Frontier: Manners and Humors of The Pioneer Days in The South and The Middle West* by Thomas D. Clark (now available as a Midland Book from Indiana University Press) are reprinted with the permission of the author. Copyright © 1939 by Thomas D. Clark.

Selections from *A History of Kentucky* are reprinted with the permission of the author. Copyright © 1937 by Thomas D. Clark.

Selections from *Pills, Petticoats and Plows: The Southern Country Store* by Thomas D. Clark are reprinted with the permission of the University of Oklahoma Press. Copyright © 1964 by the University of Oklahoma Press. (This volume was originally published by Bobbs-Merrill in 1944.)

Selections from *The Southern Country Editor* by Thomas D. Clark are reprinted with the permission of the author. Copyright © 1948 by Thomas D. Clark.

Selections from *The Emerging South* by Thomas D. Clark are reprinted with the permission of Oxford University Press. Copyright © 1961 by Thomas D. Clark.

Selections from *The South Since Appomattox: A Century of Regional Change* by Thomas D. Clark and Albert D. Kirwan are reprinted by permission of Oxford University Press. Copyright © 1967 by Oxford University Press, Inc.

Selections from *Kentucky: Land of Contrast* by Thomas D. Clark are reprinted with the permission of Harper & Row, Publishers. Copyright © 1968 by Thomas D. Clark.

Selections from *The Kentucky* by Thomas D. Clark are reprinted with the permission of Holt, Rinehart and Winston, Inc. Copyright © 1942 by Thomas D. Clark.

"Research Possibilities in Southern History" was published in the February 1950 (Volume XVI) issue of *The Journal of Southern History*, pp. 52-63. Copyright © 1950 by the Southern Historical Association. Reprinted by permission of the Managing Editor.

"Preserving Southern Historical Documents" was published in the January 1953 (Volume XVI) issue of *The American Archivist*, pp. 27-37. Copyright © 1953 by the Society of American Archivists.

"The Common-Man Tradition in the Literature of the Frontier" was published in the Spring 1957 (Volume LXIII) issue of *The Michigan Alumnus*, pp. 208-17. Copyright © 1957 by the Alumni Association of the University of Michigan.

"Americana in a State University Library" was published in the 1963 [Volume XXIII] *Bulletin* of the University of Kentucky Library.

"Travel Literature" was published in *Research Opportunities in American Cultural History*, edited by John Francis McDermott. Copyright © 1961 by the University of Kentucky Press.

CONTENTS

INTRODUCTION

The North Central Hills section of the State of Mississippi is *terra incognita* to most Americans. Even the nomenclature is misleading, for much of the section is east central rather than north central—and the hills have little altitude. It was the fortune of Thomas D. Clark to be born and reared in this area of challenging economic conditions, remoteness from urban advantages, horse-and-buggy and mule-and-wagon transportation, no rural electrification, low hills, hard work, and cotton. Fortune? A person who has not met a man like Tom Clark, and never sized up Clark himself, might superficially conclude that it was a matter of unadorned misfortune in the early 1900s to be a child and then an adolescent in such a place, where life assuredly had harsh features and where opportunities for improvement of a farmboy's lot did not seem to beckon. And yet to one who knows him or is aware of his contributions to American scholarship and American culture it was a singularly beneficial circumstance that an outstanding historian of the American frontier should have been so intimately acquainted with the realistic conditions—the pluses and minuses—of something akin to pioneer life.

Rural Mississippi between 1903 and 1928 was unlike the frontier in that most of its communities, though small, had long been settled. Its soil had yielded crops many decades before to ancestors of twentieth-century farmers. The dogtrot clapboard houses, the country stores, schools, and shotgun churches were by no means all new; many of them had long antedated the parents of Clark's generation. A further dissimilarity from much of the frontier lay in the fact that the North Central Hills area had its thousands of Negroes, even though they were not nearly so numerous as in Mississippi regions of generally richer soil—to the east in the Black Prairie or to the west in the fabled Delta.

Frontier and near-frontier conditions, however, abounded. Louisville, Winston County's seat of government and largest town, contained only 1,181 people in 1910. Noxapater, ten miles to the south, had only 311; Highpoint Village, 104, while places like Rural Hill and Flower Ridge were barely hamlets, aptly named. With slightly more than 17,000 people in the county, almost everyone was a member of a farm family. Louisville had its bank, its stores, and its newspaper office. But manufacturing plants were nowhere to be seen; youngsters, except a few who wandered "a fur piece," had no first-hand view of a factory, a rolling-mill, a foundry. The Gulf, Mobile & Northern Railway was an innovation, connecting such communities as Pontotoc, Laurel, and Hattiesburg. And the only other intruder on traditional ruralism was the lumber industry with its steam sawmill.

The Clark farm where Tom grew up was situated off to the right, or west, of the unpaved road that led southward from Louisville to Noxapater, about eight miles from the former and four from the latter. Thomas D. Clark's mother belonged to an old Winston County family that included Grandfather Dionysius Bennett—a local leader who served as a County Supervisor, a post giving him much authority in the sphere of road and fiscal operations. A schoolteacher both before and after her marriage, Sallie Bennett Clark bore seven children, of whom Thomas was the eldest. There is abundant evidence that she was the most important influence in the early intellectual development of her son. And equally certain it is that her younger brother, a superintendent of schools in Virginia, was just as influential in speeding the day of his nephew's first successes in higher education.

Tom's father, John Collingsworth Clark ("Johnnie C." to his neighbors), was a member of a family which had settled in New England after crossing the Atlantic in colonial times.

The name was spelled "Clarke" in those days, just as Bennett was "Bennet," and early Clarkes were prominent regionally and nationally as well as in Rhode Island. Eventually some of them headed south and west. Matthew Clark and two of his sons participated in the Revolutionary War, serving under George Washington at Yorktown. Over half a century later, four of Matthew's sons moved from Anderson County, South Carolina, to Mississippi near the Naniwaya Mound in the heart of the Choctaw country. Good cotton land had become available because of the departure of most of the Indians after the signing of the Treaty of Dancing Rabbit Creek. Subsequently, Joseph Bennett took passage aboard a sailing vessel from Charleston to Mobile and then went north up the Tombigbee River. Other forebears of Thomas Clark were the McGees, who hailed from Warren County, Kentucky, and the Cagles, who in an earlier migration had made their way to North Carolina from Pennsylvania. All these people had been drawn at least in part by the widespread reports of the boom or "flush" times of the 1830s, which gave Mississippi such an enviable reputation for productivity and potential wealth that there was nothing strange about seeking one's fortune there. Also, this was the era before the Civil War's destruction of southern farmers' capital—a catastrophe that necessitated the growing of an annual cash crop under the most discouraging financial handicaps.

Thomas Dionysius Clark—his first and middle names the simple, sober and colorful, classical ones of his grandfathers—was born July 14, 1903, in a big double log house, the old Clark homestead built by his great-great-grandfather. His infancy and toddling years were spent on a small farm where his parents had begun housekeeping as newlyweds. A happy, robust baby, Tom (or "T.D." as his mother called him) had a typical, rural Mississippi childhood in an atmosphere not far from pioneer life. Before many years had passed the family moved to a larger farm, and T.D. was the big brother as other children were added to the family. Certainly young Tom was not spoiled, and the chores of normal farm living became part of his daily routine. One of his first assignments was to carry cool drinks of water out to his father working in the fields. He helped in innumerable ways, and by the time he was ten he worked actively in raising cotton. T.D. resembled his father, in his teens and twenties becoming the precise image of Johnnie C. with his sire's strong chin, aquiline nose, flashing blue eyes, and coal black hair. Temperamentally, however, the boy was more like the Bennett men, for he had little of the explosiveness that gave variety to the humor and sternness characteristic of some of the Clarks.

The first country schoolhouse which Tom attended was almost within sight of the Clark house on land donated by Tom's father. The school burned one afternoon when Tom was seven or eight, and afterwards he recited his lessons in the tenant house on the place and later in a school four miles away in the White Hall community and then in a fourth school at Scott's Springs. On Sundays, with his parents, Tom attended the Methodist Church about two and a half miles north of the farm. From his father more than anyone else, he absorbed an unusual sense of moral values; from his mother, the intellectual drive which has astounded colleagues in a dozen universities.

"When my children were babies," Mrs. Sallie Clark has written, "I never rocked or sang to them to get them to sleep. I would take them in my arms, and, because I liked to read very much, I always had a paper or book in reach. Perhaps they did not understand what I was reading aloud to them, but soon they would get quiet and go to sleep. T.D. would come to listen to my reading. He had a little red-backed history book that was given to him by a close relative (I have forgotten the author) that he liked me to read to him. Before he could read he could tell all about Columbus, Washington, Lee, Jackson, Grant, and many others. He was a very inquisitive child, and I once told him that his name should have been 'Who, Why, What, Where, and How?'" Tom's own version is somewhat different. The book did affect him, he acknowledges, but it was far from straight history—being entitled *Joe: A Boy of the Wartime*. After years had gone by and he had searched widely for it, he finally found a copy in a Nashville store. "I was disgusted with it. It was the most insipid thing. But, when I was a boy, it caused me to shed tears both for the Confederacy and for the Methodist Church!"

Mrs. Clark taught her son his letters and numbers. Starting to school when he was five years old, he then knew most of his letters and could count to one hundred with a bit of help. History, legend, and romance were all around him in the North Central Hills. Had not Hernando de Soto come to the region more than three and a half centuries before? Had not Chickasaw and Choctaw Indians hunted and fished there in bygone times? And what of Grierson the raider and Sherman the burner and all the other bluebellied damnyankees in the area less than fifty years before? The village of Houston, up the line, was named for Sam Houston of Texas fame. Notorious outlaws had killed wayfarers along the Natchez Trace, which cut into neighboring Attala and Choctaw counties. And through Noxubee County, immediately to the east, ran the Jackson Military Road that invited stories about "Old Hickory" and his victories over redskin and redcoat. Johnnie C. Clark was one of numerous master storytellers in Old Winston. Small wonder that his susceptible son relished tales of the region's past.

For the boy Tom Clark history was not a monopoly of books, nor were the remote and the recent past of Winston County and its environs the exclusive domain of truthtellers and yarnspinners by the fireside or at the crossroads store. For him historic developments were also intertwined with the everyday experiences of his boyhood. When he went to town, he might see Indians, sometimes in bright calicos, along the red clay road to Louisville. These were the grandchildren and great-grandchildren of the Choctaw minority that resolutely refused to trek west in the 1830s; descendants of those warriors still had their homes near the Choctaw Agency in the next county south. Often Tom listened to candidates for county offices at the Winston County fairground or in the park at Louisville—"thoroughly enjoying all that greenhorn speaking and flights of oratory so high that there was no place they could land." Now and then he was exposed to the forensics of a Vardaman, a Percy, a Bilbo, or a Harrison. Repeatedly he heard accounts of the Mississippi farmer's plight and how true a friend of the farmer the speaker of the moment would surely prove to be.

Nearer home, and right there at home, the past and the present were interwoven. What the boll weevil did to the incomes of Mississippi farm families in 1909, when Tom was barely six, was an important part of his awareness. "We heard of the terrible plague coming our way. We caught the first boll weevil in our cotton in the white bloom. The world really fell on top of us. It was a major calamity." The iniquities implicit in high protective tariffs likewise constituted an inevitable theme of the conversations of his father's neighbors and friends. Next to the need of rain, some means of coping with the boll weevil, and freedom from bondage to the single cash crop, no boon was sought more avidly or touted more eloquently than the long-hoped-for lowering of tariff barriers. Unlike city children who merely read about such things, to a bright farm youth in Clark's part of Mississippi such topics were very real and of immediate significance.

This is not to hint that all of life was serious, or that the boy became an old man before his time. "He liked to play with his three brothers and four neighbor boys," his mother recalls. "When they were all together, there was never a dull moment." So picturesque is the mature Clark, nevertheless, that serious aspects of his growing to manhood—the realism of his background blending with the romance of his nature—deserve underscoring here lest they be overlooked. Most of the time, of course, he was either living at home or going to school. He studied mathematics, history, and some Latin and pored over a succession of Baldwin *Readers*, with his mother as the classroom teacher during three of his seven years of primary education. The larger world came into the house through the Memphis *Commercial Appeal* and the Atlanta *Constitution* as well as the *Winston County Journal*. The senior Clarks were great newspaper readers, and their son shared their interest in news reports and editorials. Tom also devoured books at home and in the "pretty good little library" of his Grandfather Bennett.

Confederate associations had a part in sharpening young Clark's historical interest. "I came up on the history of the Confederacy," he has said. Pictures of Generals Lee, Jackson, Forrest, and Wheeler were framed in his Grandmother Clark's living room, and "I was 21 years old before I knew they weren't members of the family." Reunions of old Confederate soldiers were held at various places in the county. T.D. attended as an onlooker and delighted in the gatherings, particularly when he encountered his paternal great-uncle Pinckney Cagle, which was almost every time he went. "Uncle Pink" had been a bugler in the forces of Nathan Bedford Forrest—"just a popeyed kid who ran off with his pa's horse and joined the Confederate Army." No one loved the reunions more than Uncle Pink, who was "sort of the center of them"; Pink would sing and dance and kiss the girls and swap lies and tell long truths about "Ole Forris." There the sturdy young great-nephew—eyes dancing—would warmly greet his relative, meet other veterans through the popular Pink, hear the hoary stories told and retold, and listen appreciatively as the bugler blew again and as battles and campaigns were replanned and refought.

There was an extremely long interruption in Thomas D. Clark's formal education between his twelfth and nineteenth years. After completing the seventh grade in the spring of 1915 he worked fulltime on the farm for two years. From "kinsee to caintsee" (can-see to can't-see), he assisted his father in growing cotton, sugar cane, peanuts, and corn. "The big, heavy work was in cotton." During most of 1917 and 1918, in the World War I period when the lumber industry found labor scarce, the teenager earned some cash at logging and in a sawmill about a mile and a half from home. Then on his sixteenth birthday Clark began two years' service as a cabin boy and deckhand on a dredge boat engaged in cutting a channel through the nearby Tallahaga Swamp at the head of Pearl River. Making a drainer out of small slats to expedite the dishwashing procedure, he also constructed and painted a chest where he could safely stow his possessions. According to Mrs. Sallie Clark, her son at this stage enjoyed being with the crew so much that he thought he wanted to continue on the boat. But the captain—H. L. Lewis of Paducah, Kentucky—convinced him there was no future in the job and advised him to prepare for something better.

In 1921 the eighteen-year-old Clark went by a roundabout route to Weir (pronounced "Ware"), Mississippi, where he applied for admission to the Choctaw County Agricultural High School. Thomas Arthur Patterson, the principal, asked: "Ever play football?" The erstwhile cabin boy said no. Patterson said: "You're a big, stout feller. I'll help ya." The first Monday of the school term Clark went out for football. He had never seen a game, much less taken part in one, but he played that Friday, and the team was victorious. For four years he played regularly at right guard or center. "I ran with the ball once in one game," the ex-linesman remembers, "and then my hands and feet were up in the moon."

Several teachers in the high school at Weir did much to stimulate and widen Clark's intellectual interests. One, a woman instructor in English, coached him in public speaking and encouraged him to participate in the debating club. Robert Nolan Bruce, teacher of mathematics and later chief engineer in the New Orleans District of U.S. Army Engineers, who had received part of his education at the University of Mississippi, urged his student to think of attending "Ole Miss" after high school. The school's farm was a source of vital income, with cotton choppers coming in to work under supervision. Principal Patterson had such confidence in Clark that he asked him to take charge of the farm in the spring and summer of 1922 with the understanding that, if the job were well done, the young man would be given his pick of the school tasks during the remainder of his course. All went well, and that autumn Clark chose the assignment of ringing the school's bells, relying on his own dollar watch for the time. In addition to playing football and ringing bells, serving on the student council and taking part in debates, he studied the usual high school subjects—including Latin and French—and also organized a newspaper, which published a few issues but lacked adequate financing. Patterson, benevolent autocrat who was known to his charges as "Mister Pat," continued to befriend Clark throughout the course. The younger man reciprocated in several ways, one of his more whimsical expressions of esteem being conveyed in the name he bestowed on his faithful dog—"Mister Pat."

During the summers of 1923 and 1924 Clark and one of his brothers "hired crossties made"—hauling them and selling them to the "Katy" Railroad with a guarantee of three carloads a week. When warm weather came in 1925, Clark went home to Winston County with his high school diploma and without a dime. His father gave him ten acres of land. Clark plowed it up, fertilized it heavily, planted cotton, and "cultivated it religiously." The harvest provided the farmer-student with funds to start his first year at the state university. At this time, he was twenty-two years old. Considerably more

It happened that a band and a cheering crowd met Thomas D. Clark's westbound Chesapeake & Ohio train when it reached Lexington in September 1928. Obviously, this was owing to no fame or notoriety he could claim but to the fact that Senator Charles Curtis of Kansas was another passenger arriving there. Then campaigning for the vice presidency of the United States on Herbert Hoover's Republican ticket, the part-Indian Curtis had shared a seat with the twenty-five-year-old Clark, who savored the experience and commotion. It did not take the transplanted Mississippian long to feel at ease in the hospitable Blue Grass, which was to be his home and center for scholarly investigations for the next forty years. Although Kentucky's history department was far from eminent, the university did have some excellent people—and at its head was a first-rate president with lofty standards and a strong personality, the tall and dignified Frank L. McVey.

Clark experienced no difficulty in obtaining his master of arts degree in a single year, writing his thesis on "Trade in Livestock, Slaves, and Hemp between Kentucky and the Lower South." More importantly, he made a decidedly favorable impression on McVey, who employed him not only to teach history but also to make a survey of library holdings on the campus and throughout the Commonwealth. In a sense, this was the real beginning of the development of the University of Kentucky libraries, for, when Clark went to work (as he often has remarked to friends), "there were not enough books to light a shuck." One of his early achievements lay in the acquisition of a fine serial set of United States government documents from Centre College in Danville and from the Kentucky State Library in Frankfort. Other contributions were of similar quality, for he proved to be an inspired collector.

At this stage of Clark's life, he more than compensated for the early delays in his education. He lost no time now in moving on to the doctorate, winning a graduate fellowship at

Duke University, from which he received the Ph.D. degree in 1932. The subject of his dissertation was "The Development of Railways in the Southwestern and Adjacent States before 1860." E. Malcolm Carroll, William T. Laprade, and Richard H. Shryock were three of Duke's history professors whom Clark esteemed. But the Duke mentor with whom he worked most closely, and whose guidance and friendship he valued most abidingly, was William K. ("Tubby") Boyd. There is a reference to Clark's affection for Boyd in a chapter in Part III of this volume.

Somehow Clark found time in the same yeasty period for his first experiences as a visiting faculty member. He first visited Tennessee Western State Teachers College (now Memphis State University) and the University of Tennessee, setting a pattern for a feature of his career. In after years he was to teach for a summer, a semester, or a year at a time at the University of Rochester, Duke University, the University of North Carolina, the University of Chicago, the Claremont Graduate School in California, the University of Vienna, Harvard University, the University of Wyoming, the University of Wisconsin, Kent State University, Indiana University, and Stanford University, among others. He has lectured abroad under Department of State and under other auspices at Oxford University, as well as in Greece, India, and Yugoslavia. President of the Southern Historical Association when still a young man, he was president of the Mississippi Valley Historical Association (now the Organization of American Historians) in 1956–1957 and of the national history honorary society, Phi Alpha Theta, in 1957–1959. A former Guggenheim Fellow and former trustee of the University of Kentucky, he has been awarded several honorary degrees. Few of the marks of recognition that can come to an historian have not come to him.

Professor Clark has been accompanied to virtually all the American universities where he has been invited and to most of his foreign posts by his wife, the former Martha Elizabeth Turner, whom he married in 1933. A daughter of William Waugh Turner and Ruth Dorman Turner, the future Beth Clark was in charge of the catalog department of the Woman's College Library at Duke when she met her husband. A graduate of Greenville Woman's College (Furman University) in South Carolina and of Simmons College in Boston, she was a slender girl with a winning smile and attractive manners who not only had a romantic appeal for the young graduate student but shared his intellectual interests and encouraged him in his scholarship. Her father, an alumnus of Davidson College, had sent six children through college and two to medical school during the depression. Her mother was also a graduate of Furman University. The Clarks' elder child, Thomas Bennett Clark, was born in Lexington in 1936 and their daughter, Ruth Elizabeth, in 1938. Both are now married, Elizabeth to a young historian and Bennett to an historian's daughter. Both Clark children accompanied their parents on many of their trips in the United States and overseas. And the familial ties are as strong in them as in their mother and father.

National and international recognition, accorded Thomas D. Clark from the 1930s into the 1960s, was in part a reflection of a growing awareness of his record at the University of Kentucky. Except for a few superior teachers and its intelligent president, the university was still not an impressive scholarly institution when Clark returned from Duke to resume his instructorship in depression-harried 1931. Funds were limited, classroom buildings were few and antiquated, and academic standards were still shaky. Despite Clark's pioneering efforts in his pre-Duke days, the library contained few books. Too many members of the faculty had long been content to plod along in academic ruts while doing little creative scholarship. McVey, who had shown remarkable courage in his battles on the controversial topic of evolution, was doing his best to cope with the difficult situation and—for all his dignity—seemed almost pathetically eager to welcome junior academicians whose concepts of the future approximated his own.

Instructor Clark, who in 1935 became Assistant Professor Clark, was one in whom McVey found hope and promise. A splendid lecturer, human and humorous, he became one of the campus' most popular teachers. It was not, however, a cheap popularity. Virile, handsome, searching, quizzical, he could be incisive, far-ranging, eloquent, earthy—arousing genuine interest on the part of his students, many of whom never forgot him. Nor was the day's work over when the last class ended. Appalled by the library's limitations, Clark made its improvement his special project.

A companionable man, he was never one to draw strict lines between town and gown. Thus, he interested many Lexingtonians in the development of the library and of the entire university. His willingness to speak on historical and kindred topics, in central Kentucky and throughout the Commonwealth, enabled him to acquaint citizens with the campus. Thus, too, he came to know and understand numberless facets of Kentucky's past and present from Appalachia in the east all the way to the Jackson Purchase in the west. As an associate professor and then full professor, he chaired or served on countless committees. His close friends are inclined to believe, however, that his personal influence on and off the campus has been more meaningful than all he has contributed in endless hours of formal committee work.

Increasingly, the healthy development of the department of history lay at the heart of Clark's executive endeavor. Before his arrival in Lexington, only one University of Kentucky historian had ever published a book, and no Ph.D. dissertations had been produced. While a master's degree program existed, the quality of most M.A. theses was pitifully low; it is doubtful that many of them would be acceptable today. Generally, the teaching was far from extraordinary, the scope of course offerings was limited, and the emphasis was on mere memorization instead of creative enterprise. In 1942, President Herman Lee Donovan took a long step forward when he selected the thirty-eight-year-old Clark to be the department's head. In charge from then until 1965, the dynamic Clark quite literally transformed the department from a mediocre relic of bygone concepts into one of the strongest south of the Ohio River and established its national reputation.

From the outset Clark improved academic standards by attracting other historians of repute who shared his aims and his capacity for hard work. In addition to inducing them to come to Lexington he managed to retain most of them, notwithstanding low salaries. Initially developing the department's offerings in United States history, he then reached out for scholars in European and British fields. Soon substantial offerings in all those areas were available for Kentucky students. Next the curriculum was rounded out by courses in ancient, Russian, Latin American, and Far Eastern history. With a gradually expanding budget and a system of promotions predicated on both teaching and research, Clark encouraged his colleagues to follow his own example and prepare manuscripts of significance. He believed that there is no basic conflict in higher education between superior instruction and frequent publication. In the lecture room and in the seminar, Clark is convinced, it is nearly always the productive scholar who transmits the spark of learning and the thrill of discovery to his pupils.

Recognizing the value of a university press both in encouraging research and in enhancing the scholarly prestige of the institution, Clark was an early advocate of a publishing program at the University of Kentucky and helped to persuade the Board of Trustees to set up a University Press in 1943. Clark, who has served on the Press Committee since its founding and as its chairman since 1965, was instrumental in the establishment of the press as a separate agency headed by a professional director. In cooperation with seven other scholars he wrote the agency's comprehensive publishing policy. As committee chairman he oversaw a major revision of this policy statement, expanding it to include all scholarly publishing within the University.

Great as has been Clark's professional influence on many of his twenty thousand students in successive university generations, he has gained access to infinitely more minds, hearts, and tastes through the printed page. The first of a long line of books, an outgrowth of his graduate work, was published in 1933 and entitled *The Beginning of the L. & N.* It was followed by *A Pioneer Southern Railroad* (1936), *A History of Kentucky* (1937), *The Rampaging Frontier* (1939), *The Kentucky* (1942), *Pills, Petticoats and Plows* (1944), *The Rural Press and the New South* (1948), *The Southern Country Editor* (1948), *Frontier America* (1959), *The Emerging South* (1961), *Three Paths to the Modern South* (1965), and *The South since Appomattox* (1967)—the last a collaboration with Albert D. Kirwan. In addition, Clark has edited *Blue Grass Cavalcade* (1956) and *Gold Rush Diary* (1967). His most recent work is *Kentucky: Land of Contrast* (1968). He brought out such widely read children's books as *Exploring Kentucky* (1939) and *Simon Kenton: Kentucky Scout* (1943).

From 1946 to 1962, Clark served as the editor of the six-volume series on travels in the South, which fulfilled one of his dreams. For four years he was the managing editor of the *Journal of Southern History*, then published at the University of Kentucky. In the course of his career he has contributed dozens of articles and several hundred reviews to leading professional periodicals, newspapers, and magazines. Clark's major current project is a history of the Louisville *Courier-Journal* from the era of George D. Prentice and Henry Watterson to the present. But even Clark's best informed friends and associates cannot be sure about what other projects he may be working on, and customarily he has at least two going at once. It has been humorously observed that his works emerge simultaneously from two typewriters.

From a scanning of the list of titles it will readily be seen that areas of history holding the greatest appeal for Clark have included Kentucky, the South, the West, railroads, rivers, rural life, journalism, travel, pre- and post-Civil War eras, and the American frontier. Superficially, these would seem to represent something other than an integrated pattern of scholarly concentration. When examined closely, however, the books and articles of Thomas D. Clark form a pattern or, more exactly, three intimately-related patterns reflecting a remarkable degree of professional concern, coherence, and—somewhat paradoxically—concentration within a wide range of events, developments, and trends.

Frontier America is not just the title of one of Clark's most successful books. More importantly, it summarizes what for him has been an ever-absorbing topic. And how big and broad, detailed yet inclusive, it becomes for the reader in Clark's depiction! Frontier America, in his eyes, barely begins with the usual montage of the Trans-Mississippi West with its plainsmen, mountain men, desert rats, Indians, Mexicans, cavalry heroes, and Forty-niners. It encompasses *all* frontiersmen and their families from Atlantic to Pacific and from border to Gulf—the frontier movement, the frontier spirit, frontier problems, panaceas, solutions. "Movement" may be too weak a word, "spirit" too ephemeral, and "solutions" too pat to indicate what Clark has sought to relate. The mighty forces and the immediate challenges and exasperations and hopes in the lives of history's big and little people—all are eligible for his purview.

Nor does the geographical frontier (however skillfully and ambitiously he expands it) have an exclusive hold on his talents. Pioneers of social action and thwarters of social progress alike belong in Clark's conception of frontier development. The metropolitan frontier, the middle-sized city, the courthouse town, the village, the fast-vanishing family farm, industrialization, transportation, electrical and atomic power, the locomotive's whistle shot and cinder fall, the embarrassment of plenty in the grotesque embrace of poverty—these involve pioneers less standardized than Kit Carson and Daniel Boone but pioneers nonetheless. The frontier of education, the frontier of race relations, and literary and artistic frontiers all have been reflected in the author's writings. Like his heroes and villains of valley and plain, the discoverer of fresh facts and interpretations in the open spaces of narrative and analysis is an adventuresome frontiersman in his own right.

In the totality of Clark's contribution a third type of pioneering effort is discernible. Research, for the questing Clark, never has been limited to dust-covered volumes on library shelves. Though it is probable that few other contemporary scholars have "gone to the stacks" with greater faithfulness, no one is more convinced than he that historical evidence is pervasive—in the mouse-chewed records of country stores, in the files of brittle yellowing country newspapers, in the scribbles of forgotten wayfarers, in the wit and repartee and oiliness and moral grandeur of salesman and savant, mayor and mechanic. The pages of the series on travels in the South bespeak a commendable devotion to the preservation, interpretation, and distribution of invaluable source materials. But, as the time available to even a Tom Clark has limitations, he has preferred to err on the side of inclusiveness—rather than exclusiveness—as a researcher.

Part I of this book reflects Clark's interest in the development of the frontiers to the West and the South—the trek of the settlers to new lands and the beginnings of frontier communities. He considers first the economic and political development of the communities—the Boonesborough settlement and its threat of Indian troubles, the confused land systems of Kentucky, the traffic downriver with the development of the flatboat and the steamboat, the ranchers and their cattle drives.

Always a keen observer of key institutions in frontier society, Clark has written extensively on the old country store, the small-town newspaper, marriage rituals and funeral customs, and evangelical religion. He describes acutely the colorful, though sometimes amazingly violent, pastimes of the early settlers, among them cockfighting, dancing and fiddling, community pranks, and gander-pulling.

In Part II, concerned with the Frontier of Social Change, he considers particular problems that have handicapped the South in keeping pace with developments in other regions of the country. Among the burdens covered in this section are superstitions, the "white diet" of the southerners, the lack of medical care and consequent popularity of patent medicines of dubious value, and a particularly brutal approach to justice —lynching. Racial discrimination continues to be an important problem for southerners, but Clark discusses recent changes in racial policies within southern politics, education, and economics, pointing out challenges for the future. Improvements in health, medical care, agricultural reform, development of transportation and industrialization, and urbanization have all worked in recent years to minimize differences between the South and the rest of the country, as he shows in this section.

Clark's deep concern with research—especially with the acquisition and retention of important source materials—is the theme of Part III, the Frontier of Historical Research. Revealed are the procedures he views as worthwhile for the utilization of the raw materials of history; his appreciation of the South's culture as expressed in southern literature; his estimates of what foreign and domestic travelers have revealed about themselves and America's uncommon common man; and, finally, his tenacious efforts to improve libraries and preserve important data of history.

The bases of Thomas D. Clark's perceptive exploration of the physical, social-action, and research frontiers are best comprehended when one studies Clark the man. It is probable that no other historian of his period has bent over his desk, reached into his bookcase, riffled index after index, or pecked at typewriter keys more conscientiously or more interminably. But his vast array of special interests reveals the "something extra" of his makeup at least as convincingly as traditional routines. He is a born collector—of postage stamps, political buttons, canes, campaign leaflets, maps, letters, and miscellaneous brochures as well as items with a direct bearing on the next project or the one after that. He also possesses much of the progressive spirit, exemplified in his daily life; educational, governmental, and social reform movements have found in him a champion. Next to his wife and other members of his family, the loves of Clark's life are friends and forestry. In outdoorsman's garb, at the wheel of his jeep, he tours his timberlands in Kentucky and South Carolina, recognizes every tree in the dead of winter, and revels in the budding of the springtime. Not long after his first grandchild was born, he told the infant's mother: "As soon as you have that boy in hardsole shoes, I'm going to steal him and take him to the woods and make a woodsman of him!"

Himself at home on the land since his earliest memory and eager to acquaint youth with joys inherent in the outdoor living he relishes, Tom Clark looks back to pioneers of past decades and centuries through the eyes of a latterday pioneer. He has always had an affinity for people—for simple, honest, rough people at least as much as for sophisticates or would-be sophisticates. Most frontiersmen were farmers after the initial stages, and Clark knows farm life from cockcrow on. He has visited and dwelt in the places he writes about—absorbing what is genuinely indigenous, bedding down in a sleeping bag in woods and mountains, boarding a boat for the winding voyage down the Ohio and Mississippi rivers. Thus, conventional primary and secondary sources are complemented by acute, shrewd observation and by vigorous literary exploitation of humanity, nature, and their rich offerings. Small wonder that from his books and articles, and from the representative selections in this volume, the clear impression is conveyed that Clark judiciously assesses his frontiers because his feet are on the soil and the earth is in his hands.

HOLMAN HAMILTON
Lexington, Kentucky
March 4, 1968

PART I. THE FRONTIER WEST AND SOUTH

CHAPTER ONE

WESTWARD EXPANSION

THE SOCIAL MEANING OF THE FRONTIER Frontier expansion in America closely resembled the roll of the sea. It broke, billowed and eddied against the various physical and social barriers which it encountered. The pattern of expansion was never uniform over any considerable geographical area, nor within any large segmented part of the more localized social organization. The movement bore telltale marks of the traditional origins of peoples and institutions—the flavor and coloration of the peculiar traditions of continental Europe, England, and the eastern Atlantic Coast. The frontier path was strewn, like that of a vast glacier, with the remains of older cultures, easily identified by their peculiar natures and characteristics. . . . When settlers came in contact with woods, prairies and plains, they started life anew at elementary levels. Social and economic advances were almost always achieved from the same simple beginnings. The frontier was the place of trail and ground breaking in new country, and of establishing afresh social and political institutions. Settlers coming into contact with the vast areas of virgin lands and mineral resources behaved much alike, whether in the pine lands cotton belt or the mountainous gold diggings. . . . The safest general observation to be made about American frontier history is that it is variegated, erratic, colorful and spacious. It combines the broad interpretations of both human and national history with the most fragmentary details of local history. In its broader meaning the history of the frontier is the account of the molding of people of diverse origins and motives into a fairly homogeneous national group. In its more localized implications, it is the story of thousands of individuals, tiny communities, counties, towns, and sections making primitive beginnings and growing into mature and permanent political, economic, and social institutions. . . .

Never before European exploitation of this continent did civilized man undertake to bring so much virgin territory under his control in so short a time. To reduce his thinking about American geography into a workable formula was a complex undertaking for the European. This accounts in part for the different European approaches made to the American continent. Spaniards and Frenchmen commonly sought immediate returns from the land, breaking trail for unbelievable distances. Englishmen on the other hand approached the continent with some degree of hesitancy. They were reluctant to sever their lines of communication with home until they had gained a foothold along the coast. . . .

Distances and contours of terrain were important in determining the distribution of population on the continent. At the same time, the great expanse of land isolated large segments of American society. Out of this grew a spirit of provincialism which had both domestic and international significance. The varied characteristics of the North American continent produced a basic, if not unique, political problem for Americans. This was sectionalism, with its special interests which made compromise necessary in every major political issue that involved making general laws for an expanding country. . . .

Obviously land was the most important economic factor in the westward movement, but its social meaning surpasses its economic importance. It played a role in the political and psychological reactions of settlers. Participation in politics in some instances was based upon landholding, and in others ownership of land gave a sense of permanence. It was much easier to exercise an effective voice in political affairs and to seek office if a man owned land. Psychologically, land ownership brought with it definite local prestige and a degree of stability and security. For many European immigrants moving on to the American frontier, the ownership of land meant the difference between the old life of uncertainty and penury and a new life of permanence and economic promise.

(from *Frontier America*)

FRENCH AND BRITISH SETTLERS In 1755, the cartographer and surveyor Lewis Evans wrote that "between 4 and 10 degrees longitude west from Philadelphia there is a spacious country which we call Alleghaney from the name of a river which runs thro' it and is the main branch of the Mississippi. . . . In this country all our Indian trade centers . . . the most of our return is Deer Skins. The Indian traders have had great credit with the merchants." Evans perceived that English expansion had reached the threshold of one of its great frontier landmarks —the immediate trans-Allegheny region. The year 1750 was in some respects one of fairly well-defined demarcations; it marked the beginning of a new phase of western expansion and the approaching end of international rivalries for peltry and land in the Ohio, St. Lawrence and Great Lakes area.

Certainly the great triangle of land outlined by the Ohio-Mississippi-Great Lakes-St. Lawrence was not unfamiliar to white men. Since 1606 the French had been moving either towards or across this area. Between 1668 and 1682 Robert Sieur de LaSalle had intermittently explored the Ohio Valley and traveled down the Mississippi to the Gulf Coast. Subsequently other traders, explorers, priests and military officials were abroad in the rich lake-shore and river-valley country to promote private and French governmental interests. Many of them came to save souls; others dreamed of making personal fortunes.

The early decades of the eighteenth century saw the French begin a pincers movement across the western country. Working down the Great Lakes chain from Quebec and Montreal,

French explorers and traders made their line of invasion along lakes Ontario and Erie to Detroit, down the Maumee River, the Wabash, and then down the Ohio and Mississippi to Natchez and New Orleans. French outposts along this route became landmarks in frontier history; along the lakes were forts Frontenac, Niagara, Detroit, Michillimakinac; down the Maumee-Wabash passage were Miami, Ouiatenon and Vincennes; westward, on the Mississippi, were Kaskaskia and Cahokia.

From our perspective of American history it is now evident that the French made one of their most serious tactical blunders in their plan for fortifying the frontier against English intrusion. Although it was doubtless good strategy for them to develop a strong backwoods cordon around the slowly expanding English colonies, such a restraining wall had to be tight and strong to check the push of settlement from the east. Backwoods geography offered the French three natural lines of traffic and defense. The first might have been the Lake Erie-French Creek-Allegheny-Ohio-Mississippi River passage; the second lay along the Lake Erie-Miami-Ohio-Mississippi route; and, the third and more distant one was the Lake Erie-Maumee-Wabash connection to the Ohio and Mississippi rivers. The first, or Ohio passage, was direct and in closest proximity to British activity. It would have brought the French line hard against the colonial boundaries of England and would have checked the eastern competitor at his own back door. Travel down the Ohio was both direct and relatively fast and safe. There were disadvantages, however, in making the long portages from the site of the future Presque Isle by way of French Creek to the Allegheny River and into the Ohio. Transportation woud have to be greatly facilitated for the route to become efficient. Garrisoning and protecting this tight frontier would involve considerable manpower and eternal vigilance, with a constant threat of border warfare hanging over the French. Added to this would be the tedious job of maintaining a dependable alliance with the Indians.

In 1701, Detroit was founded on the Detroit River between lakes Erie and Huron, and nineteen years later forts Miami and Ouiatenon were planted on the Miami and the Wabash. About 1731, Vincennes was located on the east bank of the Wabash in what is now southern Indiana. Choosing the Maumee-Wabash line placed the French between 350 and 500 miles west of the immediate point of contact with the westward-moving English. This decision left a large area of highly fertile Indian country open to hostile Indian traders and land speculators. It also left an important segment of Indian population exposed to the seduction of traders and their goods, from Pennsylvania and Virginia. The wide margin of territory also gave the British an opportunity to gain a foothold across the mountains without immediately facing armed conflict with the French. British adventurers and traders quickly used this geographical advantage to promote their commercial interests. Proof of their success were the major Indian trading posts of Logstown, the Shawnee towns, Pickawillany and its associated Twightwees posts; and there were by 1750 well-worn trading paths into the interior. Journals of Christopher Gist, Conrad Weiser and Frederick Christian Post give good first-hand views of this area in the 1750's. Activities even west of these posts showed how far the trading frontier was in advance of the colonial settlement line. It was, in fact, so far in advance that it was already threatening to breach the French frontier line along the Maumee and Wabash rivers.

The French moved rapidly across the trans-Allegheny frontier, whereas the British colonials moved slowly. The French did not delay their advance by establishing a front of agricultural and commercial settlements. The British, on the other hand, hesitated to leave the coast and the eastward flowing rivers. Their economic philosophy was conditioned to a combined land and maritime commerce. . . . Periodic samplings of the settlement lines throughout the seventeenth and early eighteenth centuries show a slowly spreading movement inland along the Atlantic coastal shelf. This was no surging tide of settlers pushing forward feverishly to exploit new lands and to engage in rich Indian trade for the sake of taking quick profits and getting out. Rather it was a leisurely spreading but highly absorbent roll forward which penetrated and colored all beneath it.

(from *Frontier America*)

BOONESBOROUGH: AN EARLY SETTLEMENT Gathered on the narrow Sycamore Shoals Island in the Watauga River in East Tennessee, the proprietors of the newly formed Transylvania Land Company passed out the last of their gaudy trinkets to their Indian friends. For several weeks the Transylvania proprietors, led by the ingenious Judge Richard Henderson, had dazzled the eyes of the Cherokees with $10,000 worth of fancy baubles. In return for these articles, the whites asked that the Indians trade them the vast stretch of wilderness territory which lay between the Alleghenies and the Ohio, and south of the Kentucky River and north of the Cumberland. One friendly conversation followed another, and the gracious Henderson used all his excellent persuasive powers to get the chiefs to give up this part of their hunting ground. All but one of the Indian leaders consented with enthusiasm to the exchange. One young chieftain, Dragging Canoe, was in a surly mood. He realized that his people had been too hasty in selling their lands. Stamping his feet and pointing toward Kentucky, Dragging Canoe muttered prophetically through his teeth to Henderson: "You have bought a fair land, but you will find its settlement dark and bloody!"

In the first flush of success, Henderson and his colleagues were not too much disturbed by the ominous warning of the surly young chief. . . . A week before . . . Daniel Boone and a party of twenty-nine companions started for the Kentucky River to begin a settlement. . . . Before the party could reach its destination on the Kentucky River, Captain William Twetty and a Negro slave had fallen victims to the Indians' arrows. . . .

Boone and his companions traveled up the Kentucky River from the scene of their disaster. Near the mouth of Otter Creek the Kentucky straightens out into a long and placid stream. The steep river hills which hover all the way down from the mountains fall back on the south side in a protecting elbow below the mouth of the Otter. Here was a safe place to erect a fort. There was fresh water in abundance, and near by was a salt lick. Roaming over the prairie were buffalo. This truly was a land which possessed all the advantages a frontier settler could desire. . . .

Quickly, upon his arrival, Richard Henderson located a new fortsite. . . . He, perhaps like Boone, lacked complete appreciation of the importance of terrain in the location of a fortification. His plans, however, of Boonesborough Fort are those of a thoughtful man. Henderson took great care with important protective architectural details. Spaces between the cabins were filled in with a strong puncheon wall. There were projecting walls out from the second stories of the blockhouses, and the roofs of the intervening cabins were slanted inward. Once the fortress was begun at Boonesborough, it became a symbol of permanence of white settlement in the Kentucky country. Here the white man was to fight many of his hardest battles for the possession of the land. . . .

A dark cloud was to hang over the West in the immediate years following the establishment of Boonesborough. As a part of "rebel" Virginia, Boonesborough and Harrodsburg were to become in fact the revolutionary back doors of the eastern seaboard. Three hundred miles west of the upper Piedmont, the crude puncheon walls of Fort Boonesborough were to withstand the savage assaults of the British and their red-skinned allies. Even before the end of 1775 Indians were raiding the country around Boonesborough. Two settlers were killed, and warlike signs were becoming more evident every day. At Harrodsburg, George Rogers Clark was beginning to make a plan to stop the Indian menace to Kentucky by procuring Virginia aid.

Before Clark and his stalwart companion could get back to Virginia to lay their claims for protection before the legislative assembly, the Indians were to come again to Boonesborough. On the quiet Sunday afternoon of July 14, 1776, the Kentucky River fort was stirred from its Sabbath lethargy by the kidnaping of Jemima Boone and the Callaway girls. One of Jemima's feet had been injured by a cut from a cane, and she and Elizabeth and Frances Callaway had gone for a canoe ride on the Kentucky. The three young girls had paddled downstream and then had drifted toward the opposite bank, which was shaded by a heavy growth of underbrush coming down to the water's edge. When the prow of the canoe eased in near the bank, a Shawnee warrior rushed out, caught the buffalo-thong tug and started ashore with it. Behind him were four other warriors. . . .

When it was discovered back in Boonesborough that the girls were gone, there was great excitement. John Guess swam across the river under the immediate danger of being fired upon by Indians in ambush and rescued the canoe. Daniel Boone took to the woods barefooted. When the cry went up that Jemima Boone and the Callaway girls had been captured, the gallant Samuel Henderson was shaving. He had shaved one side of his face and was about to begin on the other, but he had no time to finish. . . .

Across the Kentucky, Boone was able to pick up the trail of the savages and the girls. Quickly he mapped out a plan of strategy. One party was sent directly to the fording place at the Blue Licks on the Licking, and a second followed closely upon the heels of the kidnapers. Night came before the searching party got far on the trail. Again the courageous John Guess volunteered his services, and went back to the fort to secure buckskin woods clothes for the party, and a pair of moccasins for the barefooted leader.

Relying upon the keen woods instinct of Boone . . . the searching party moved quickly behind the Indians. Tracks ahead of them began to appear fresher. Then there was the still-warm carcass of a freshly killed buffalo. A little farther on was the wriggling body of a snake which had just been killed. The trail disappeared abruptly. Boone, long experienced in the habits of the savage in the western woods, read accurately the meaning of this sign. The Indians were hungry, and they had waded up the middle of a near-by clear-water stream to a place where they could cook their buffalo meat.

Moving cautiously along the creek, the searching party found Boone's judgment to be correct. There were the five Indians about the campfire, and the girls were seated near by. The two younger girls were resting their heads in Betsey Callaway's lap. Prematurely one of the whites fired his gun at the Indians. Shots from the guns of Boone and John Floyd knocked down the sentry and the Indian cooking the buffalo meat. The others fled into the brush, but before they ran for cover one of them threw his tomahawk at Betsey Callaway's head. The men from Boonesborough were highly excited over the capture, and before they could be calmed one of them had almost knocked Betsey Callaway's brains out with the butt of his rifle. He had mistaken her, with her dark complexion and head tied up in a bandanna, for an Indian.

The rescue of the kidnaped girls was a tender affair here in the wild Kentucky woods. Samuel Henderson, with two more days' growth of beard on one side of his face than on the other, was there to rescue his financée, Betsey. Within a month after they returned to the fort they were married. Too, Flanders Callaway and John Holder, gangling boys, romantically rescued from the clutches of savage warriors their fourteen-year-old sweethearts, Jemima Boone and Frances Callaway. It was with a high spirit of triumph that the bedraggled rescue party delivered the three girls back at Boonesborough.

This was the famous year of the "three sevens," and it was to be a trying one for the people at Boonesborough. The man power had dwindled to an insignificant number. Food was scarce, and the continuous danger of Indian raids kept the settlers from properly tending their fields and gardens. News came in throughout the year that the Indians were menacing the settlers all up and down the Kentucky valley. Bread-stuff became exceedingly scarce, the supply of gunpowder was exhausted, and in the dead of winter salt gave out. It seemed that the ragged, half-starved band of settlers hovering about the smoldering fires in the Boonesborough cabins would have to give up and go back to their friends across the mountains. Again it was the indomitable will of the old woodsman-dreamer that saved the day. Boone had not wavered in his purpose since the day he wrote Henderson, in April, 1775, of his intentions to settle in Kentucky.

(from *The Kentucky*)

LAND SYSTEMS OF KENTUCKY Kentucky's land system was in a serious tangle at an early date. . . . Virginia's western land laws were weak, because they did not provide for the supervision of private surveys. Each claimant prided himself upon his ability to recognize good land, disregarded previous surveys, and proceeded to the business of laying out his claim by personal choice. Under the haphazard system of surveying, numerous small plots of ground remained unregistered, and land speculators immediately issued blanket claims in order to secure possession of these neglected plots. Grants of the eighteenth century were not unlike present-day claims, for many of the abstracts rested upon the knowledge of some individual who professed to remember the boundaries of the original claims. In many Kentucky counties today, title lawyers have to walk over the entire area of a tract in order to get a definite notion of its shape, size, and location. Markers for land lines have always consisted of such unstable guides as trees, rocks, streams, and oftentimes houses. Accordingly, the only reliable and scientific guide the land owner has is the surveyor's chain. . . .

Many of the large estates of central Kentucky were created from numerous smaller claims, for the purchasers of the larger plantations, in most instances, were unwilling to brave the rigors of the frontier. They waited until the plantation home was completed before moving their families into the West. Overseers and slaves were sent ahead to clear land, build houses, and transport the family property from east of the mountains to the new home. . . .

In a political sense, the institutional growth of Kentucky dates from the formation of Fincastle County in 1772. This county was created by Virginia as soon as it was apparent that the western country was to be settled. With a rapid increase in the western immigration, it was soon found that the authority of Fincastle County, which included all of Kentucky, was quite inadequate. Kentucky County was created in 1776. . . .

(from *Frontier America*)

BOOM POLES AND PADDLE WHEELS Center of western commercial activity were the rivers. River life from the beginning was vigorous, and it was among the boatmen that such terms as "Kentucks," "red horses," "screamers," "buckeyes," "half-alligators," "half-horses," "children of calamity" and "howlers" originated. These were strong terms, but they were expressive of the unrelenting hardships combated by boatmen.

From 1775 to 1860 the Mississippi River and its tributary

streams were channels in which thousands of boats of every description floated southward to markets. First in order there were the pirogues, bateaux, canoes and skiffs. As pioneers moved westward to settle Kentucky, Tennessee, Ohio, Indiana and Illinois they used flatboats, arks, broadhorns, rafts and keelboats. On these crude and clumsy craft an empire floated to a new home west of the mountains. Families floated down the river from Pittsburgh to begin life all over in the Mississippi and Ohio Valleys. . . . Far more settlers floated westward than trudged over the Wilderness Road.

While peaceable citizens were floating slowly to landings in the new settlements, there came with them a procession of banditti. James Flint in his letters says that the Ohio River was an open thoroughfare on which a constant throng of bandits floated, under cover of night, to the western communities. There were horse thieves, jailbirds, counterfeiters, black legs, boat-wreckers and scalawags of no specific classification. These cowardly rascals came into the West without their true characters being known, and without anyone's taking too much trouble in advance to investigate them. Some of these knaves proceeded to throw off all moral restraints in the new country where law-enforcing agencies were either poorly organized, or within their control. If one of this fraternity of cheats landed in jail, he remained there as long as he was satisfied with the accommodations, and then broke out and put off down the river to a new field of nefarious endeavor.

There were, also, those hardy individuals, many of whom could scarcely name the place of their birth, who followed river-boating as a trade. They learned by constant association with the river about the snags, shoals, eddies and sandbars. They mastered the art of steering their craft clear of Indian attacks along the west banks, a danger which was ever present until Wayne's victory in 1794. These professional rivermen became distinct characters in a land which had already become famous for its rugged personalities. They were boastful of their prowess with pole and paddle, and they believed steadfastly that they were "some" when it came to dealing with boat-wreckers, cheating gamblers, and bandying prostitutes from Pittsburgh to 'Orleans.

It was generally conceded that Kentuckians, Buckeyes and Hoosiers were past-masters in the use of poles and at handling clumsy ill-shapen rivercraft which floated southward with the current and were loaded to the gunwales with heavy plunder. The French, however, were more temperamental and they mastered the more exact science of the paddle. A Frenchman could take a pirogue and journey from the headwaters to the mouth of a river without serious mishap, while a Kentuckian, Hoosier or Buckeye could not even "mount" this type of boat without a ducking.

Often in traveling down the Ohio and Mississippi Rivers, boatmen were caught in blinding fogs. These were frightening because there was danger of butting into another craft, or of being snagged or beached. To keep from colliding, boatmen blew their long tin horns continuously until the cloud lifted. When other boats were known to be in the vicinity, these horn-blowing boatmen kept up a din that would have put the idiots of bedlam to shame. Alexander Wilson wrote a friend in 1810 that he had stood on the bluff overlooking the Kentucky River on a foggy morning, and was highly entertained by the terrific furor created by the boatmen blowing their horns. . . .

It is little wonder that the water fronts at Pittsburgh, Wheeling, Cincinnati and Louisville became veritable hells, because rivermen who had wrestled with every conceivable hardship on the river relaxed by taking in stride the fastest entertainment the towns offered. These rivermen celebrated their arrival at the various meccas of entertainment with a sense of taking the pleasures at hand instead of looking forward to either economic or celestial security. Hard pulling on oars and poles, a boiling sun, heartless snags, eternal sandbars, swirling eddies, and a stubborn current were trying. Timid souls never succeeded on the river because they wavered, and in wavering, they were lost. . . .

Drifting around the wide sweep of river which is Giles' Bend, men who had struggled with their boats came in sight of their first down-river stopping place, Natchez. They saw not staid and dignified Natchez which sat atop the foot of the Chickasaw Bluff with its churches and "decent society" like a plume atop a militia colonel's hat, but more alluring and exciting "Natchez-under-the-Hill." Danger, at least from the river, was behind the rivermen, and here they found a market for their produce, and fun which ran the whole category from drinking freely of raw liquor to alluring and painted Delilahs who had "entertained" and fleeced a whole generation of Kentuckians, Hoosiers, Buckeyes and Suckers. "Natchez-under-the-Hill" in its heyday would surely have put to shame those hellholes of antiquity, Sodom and Gomorrah. Modern eighteenth and nineteenth-century vice showed a "marked development." This town on the Mississippi was located at at the foot of the great bluff which overshadowed the river. There was one main street which ran from the road ascending the "hill" to the water's edge toward the bight of the great Giles' Bend. Lining either side of this muddy thoroughfare were rows of wooden shanties which were alternately gambling houses, brothels and barrooms. The sunken sidewalks were blocked day and night with fashionably dressed dandies from the plantations back of the hill, rough, crudely dressed river bullies who smelled of a hundred days' perspiration, sailors and foreign merchants, and tawdrily arrayed, highly rouged and scented females who could not recall the day of their virginity. Life in the underworld was cheap, gamblers cheated at cards and shot protesting victims without mercy, boatmen, blear-eyed with bad whisky or green with jealousy over deceptive whores, bit, kicked and gouged one another.

The town under the hill knew no God, no law, no morals. . . .

Just as the ark, the broadhorn and the keelboat supplanted the pirogue, the bateau and the canoe, the steamboat eventually drove the smaller craft from the rivers. . . . The coming of the steamboat to the western waters influenced greatly the movement of commerce on the rivers, and changed the whole society of the western country. Western Pennsylvania, Virginia, Ohio, Kentucky, Indiana, Illinois and Missouri farmers produced vast quantities of agricultural products which they now hurried away to rich southern markets. There were flour, corn meal, pork, bacon, hams, salted beef, apples, cider, dried apples, peaches, salt, iron, cotton bagging and rope, and slaves; from Ol' Kentuck and Pennsylvania there was red liquor! Most of the early steamboat crews were ex-flatboatmen, and they set the precedents for steamboat conduct. Captains had poled Kentucky boats along the river or had served as patroons on keelboats, pilots learned about the river from the decks of flatboats, and machinists learned their trade as they traveled. There was a hierarchy of authority on board, at the head of which stood the captain. Most of these officious gentlemen were rivermen who had come up through the ranks, and their ability to knock a deck hand down surpassed their capacity to carve gracefully as the head of the boats' tables. If a passenger irritated these dignitaries, and that was easy to do, he was put off at the next landing. Arguments between captains and woodchoppers sometimes took a nasty turn. Rifles were kept loaded and conveniently located behind cabin doors in case arguments over wood arose. The poor swamp dwellers were often treated by the boatmen as though they were entirely devoid of human sensibilities.

(from *The Rampaging Frontier*)

WILLIAM ASHLEY, MISSOURI TRADER William Ashley, perhaps the most successful of all the native traders, typified much of the personal element in the history of the frontier. He was a Virginian who, like Stephen Austin and others, had followed the promise of fortune westward to Missouri. In Missouri, Ashley engaged in the manufacture of gunpowder. Here he became associated with Andrew Henry, and during the early years of the 1800's these men heard much of the profits to be made in the fur trade. Like Virginians everywhere, Ashley became a militia officer and participated actively in local politics. Passing in and out of St. Louis he came to know many of the trappers and traders who came to its market. When Ashley entered the fur trade with Andrew Henry, there was already a distinguished group of experienced river and mountain men congregated in and about the western market. . . .

Ashley and Andrew Henry teamed up to trap in the mountain beaver streams. When they led their company out of St. Louis in 1822, it was the largest organization of American trappers to date to enter the field. This new band was to make some interesting innovations in trading practices. Ashley soon depended more upon the free white and contract trappers than the Indian hunters. He was not to establish himself, however, until he had undergone some harassing experiences with the Indians. On his first journey upstream some of his men were killed in Indian skirmishes. The company lost many horses and furs to marauding bands, which reduced its opportunities to make profits. Apparently the appearance of so many white men in Indian country stirred the Blackfeet and Arikaras to new efforts at resistance, and Ashley was to reap the harvest of their ill-will.

On his second journey up the Missouri, William Ashley got a full taste of Indian violence. When his keelboats, *Yellowstone* and *Rocky Mountain,* reached the Arikara villages, the Indians undertook to rob and kill his men. First making a show of friendliness, they sold him horses and engaged in trade generally; one of the chiefs even invited Ashley to visit his cabin. So well did the Indians conceal their real intentions that the sun set on a scene of peace and goodwill, but before morning those of the white party who had camped on the beach were caught in a heavy attack. The Indians created pandemonium among their visitors by outnumbering and outmaneuvering them. Before Ashley's company could effect a retreat, thirteen men had fallen and eleven more were badly wounded. General Ashley had made several tactical blunders, in addition to allowing himself to become over-confident in the face of so much pretended friendship. Leaving his men overnight on the beach next to the villages was an act of folly which cost dear, but nothing he did hurt more than presenting himself before his men as a reluctant warrior in battle. The fight with the Arikaras taught the white traders once again that the upper Missouri Indians were not to be trusted. Traders from St. Louis were to face situations comparable to that which had arisen with the Arikaras many times in the future, but because of Ashley's sad experience they knew that a show of friendship meant disaster in the end. . . . The St. Louis traders' activities were highly successful after 1823. Parties under the leadership of Henry, Fitzpatrick, the Sublettes, Smith and Provost returned to the first major rendezvous in 1825 with rich caches of fur. They had combed the mountain areas around the headwaters of the Missouri for new beaver grounds, had crossed the Great Divide and trapped at the headwaters of the Columbia, they had followed the Snake to its junction with that stream, and had explored numerous other stream courses which were to become well known in Rocky Mountain history. To carry on a successful trade Ashley was forced to seek a new route to the trapping grounds to avoid the drudgery of the upriver pull in boats and the treachery of the Indian villages. He introduced the pack train to bring trade goods to the rendezvous and to carry furs back to St. Louis. By following the overland route along the North Platte he bisected the great triangle of the

Missouri and cut off at least five hundred miles of the journey. Following this route, he opened a new passage to the Rocky Mountains and the important fur-bearing streams, and outlined the great trail followed not only by traders and trappers going to the mountains, but also by settlers in subsequent years on their way to Oregon.

In three years William Ashley made a modest fortune out of the fur trade and retired to St. Louis to engage in merchandising and politics. When he left the trade in 1826, he sold his Rocky Mountain Fur Company interests to three of his men, William Sublette, Jedediah Smith and David E. Jackson. Some of Ashley's traders, including Smith, secured large quantities of cheap furs from Indians and trappers obligated to the Hudson's Bay Company. When he returned to St. Louis after his last rendezvous, he was able to claim the greatest cash income made by any individual trader to date.

(from *Frontier America*)

CATTLE TRAILS ON THE FRONTIER While the Mexican War was being fought, the early Texas cattlemen found a ready market for much of their beef, and some historians cite this as the beginning of the range cattle trade. By 1861, and the outbreak of the Civil War, a promising cattle industry in the Southwest had made a good beginning. Already trail herds had moved northward to Ohio and other northern markets. Edward Piper took a thousand cattle to Ohio from Texas in 1846, and in 1859 John C. Dawson drove a herd to the Colorado gold fields. The wild cattle and the grasslands of southwestern Texas were attracting an increasing number of cattlemen. Four years of Civil War created a demand for both meat and leather, but at the same time disrupted delivery of cattle to market. Some herds were driven across the Mississippi River to the Confederacy, but occupation of that stream by Yankee gunboats interrupted this trade. Some herds of wild cattle were assembled and driven northward to the virgin ranges of Kansas and Nebraska and were then started in search of buyers. But sales of beef cattle from 1861 to the end of the Civil War scarcely touched the great herds that roamed the plains without molestation. For four years wild cattle multiplied and fattened in Texas. A shortage of men and the distance to the northern and northeastern markets defeated the idea of immediately driving herds in that direction. By 1865 it was estimated that there were 3,111,475 head of cattle in Texas. No one, of course, knew how many cows there were among the wild and untended herds, and the precise figures given in the various sources of information can be little more than statistical whimsicalities.

The end of the Civil War brought both a supply of drovers and a sharp increase in the demand for meat. Cities of the East and Middle West had grown in size; increased industrialization during the war had developed a cash market for meat; and military and Indian purchasing continued good for a considerable time. Steers which could be bought on the Texas range for as little as three or four dollars could be sold at prices ranging from twenty-five to fifty dollars. Transportation costs ran around four dollars a head in the early drives. Moving cattle from range to market, however, had its serious drawbacks after 1865. The transcontinental railway systems were still in the organizational stage. Only the Union Pacific was actually started across the plains; consequently the early trail herds had to be driven into Missouri and Illinois with St. Louis and Chicago as final destinations. To reach railheads which connected with these cities involved a drive of eight hundred to twelve hundred miles across dry country, through Indian territory, and over the farming lands of western Missouri. It was a tossup whether Indians or farmers were more hostile. . . .

The early Texas drives had resulted in frustration for the cattlemen. Unless they could find a market for their stock removed both from woods and settlers, they were finished almost at the start. No one realized this more than the three McCoy brothers who bought Texas cattle for the midwestern and eastern markets. Joseph G. McCoy set out to solve the problem of a stable market center for the Texas ranchers. He first sought land for pens and sidings in Junction City on the Kansas-Pacific; and when he was forced to look elsewhere, he met with the officials of the Kansas-Pacific in St. Louis to get their assistance in locating and equipping a cattle market. These short-sighted men were unwilling to take a chance, and once again McCoy was forced to go elsewhere. He called on the haughty president of the Missouri-Pacific and was summarily dismissed with insulting rudeness, an act which McCoy believed kept St. Louis from becoming the great packing center of the United States.

Upon being turned down by the two most important railroads, McCoy made successful proposals to the struggling Hannibal and St. Joseph road which connected the Missouri River by way of Quincy with Chicago. He then visited central Kansas to select a suitable place to establish a trailhead. Solomon City and Salina refused to tolerate the idea of stock yards. Finally McCoy selected Abilene, a struggling, dirty prairie village of a dozen huts that had neither life nor civic consciousness enough to protest against the smell, dust and iniquity of the Texas cattle trade. Before Abilene, located later on the Kansas-Pacific, could be converted into a cattle town, it was necessary to construct pens and sidings, a public facility which the citizens of the town could hardly be expected to support. When the Abilene market became a certainty, McCoy dispatched W. W. Sugg, an experienced trail herder, out to the plains to spread the news. Within a short distance of the new town there were several herds wandering around with no place to go. Sugg's news was cheering, but there was question as to whether or not it might be a rustler's trick to catch unwary cattlemen. The first herd driven into Abilene had been brought up from Texas by a ranchman named Thompson and sold to Smith, McCord and Company. A second consignment was driven to Abilene by Wheeler, Wilson and Hicks. On September 5, 1867, the first train of twenty cars of cattle departed for Chicago, and before the year ended a thousand carloads had been sent away to the Great Lakes market.

Not all was smooth sailing for the cattlemen. Many eastern buyers had well-developed prejudices against western stock and even refused to pay cost on shipments. Railway cars were ill-adapted to deliver their live cargo in good condition. It took considerable organization and boosting to establish the western cattle trade on a profitable basis. Before this first railhead town had more than settled down to steady operation, both the railroad and the cattle industry shifted farther west, but already Abilene had become a magic name in pioneer range cattle history. . . .

The great roundups of the cattle country were immensely exciting events. All the cattle from a given range were driven to a central point for sorting and branding. Neighboring ranchmen and their outfits gathered at central points, selected captains of the roundups, chose herding grounds and then set out to bring in the cattle. Once the cattle were driven into the chosen grounds, the man on whose range a roundup occurred was given the first choice or cut of the cattle. Then the remaining animals were sorted out and claimed by other owners. There was much hard riding and joking, with kangaroo courts doing big business, and generous amounts of food being consumed. The company abided carefully by range-made laws, and captains were serious leaders who performed their duties with great care. The roundup was the plains' version of the logrolling and houseraising of the eastern wooded frontier.

Trail driving to railheads and northern grass lands had a remarkably short history—approximately from 1866 to 1886—

yet it played an important role both in national economy and in frontier expansion. News that there was money in cattle attracted scores of speculators to the West. Many of these sought wealth by the investment of small amounts of capital. With one good drive a cattleman could accumulate a comfortable nest egg of wealth. A drover could buy Texas range cattle for five to fifteen dollars a head and drive a herd of twenty-five hundred north at an approximate cost of a dollar a mile. In the northern market these same cattle sold from twenty-five to fifty dollars, leaving a substantial profit. Many dreamers trailed paper herds northward at enormous imagined profits, but when they tried the actual operation they discovered that they had overlooked the realities of the situation. . . . By 1886 the first phase of range cattle history was drawing to a close. Several new developments were blocking the trails and preparing the way for the confinement of grazing activities to set ranges and pastures. Farmer-settlers were beginning to advance rapidly from the lagging frontier of the eastern border, planting wheat on the old buffalo range and building highways, villages and towns where the trail herds had grazed. Schools, churches and courthouses crowded town squares and main streets where saloons and brothels had flourished. Even Abilene, Newton, Big Bend, Dodge City and Ogallala succumbed to the influences of civilization. Trail herds no longer came to them in booming clouds of dust; instead reapers felled waving fields of golden grain into rows of bundled shocks. In the enclosed pastures the chunky short-horned steers had forced the hardly old longhorn to surrender. It was meat and not trail stamina and color that the newer generation of beef eaters in America and Europe were demanding. The old days of *laissez-faire* ranching and herding were all but memories. Cattle ranching as an organized and confined industry had expanded over the entire plains area from Texas westward to Arizona and New Mexico, and from central Kansas to Colorado and northward to

Wyoming, Montana, Nebraska, and the Dakotas. Sharp competition had developed for grazing lands. The more cattlemen moved into the country, the more important it became to acquire possession of large blocks of range. A ranchman could homestead 160 acres in his own name, and he could get each one of his employees to make an entry for a quarter section. Sometimes these co-operative homesteaders located their claims so as to box in blocks of public lands, making them well-nigh useless to outside homesteaders and purchasers. Finally, a ranchman could purchase public lands outright, but however he acquired a claim to land, he became as much a part of the established order of the new civilization as the settlers at the plow handles and the store counters.

(from *Frontier America*)

ROUNDING OUT A CONTINENT Expansion of the national population, the rise of industry and the growth of American cities checked, if they did not halt, the frontier movement. Youths who in other years would have escaped social and economic competition in older settled communities by moving westward then turned their steps toward the expanding cities. Wage-paying factories, packing houses and offices opened new opportunities to rural and farm youths. Cities such as Chicago, St. Louis, Dallas, Omaha, Denver, San Francisco, Seattle and Portland in time drew millions of agrarian migrants to their factories and service industries. Later the great automobile manufacturing centers on the Great Lakes were fed by burgeoning streams of rural workers. The bright lights, the sidewalks, places of amusement, and the relative assurance of steady pay checks drew people away from the hard regimen of the land.

By 1890 the great American heroic figures of the past were having to take back seats. The hardy frontier scout, United States marshal, badmen and women, Indian braves and border army officers were being supplanted by bankers, inventors, scientists, packing-house overlords and railroad tycoons. The American economic complex was becoming too intricate to be translated into the simplified vernacular of a frontiersman who understood only the horizontal pattern of frontier economics. Changes in America after 1890 created almost as many approaches to an interpretation of meaning of the frontier in its inverted order as have the various academic hypotheses themselves. Possibly the most certain thing which can be said in this connection is that the change which came after 1890 offered a sound perspective from which the whole frontier movement could be viewed.

Again the westward movement may be compared with the waves of the sea at ebb tide. They broke across an uneven coastline in violent breakers, or rolled gently out into wide estuaries. Whatever an abstract statistical pattern revealed to the census taker in 1890, the frontier was still a fact. In Appalachian America, for instance, the movement was held in suspension until after 1920. Virginal survivals of frontier patterns tended to set that region apart from the rest of the country in the first quarter of the twentieth century. Not until the advent of improved roads and the Tennessee Valley Authority did changes destroy the old patterns. This was true elsewhere in the West. But generally the frontier movement as a great physical force in national growth was halted by the turn of the century.

Just as there was no precise moment when the great westward movement had its beginning, there was none when it ended. The westward movement involved both physical and spiritual forces. It was a movement of people struggling across the land planting farmsteads, ranches, counties, towns and states. They created folk legends and heroes as they went, which were landmarks of their travels. It was a movement which brought the nation to the full physical realization of its great potentialities in land and resources. At the same time it was a motivating spirit which developed a keen sense of progress and sustained a belief in the essential capacity of the American to accept large challenges with abiding hope of success.

There are frontiers today, but they are not free land frontiers. Whether in expanding city limits, opening new power and irrigation projects, combatting debilitating diseases, marketing new automobiles and merchandise, or staring at the moon as a possible new place for colonization, the ebullient American accepts his new problems as a frontier challenge. The transition from land to industry, science, merchandising and international relations has been as subtle as the changing of the seasons. Spiritually the frontier survives in the American outlook, in the language, in the sense of space, and most of all in a basic national confidence in its resourcefulness.

(from *Frontier America*)

CHAPTER TWO

THE DEVELOPMENT OF THE FRONTIER COMMUNITY

MARRIAGE AND THE HOUSEHOLD Three moments in frontier life created excitement. These were birth, marriage, and death. The first of these was more momentous to the person being born than to his family and neighbors, except that his presence swelled the population. Not so the latter two. A marriage, unless it was a hasty affair, was most often a happy community occasion involving quiltings, house-raisings and warmings, a wedding party, a dance, an infare—all of them offering excuse for entertainment to the community. No set formula was followed in marriage since conditions varied with place and circumstance. Both the housewarming and the wedding dance were boisterous. Houses were "warmed" with *bran* dances in which corn siftings were spread over the floor so that the oily germ of the kernel was pressed into the wood, making it smoother and more tolerable as a living room. This frontier term has been thoroughly corrupted by the modern and synthetic hillbilly radio bumpkins who talk about "barn" dances. The frontiersman would have derided the idea of dancing in a barn, and historically the term "barn" is nothing short of an egregious typographical error. Weddings were accompanied by much drinking, some drunkenness, and much folksy joking and suggestive pranking. Infares were "day after" dinners served in the groom's home where young couples were set up on their own. New couples started life with only the basic utensils and tools; they had no furniture which could not be made with an ax and a drawing knife. . . .

The institution of marriage often presented a dilemma to frontiersmen. It was not unusual in some places for settlements to be far distant from communities where legal marriages could be performed. Often this problem was solved by common law matings, many of which were later regularized. Among the first laws considered by the early legislatures were those governing marriages. Designated persons were authorized to perform the ceremony, and provisions were made for keeping marriage records. As new counties were established, the recording of marriages was made mandatory by the granting of licenses. Legislatures assumed the right to establish marriageable ages and to grant divorces. Because there were fewer females than males, the marriageable age for females was generally lower. Girls were legally marriageable at fourteen and boys at sixteen or seventeen.

There was a certain spirit of gallantry about the laws granting divorces in which the woman's side of the case apparently received the more generous hearing. Almost constantly, early newspapers, and occasionally handbills, told stories of both men and women shirking the responsibilities of marriage. Unfortunate or hasty marriages commonly resulted in divorce, and sometimes cases of bigamy were exposed. Bigamy occasionally resulted from a belief that a husband or wife had died as a captive of the Indians. Such was the case of Rebecca Boone's marriage while Daniel was a captive of Chief Blackfish. Sexual irregularity prevailed, of course, but generally speaking, illicit love and illegitimacy of childbirth were scorned. A woman who gave birth to a child out of wedlock perhaps did not suffer entire social ostracism, but she did lose social caste. Again, bastardy was an early subject of legislation. The frontier was rather conservative when it came to preserving the ideals and integrity of the family unit as the central social force in frontier expansion.

(from *Frontier America*)

THE COUNTRY STORE Robert Somers, an English traveler in the United States in 1870, stumbled along the muddy streets of Atlanta. Five years before, the town had been prostrate from Sherman's raid, but now this traveler could detect little of its story of destruction. As he walked down the bustling, partially completed streets, Somers philosophized that "one receives at every step a lively impression of the great power residing somewhere in the United States of filling the most distant and unpromising places with wares and traffickers of all kinds." Opening onto the sidewalks, the store doors overflowed with goods from everywhere. Piled upon the rough walks were "northern notions" from New York, Baltimore, Cincinnati, Chicago and Boston. New York oyster saloons were crowded with hurrying people, and their doorjambs were piled high with empty oyster shells shipped in from Savannah and Charleston. Drummers swarmed over the town displaying the very latest in patented devices, and at nights they were crowded into stuffy hotel rooms where they carried on their poker playing and eternal yarn spinning.

In one wholesale house the Englishman halted to inspect the wares of an imaginative agent of a Yankee manufacturer. Before he could begin his inspection of the goods, he was regaled with a long dissertation on the new safety kerosene lamp. It was the most perfect device to come from the lampmaker's shop. Safety, in fact, was its cardinal virtue. Already drummers had sold much of the rural South on the idea of using patent lamps, but there had appeared a serious drawback. Everywhere it was said that the new lamps were dangerous. Leaning back against hundreds of kitchen walls in homemade hickory chairs, dramatic bumpkins repeated to their neighbors hair-raising stories of exploding lamps. Flimsy pine-plank houses burned to the ground in a twinkling of an eye, all due to the use of kerosene. . . .

That morning the querulous English traveler saw the true symbols of the New South: Atlanta, a newly patented safe kerosene lamp, and piles of goods in wholesale houses for the southern country stores. It was not so much a matter of mystery that quantities of goods were found on the Atlanta market as was the fact that these goods were effectively put into channels where they were sold directly to small customers. Actually the English visitor had picked the mercantile story up in the middle. He understood neither its beginning nor its end.

Already the shadow of reconstruction was showing its outline. The old system of southern economy was in an advanced stage of deterioration. Large plantations were being broken into smaller units, and communities predominantly yeoman became more important factors in southern civilization.

Immediately after the war numerous villages and towns came into existence almost overnight. Crossroads stores popped up like mushrooms. Small purchasers were far removed from the source of goods. No longer were there plantation owners and factors who moved in supplies in large quantities. The whole picture of trade was changed.

As large landholdings were broken up into moderate farms, there was an increasing demand for merchandise in smaller individual quantities. Southern people found themselves isolated; they had to have stores near by, and "near by" to the postwar southerner meant the maximum distance which could be traveled in a brief space of time by a Negro boy on a mule.

Merchants who formerly supplied the southern trade through middlemen or factors were now concerned about the convenience of the stores to their customers. Drummers in two-horse buggies struggled over the miry roads of the South in search of crossroads where prospective customers could begin storekeeping. Their unexpressed motto was "A store within reach of every cabin in the South." They were agents of the new industrial age. For them, reconstruction was not alone a matter of political and social change.

Manufacturing companies and wholesale houses constantly sought new outlets for their goods. They were anxious to supply both stock and capital if bright young men would open stores in their communities and get the local business. In every section railroads were being built, and as their lines were extended they needed both freight and freight agents. Selecting strategic points along their newly built lines, company representatives encouraged the building of warehouses, stores and railway stations. At Dewey Rose, Georgia, railroad officials encouraged young T. J. Hewell to open a store, and when he demurred that he might go broke, he was asked if he had money. When he said, "No," the promotion agent asked, "How in hell can you go broke when you ain't got nothing?" This young Hewell had never pondered. At any rate such a philosophy evidently put the proposition in a new light, for soon a long-barreled house was serving a thriving trade as both freight station and store.

Elsewhere in the South stores were springing up in almost every location where there were enough people to buy a profitable quantity of goods. These crossroads emporiums of cheap merchandise rapidly became symbolic of the creation of a new southern economic system from the wreckage of the old. Perhaps no other southern institution more nearly embodied so much of the intimate story of the New South.

Plantation owners, army sutlers, adventurous ex-soldiers, Alsatian Jews and enterprising native yeoman sons opened stores. Sidney Andrews, a northern newspaper reporter, saw northern men coming south with their stocks of goods and capital to begin new businesses.

The Union Army took men across the South, and many of the soldiers saw in it a land of opportunity. When the war was ended they came back to cast their lot with the region which they had helped to over-run. Already, in many instances, they had established pleasant relations with the people in the community and upon their return they were able to make a quick start. At Glymp's store in South Carolina a New Jersey Jew spotted an opportunity to make a fortune, and hardly had the surrender occurred before he was back. He bought the old stand which had been started in 1845 and expanded it into a big general merchandise store. . . .

Many of the southern stores had their beginnings in humble peddler's packs. Alsatian Jewish peddlers bumped over impossible roads in one-horse wagons loaded with lines of cheap goods, or in winter floundered in bottomless mudholes to reach their customers. Sometimes they came on foot with packs strapped securely to their weary backs. These peddlers were postwar counterparts of the shrewd Yankees who had once swarmed over the land with their numerous gadgets, tin pans, buckets, clocks and shoes. The Jews were of a similar humorous turn of mind. Also like the Yankee they had their eyes fastened on the main chance, but unlike him they were unable to whistle through their teeth in the face of adversity.

Southern country folk found these peddlers interesting. They laughed at their strange European accents and the bargain-driving shrugs of their shoulders. They made them the butts of crude practical jokes, but always their visits were welcomed and exciting. Nothing brought a rural family quite the same thrill as having a peddler open his pack before the fireplace. Beds were pushed back, chairs squared around, and the peddler was given a place of honor in the middle of the floor. With a flourish he undid his stout leather fastenings, and then rolled back the awning-striped cover of his pack to expose his wares. With subtlety he placed his bright-colored cloth in the first bag to be opened, and in one deft movement revealed its colorful bolts of goods. When his canvas roll was opened there came a rush of smells. Odors of sachets, cheap perfumes, soaps, leather goods and spices filled the room. It was like bringing a store right up to the most isolated country hearth. . . . For many years the southern people had been forced to do without consumer's goods. During four years of war when stocks were exhausted and could not be replaced, most of them were unable to buy even the most commonplace and necessary goods. When the war ended, these customers were again ready buyers. Most southerners were without money, but as a result of the lien laws recently passed by the state legislatures, they were able to purchase astounding amounts of merchandise. Everywhere there was an anxiety to buy new goods, even if buying meant going hopelessly into debt; large piles of goods stacked on the Atlanta, Mobile, New Orleans and Charleston shelves and sidewalks melted overnight. Where there had been one store before the war, there were now ten. A flush postwar market had created thousands of outlets.

Of course the Negro, hampered by both war and slavery, had felt the pinch even more than the white man. Now the freedom of going into a country store and looking over its crowded shelves was for him nothing short of a trip to heaven. Long shelves of bright-colored goods and piles of fat meat; the smell of lard, the rich, heavy overtone of tempting salt herring and mackerel spiced with the celestial odor of sardines and cheese; the mouth-watering sight of big boxes of crackers and tantalizing glass jars of long sticks of striped candy were entirely too much temptation for the impractical man of either race. Political rights and freedom meant nothing in the face of this maddening intoxication. Quickly Negroes became the stores' best customers, buying what they wanted rather than what they needed. . . .

Louisville wholesale distributors, for instance, were quick to realize that the southern trade was a rich plum. If only they could hold the "Cincinnati Yankees" off until they thrust their powerful Louisville and Nashville railroad southward, prosperity would be assured them. During the war the city had been under the control of the Union Army, but now it was the best rebel city outside of Richmond. George Prentice's *Journal* spread the cheering news that Kentucky had plenty and to spare. The editor of the Barnwell (South Carolina) *Sentinel* published the fact that "Kentucky had an enormous surplus of corn and meat this season, and she intends to give liberally of them to her suffering brethren in the South. For this purpose societies are being organized throughout the state, and before the close of the year we hope to hear of one in every county." . . .

Poor roads and a lack of railways encouraged new stores. Back of this, however, was the demand for an agency which could exchange small quantities of goods for equally small amounts of diverse rural produce. At the same time cotton selling and buying was now removed from the larger towns and cities to crossroad villages. Reconstruction credit legislation forced upon the country merchant the necessity of buying produce of every sort. Thus it was that the stores became not alone sources of supply for merchandise, but likewise community markets for almost everything that could be sold for a profit. . . . The stores of the southern countryside quickly became the heartbeat and pulse of a good portion of American business. In their own communities they were centers of every sort of neighborhood activity. Everything of importance that ever happened either occurred at the store or was reported there immediately. If a man got shot he somehow arranged to have the shooting take place at the store, or if he wished to give an enemy a first-class flailing, he usually found him on the store porch along with a highly appreciative audience. When he wished to "cuss" the government or to complain at the Lord because of the perfidy of politics and weather conditions, there was no place like the hitching ground around the store. No other place, not even excepting a country church ground, the polls or a saloon, ever offered quite the same golden opportunity to get drunk. When a man's wife was about to give birth to a baby he bought from the country store twill or birdseye for diapers, flannel for gowns, bottles, black rubber nipples, scraps of unbleached domestic for "sugar teats," and plain goods for long dresses and caps. When his aged mother died he rushed a messenger off to the store with a note to buy her a shroud and metal fixtures for her homemade coffin.

As one old-timer boasted, his store was "where we put clothes on anything that had a back to wear them between the cradle and the grave, crowded their feet into something to keep them off the ground, and rammed food down everything that had a gullet to swallow it."

(from *Pills, Petticoats and Plows*)

THE COUNTRY NEWSPAPER The position of country editor demanded a man of competent judgment. It was his responsibility to know what was happening in his community and to report the news with reason, humanity and intimate understanding of local background. The editing of a country paper was an extremely important function, and an editor had to be able to use "nice judgment and discrimination" so as not to strike down innocent people who appeared to be something they were not. He had to develop with care the delicate instruments of public opinion and community pride. After 1865 the country paper was to herald, in its own inimitable way, the rise of a new South.

When the Confederate troops straggled home from Appomattox, only 182 tattered weeklies had survived the conflict to greet them. Even the appearance of these impoverished papers dramatically documented the ravages of war. Greasy homemade ink spread a dark, discoloring film from one impression to the next. But these little journals boldly assumed the task of welcoming a new age in the South. Among the many institutions that contributed to the rebuilding of an exhausted land, one of the most important was the rural weekly newspaper. . . . The scope of the newspaper became as broad as Southern life itself. True, a vast majority of the papers established after 1865 boldly asserted their intention of upholding the principles of the Democratic Party. Occasionally this vigorous declaration was challenged by papers sailing under opposition banners and proclaiming the virtues of Republicanism. These were usually operating safely in solid Republican districts or were seeking favors from the hands of radical state officials, and their number was never great. Among the partisan papers the whole confused process of Reconstruction was bitterly contested. Democrats spoke of Republicans with contempt, and the badgered Republicans snarled back like frightened animals. Political rivalry was not new. Whigs and Democrats had battled before the war, and Republicans inherited some of the Whiggish fight.

It was important, however, that the new-type country journal reduced its emphasis on politics and extended its coverage of social and economic affairs. In an age when transportation and communication facilities were being improved and expanded news took on a more vital importance. The demand for human-interest matter grew as rapidly as the number of new papers. Even the most isolated rural community developed an awareness of new social relationships, and of the active part county and state were playing in national growth. With this changing sense of national importance, Southerners took a certain pride in their localities and wanted to see them against the background of the rest of the South. The printed page was able to work wonders in giving the community a sense of importance.

But the feeling of membership in world and national society was hedged about with difficulties. It was paradoxical that as the world about the South grew smaller, Reconstruction caused Southern rural areas to grow in many respects more and more isolated. Antagonism toward the dominating national political system contributed to this condition and a sense of loyalty to immediate political alliances tended to focus attention on the precinct and county. As one Southern editor said, it mattered less to the Southern people whom the Radicals sent to congress than who was to conduct the county affairs. Thus at a time when industry and business in most areas were becoming nationwide, in Southern communities they were being constricted into tight local limits. . . .

As to news, the editor of the rural South was called on to supply only a purely local brand. The field of national and world news was not for him. By the time he could publish stories from distant places his material was stale. His responsibility here was that of abstracting the dailies and boiling down world news into concise opinionated editorial statements. Country readers were as much interested in what the editor thought as they were in reading the stories themselves. They expected him to read the daily papers and write in his weekly a suitable attitude toward the news of the outside world. An attitude was all they required. . . .

The Southern common man lived simply and his interest was centered in the trivial happenings about him. It was to serve this everyday demand for local news that country papers resorted very early to the publication of names whether they made big news or not.

It was good practice to publish every birth, marriage and death, and to print obituaries in great numbers. It was part of the gloomy ritual of death in the South not only that a deceased individual be buried decently but that his memory be embalmed in printer's ink in a long and mournful obituary. Nearly every community contained at least one "literary" figure who could combine eulogy, sympathy and poetry in an expression of public sorrow. Even babies who lived scarcely long enough to be named were given publicity through expressions of sympathy for their parents. Country papers brought considerable peace of mind to bereaved families.

The sting of death was materially lessened by publication of eulogies. These were features which readers clipped and preserved in scrapbooks for future generations to read. In fact, there were the morbid clippers who pasted every obituary in their scrap books whether they knew the deceased person or not; the grandiloquent praise of the dead satisfied their desire to be so remembered by the paper when they passed on.

Newspapers performed endless services in the vast field of human relationships. Perhaps none was more appreciated than the link they formed between persons who migrated to other parts of the country and their old communities. An army of homesick immigrants wrote long letters to local papers in which they described conditions in their new homes and inquired about persons and matters which they had left behind. The editorial shoulder was always a willing weeping post where the detached and lonely subscribers could rest their weary heads. They always found the editors willing to print even passable letters, and editors found nostalgic readers good subscribers from whom they collected important extra revenue.

There was no tie with a man's past which remained so constant and voluble as the country paper. It was a friendly, sympathetic weekly letter from home which revealed the activities of the whole community and which recorded the degrees of change more effectively than was ever possible in personal correspondence. Editors appreciated this fact, and they often ran special features to attract the attention of distant readers who had lost interest in detailed personal happenings. By doing this they converted their papers into pleasant doorways through which the reader was admitted to the historical past.

(from *The Southern Country Editor*)

GO TELL AUNT LYDIA Two faces beamed benevolently at millions of American country newspaper readers. In fact, it is possible that these portraits were printed more often than any others in the country's history. They were Lydia Estes Pinkham and W. L. Douglas, the famous three and four-dollar shoeman. Lydia Pinkham became a famous woman, so famous in fact that a respectable amount of space is given to her in the august *Dictionary of American Biography*. She might easily be called a matron of panic. She was born in 1819 when the nation was feeling the pangs of postwar deflation, the daughter of a Quaker family. As a young woman she taught school and then married Isaac Pinkham, a builder and operator, in 1843. As Mrs. Pinkham, she compounded tonics from herbs which she found about her home in Lynn, Massachusetts, and gave them to neighboring women to relieve them of suffering from lacerations and weak backs. She had come to recognize the fact that the milestones in feminine health and life are filled with horrors, and she was interested in bridging the chasm from youth to womanhood, and from womanhood to the more matronly phases of life.

Mrs. Pinkham began a most successful career. Isaac Pinkham's real-estate business felt the pinch of 1873, and three years later the family was financially stranded. Mother Lydia was an ingenious soul, and in that strenuous period of 1875 she recalled her herb pot and suffering womanhood. This time it was to be for a modest price that she ministered to her ailing sisters. A job printer was hired to prepare labels, and her enterprising son Daniel went away to Boston, New York and Brooklyn to apprise the debilitated females in those places of the modern miracle of Lynn. In 1877 Daniel proved himself a master entrepreneur. The Lydia E. Pinkham Medicine Company began its long career of newspaper advertising. Its founder, however, did not live to see the business a success. She died in 1883, and her famous formula passed on to her sons to yield them snug fortunes.

The benevolent countenance of the saintly woman of Lynn smiled with gentle and motherly benignity at every female approaching puberty and promised to remove successfully the galling sting of womanhood's badge of original sin. In short, there were few female ailments from the cradle to the grave which this benevolent mistress of the herb pot could not cure. Her countenance was an epitome of American maternal love, and her advertising line was a famous chapter of American economic freebooting. She could easily have passed for the nation's mother of 1882, or as a crusading reformer seeking a second chance for wayward girls and motherless boys. Scarcely a country newspaper in the South was without her picture and her message. The year she died it was estimated that her portrait adorned the advertising columns of 6,000 journals.

Publishers wondered in the long hours when they were setting type by hand if there was such a person as Lydia Pinkham. The editor of the Burlington (Vermont) *Free Press* took it on himself to check this for the 5,999 other papers which bore her angelic countenance. In Lynn he found her at 225 Western Avenue in a bright and pleasant home. She appeared a trifle thinner than her portrait but just as sympathetic with her simple and trusting clientele. Pointedly she told the Vermont publisher that she spent her time answering letters from women who sought advice. She felt it her duty to mother every female with a pain, and she was happiest when immersed in the great care and labor of her mail. She answered on an average one hundred letters a day and kept two secretaries busy taking dictation.

So the fabulous Lydia E. Pinkham was described to the country press everywhere. In later years when the United States Congress became interested in the truth of medicinal advertising, the Lydia E. Pinkham Company must have become somewhat conscience-stricken. From time to time since 1883 it had published intimate notes about the personal activities of its patron saint. She had been pictured as a scholarly woman searching steadily into the diseases of the female organs. Once an enthusiastic copy writer boasted that she had had more training in the treatment of women's diseases than any doctor in the world.

The company was subtle in advertising its compound. After her death in 1883 the weekly spreads were made to read in such a way as to leave the impression that Lydia E. Pinkham still lived. In 1905, however, this misrepresentation was brought to light in Samuel Hopkins Adams' articles in *Collier's Weekly* exposing "The Great American Fraud." Quickly the country papers carried an advertisement which gave a partial biographical sketch of the founder. It was indirectly admitted that Mrs. Pinkham's daughter-in-law had worked with her and had taken over the task of answering the intimate letters which poured into the company offices. For twenty-five years young Mrs. Pinkham had written to women who doubtless believed they were communicating directly with Mother Lydia whose portrait had appeared with regularity above the admonition to address their pleas to her!

Lydia E. Pinkham's company was the most consistent of the hundreds of medicine companies that advertised in the country papers. It had contracts with ready-print distributors, and few if any issues appeared without the conventional advertisement displayed in a prominent place. Just as it was one of the most consistent advertisers after 1877, it was likewise one of the most appealing to suffering womanhood in its extravagant materials. Appealing to women who were denied medical care, it promised them impossible relief from their suffering.

The nostrum, it was claimed, "revives the drooping spirits, invigorates and harmonizes the organic functions; gives elasticity and firmness to the step, restores the natural lustre of the eye, and plants on the pale cheek the beauty of fresh roses of life's spring and early summertime." This just about covered the range of desires for a vast majority of women. If a fair dose of Lydia Pinkham's Compound, which was said to contain

20 per cent alcohol in 1905, could do it, was not that all right? Who could object to befuddled womenfolk taking a mild toddy, with some herbs for good measure? At least the public was spared the ordeal of having senators and congressmen recommend it from personal use.

There was more to the Pinkham story than bloom on the cheek and luster in the eye. To worrying females it promised children by rearranging their reproductive organs. Letters told of women in Iowa and South Dakota who had overcome the humiliation of barrenness. A Mrs. E. F. Hayes of Boston testified that Lydia Pinkham's Compound had cured her of a fibroid tumor which had baffled the skill of Boston physicians. By mail the "ghostly" Lydia had been able to prescribe the proper cure. Mrs. Hayes agreed to answer any and all letters asking about her case. "Mountains of gold," it was said, "could not purchase such testimony." To prove the validity of the testimonial, if not the cure of Mrs. Hayes' fibroid tumor, the medicine company offered to pay $5,000 if it could not produce the original letter.

The Cheney Medicine Company placed extensive advertising. It produced the famous "red clause" contract which provided that advertising could be canceled in a paper if the state passed a law detrimental to the nostrum seller's best interest. It was a brazen attempt to restrain the press from any crusade for pure-food and drug acts. An editorial construed as unfavorable would make a paper suspect.

Among the most active users of the country press was Dr. S. B. Hartman's Sanitarium of Columbus, Ohio. It advertised Peruna which was said to relieve almost every ailment that afflicts mankind. It contained 28 per cent alcohol, and its critics asserted that its victims were legion. Public officials . . . were quoted for weeks on the beneficial results which they had experienced from taking the medicine. . . . Dr. J. T. Ensor, postmaster of Columbia, South Carolina, and late superintendent of the state insane asylum, found Peruna a lifesaver for his large family; perhaps its general effects had helped to bring about the change in jobs for him! Governor W. J. Northern, a Georgia Populist and famous livestock farmer, expended a part of his literary talent in telling ruralites that he too had drunk deep at the Hartman wellspring of health.

Nearly all the medicine companies ran advertisements in series. . . . From Civil War times on to the first decade of this century, the medicine companies subsidized much of the free press. At first it was the bitters trade seeking a Reconstruction patronage by recalling the days of struggle. Already the quacks had learned to play upon political and social prejudices. One ingenious advertiser claimed that his product was the South's own. It had been used throughout her armies with amazing results. Attention was attracted by the picture of a Confederate soldier whose face bore a marked resemblance to Stonewall Jackson.

In keeping with times when Confederates straggled home years after the war to reclaim wives whom they had deserted, the bitters people advertised their wares as the stuff which kept women young.

There was the case of John who had loved and cared for a delicate wife in ante-bellum days. When the conflict began, "no persuasion could induce him to abandon his fighting propensities. He craved Yankee meat." John kissed his nervous and anemic wife good-by and went forth to do gallant battle. During the first year of the war he heard a rumor that his fading blossom at home had departed this life. Years after the struggle, John thought of home. "Oh," said he, "that sweet flower, so beautiful in failing, has gone, but I will stroll the walks where once we were so happy." At the door he was greeted by a full-bosomed and rosy maiden who screamed and fell headlong into the old Johnny Reb's arms. "My dear wife," gasped Johnny, "what has produced so great a change in you?" In one glad but tearful whisper, she said, "Dromgoole and Company's English Bitters." . . .

Children were given narcotic-laden pacifiers which kept them quiet—but impelled them into a life of physical and nervous ruin. Parents were advised that they could rescue their offspring from croup and pneumonia by administering cough drops and ointments prepared by the great scientists of the proprietary-medicine trade. They were shown pacing the floor at night with limp children, and underneath the picture of woe a dramatic legend spoke of the saving powers of One-Minute Cough Drops, Teethina, McGee's Elixir or some other infanticide which was available for remarkably small sums of money. . . .

There was no disease that could not be cured. The surgeon's knife was a thing of holy horror. Cancer did not necessarily have to kill; Swift's Specific and a dozen other nostrums would cure it. Consumption could be as slight an ailment as a strawberry rash when treated with Allen's Lung Balsam, Dr. Pierce's Golden Medical Discovery, Ayer's Cherry Pectoral, Shiloh's Consumption Cure and many other varieties of bottled brown liquids. In all seriousness a Dr. Williams advertised his "Pink Pills for Pale People." They put real stamina in the corpuscles, a blush in maidenly cheeks and snap in the step. "Any girl can tell, and a physician who makes a test and is honest can see red corpuscles doubled. . . ."

It was strange that such implicit faith could be placed in testimonials prepared by quacks and illiterate patients. Perhaps nothing begets success like proclaimed success. The allegation of cures was accepted as sufficient evidence. It was all part of a meaningful chapter in American social history. The South was not alone in its gullibility. The nostrum maker worked the entire country. He was careful, however, to regionalize his appeal. It was not worth while to advertise chill tonics in Minnesota or chilblain remedies in Louisiana.

The Southern market was a particularly good one. A woeful lack of medical care prevailed there, and what was available was little above the level of some of the "doctors" who advertised their cures in the papers. The ills the medicines were said to cure were those of people overworked, poorly nourished, subjected to hard weather conditions, victims of bearing too many children and of bungling midwives. They were uneducated and without knowledge of scientific therapy. They looked on medical treatment and surgery as a sort of extreme unction, and they were reluctant to subject themselves to it. . . .

Publishers yielded to an insidious practice which should have disgraced them even with their undiscriminating readers. Agreeing to locate advertisements in advantageous places, they agreed also to carry a certain amount of material in "home-set" print in the news and editorial columns. . . .

Fully 80 per cent of the country papers were desecrated by medicine advertisements. It took a ravenous reader indeed to stomach them. They carried so many notices of *certain* cures for insidious diseases that they became nauseating. Editors who made the proud boast that they were publishing pure and innocent family newspapers did so in the face of the outrageous quality of their advertising. Scarcely anything could be more repulsive than to have chapter after chapter of female troubles spread out for the public to see. . . . In this brazenness is revealed a curious psychological inconsistency on the part of both editor and reader. Had an editor attempted to discuss in original copy some of the subjects covered in medicine advertising, he would have been ostracized by his patrons and possibly his paper would have been bankrupted by irate withdrawal of support. No editor would have dared to refer himself to the fact that certain matrons were suffering from fallen wombs or disarranged organs, or that some petite miss was having trouble of an equally intimate nature. . . .

A few discriminating editors refused to let medical advertising appear as reading matter and either limited or excluded altogether the more blatant frauds. Where this occurred the quality of journalism was high. Perhaps no single phase of journalism reflects the dangers of uncontrolled and unregulated enterprise better than the abandon with which fraudulent nostrum sellers robbed the public from 1865 to 1905. Only the most reckless defender of that period of unscrupulous advertising could say that had it not been for this source of revenue the country never could have developed such a widely dispersed press. That would obviously deny a sense of proper values.

From 1900 to 1906 the so-called muckrakers and an important segment of the national press expended great energy to expose the patent medicine quacks. Little or none of this important campaign was publicized in the country papers. In a large number of cases the famous "red clause" provisions had silenced the editors. Equally significant is the fact that a remarkably small amount of publicity was given the passage of the pure food and drug acts. While this legislation was driving free-spending advertisers from the flesh pots of weakness for patent medicine, some editors were too timid to express opinions.

As early as 1895, a bill was introduced in the Tennessee legislature which proposed that compounders of patent medicine print the ingredients on their labels. This caused a minor battle among the editors of the state. There were those who contended that this was a free country, that men had a right to their trade secrets and that any attempt to make them reveal these secrets would be tyranny. One editor with more wit than social consciousness said, "The Memphian is right. When a compounder gets together some good bitters and bad gin that will fill in the morning a long felt want in the stomach of a prohibitionist, the originator of the drink should not be compelled by law to give the Scnapp away."

After 1906 the country press grew bolder. It spoke with

more freedom on narcotics and was a little more circumspect about advertising. Those self-respecting editors who sought legitimate local advertising and freed themselves of the Eastern and Chicago advertising agencies were able to publish effective papers. Once the ready-print pages were attacked by the state press associations, and organized editors began writing uncomplimentary editorials about those rugged individualists who wished to continue to receive the frugal handouts of the agencies, the country journal became a less offensive advertising medium. More significant was the reflection of a growing medical profession, and a semi-intelligent attitude toward more adequate public health care for the Southern common man.

(from *The Southern Country Editor*)

THE FARMER'S ALMANAC Equally as universal as the medicines, and more generally popular, were the indispensable pair, the *Ladies Birthday Almanac*, and *DeVoe's Daily Weather Forecast and Calendar*. The *Birthday Almanac*, first published in 1890, rapidly became a southern institution. From its first issue it contained tables of the chronological cycles, the seasons, holidays, fixed and movable festivals, eclipses, time of rising and setting of sun and moon, and the signs of the zodiac arranged about the disembowled figure of a man. Each month was listed separately with two pages of detailed weather and seasonal information. The monthly chronology was arranged so as to give weather signals, zodiac signs, standard time changes, and birthday and Biblical proverbs and references. At the foot of the column was the DeVoe weather chart presenting a general over-all long-range weather prediction for each month.

Mixed in with the weather forecasts were proverbs and bits of miscellaneous historical information. On page two there was an anniversary table which served the purpose of a short chronological encyclopedia. For instance, almanac users were told these facts: "April 1, April Fool's Day;" "April 13, Thomas Jefferson's Birthday;" "May 13, Settlement of Jamestown, 1607;" and "June 3, Birthday of Jefferson Davis, Confederate Memorial Day in Tennessee." Scattered through the book were words of ancient wisdom—"Plant your taturs when you will, they won't come up until April," "Till April's dead change not a thread," "Whatever March does not want April brings along," "The more thunder in May, the less in August and September," and "Be sure of hay 'til the end of May." Added to these folk proverbs were daily scriptural references in keeping with the season.

Weather predictions and chronology of both the *Ladies Birthday Almanac* and the weather chart were the work of Professor Andrew DeVoe, an amateur meteorologist of Hackensack, New Jersey. Professor DeVoe made weather a profitable hobby. He worked out a system by which he believed he could make successful long-range weather predictions by the relative positions of the earth and sun. Weather he felt was governed by the angles of the earth because they in turn determined the eclipse. That he was successful in forecasting weather events was attested by the fact that he predicted both the Galveston Flood and the Florida Hurricane. These forecasts brought the almanac and weather chart maker much newspaper publicity and established him as something more than an amateur in meteorology.

"The Cardui Calendar and Weather Chart" was equally as famous as the almanac. Professor DeVoe transferred his chronology and weather forecasts to the shoulders of the large calendar face. Figures of the calendar were in bold black-face type inside large red-lined squares containing sufficient blank space for miscellaneous notations. Smaller red script lines underneath the numerals gave notices of religious holidays and sun and moon changes. But of equal interest was the fact that many significant anniversaries in southern history were recorded. These included arbor days, famous southern battles, the birthdays of southern statesmen and military figures, and days on which there was to be no rural free delivery.

The large blank spaces around the bold black letters of the calendars became places for making notes of all sorts. Breeding records of livestock, the setting of hens, and the births and farrowings of calves, colts and pigs were recorded there. Often purchases from the stores were set down in the squares on the proper dates. Time records of wage hands were written on the calendars. Women sometimes used the squares for the purpose of keeping check on their menstrual periods. For those who dreaded pregnancy the calendar's stories became a mild sort of torture. For those who became pregnant the notes kept the date of expected confinement in mind. Because of these business and intimate personal data, the DeVoe Weather Chart and Calendar was often left hanging on living and store room walls for several years at a time.

Calendar headings were cut so that specially printed cards bearing merchants' names and business legends could be inserted. From choice of stereotyped headings, merchants selected one which suited their business and it was inserted in the calendar. In 1904 the calendar manufacturers advertised that a single merchant the year before had ordered 7,000. "Business men," said the circular, "have for years sought in vain for such a Calendar. We now put it in your easy reach." Storekeepers were told that "you can find no better investment than to put out as many of these calendars as possible. Do so and each one will be making you friends and customers every day in the year. . . ."

Perhaps Professor DeVoe's weather charts have been more influential between 1890 and 1920 in determining the planting and cultivating of crops than have been many of the southern county agents. In matters of agriculture where the exact date was a factor, the DeVoe chronology was always at hand.

Many farmers depended upon the changes of moon and sun time, especially moon changes in planning their planting and harvesting activities. Realizing that the almanac was a factor in farming, the editor advised farmers that he could not devise a chart of plantings of a sufficiently simplified nature to make it practicable, and he advised them either to consult their county demonstration agents or write their congressmen for information. Even though the almanac has lacked a planting guide, it has remained a farmer's handbook.

(from *Pills, Petticoats and Plows*)

DEATH ALWAYS CAME AT NIGHT In January 1893, Nathan Long of Marengo County, Alabama, with a hand bound down in grief drafted a sorrowful note on yellowing tablet paper to his furnishing merchant. His mother was dead and Nathan, a dutiful son, prepared to pay a last and dignified tribute to her memory. His humble note was a classic in the simple affairs of death in the South. "Ples send me a cheap coffin and some Bleatching a Bout what you think will Beary a Body in something like a sheet My Dear old Mother is Dead i am Poor But I wants to Beary Her I will need a Bout 6 yds to mak a sheet for Her and Charge them to me." In a postscript the affectionate Nathan summed up the morbidity of death in his isolated community. "Ples send me a par stocking to Put on Her feet."

A wrinkled weary old soul had found the upswing of winter too hard for one of her years and had given up the struggle. It was difficult for Nathan to start the spring under the handicap of added expenses, but he wished to extend the last full measure of filial devotion. A simple coffin "on the credit" cost ten dollars. Six yards of shoddy bleaching for a binding cloth cost seventy-five cents, and a pair of grayish-white stockings for the aged calloused feet which in life had seldom known such comforts was twenty-five cents more. The total cost of the old lady's funeral was not great, but even so in the panic year 1893 it required half of a big bale of cotton to pay the bill in October.

Scattered among the pine hills of the rural South are the sprawling graveyards. They epitomize a gaunt struggling death which gives a grievous ring of truth to the psalm of finality that "from dust thou are to dust thou returneth." Broken tombstones deeply etched with fragmentary biographies and trite phrases and verses of solace and hope bear mute testimony to the closing phases of a way of life. . . .

This inanimate document coupled with vital statistics, and the history of diseases prevalent in the region reveals an important facet of the picture of rural southern life. Death has ever been a subject of primary interest in the region, and around it has developed a huge volume of folk history. In the confused years of the late sixties plans for the decennial census of 1870 provided that the published findings should contain an extensive section on life and death which would go beyond the highly formalized statistics of earlier reports. Long categories of diseases were given for the states, and deaths were catalogued by newer classifications. Diarrhea, enteric and intermittent fever, measles, whooping cough, childbirth, croup, consumption, skin diseases, scalds, burns, cholera infantum, malaria and general debility were given high places among major causes of southern deaths. Out of the chaos of the times and the gross inaccuracies of the census takers' reports there comes a pattern of some significance. In graphic varicolored charts, disease and pestilence were spread forth on the face of the national map. Many of the areas of the Confederate states were stamped in heavy colors to indicate that pneumonia, malaria, croup, measles, consumption and debility were fatal.

For the succeeding decennial reports, planners of the census gave careful attention to the state of health in the nation. Decade by decade the picture was made more intelligible by expanding medical knowledge and more detailed classification. There were not only the old stand-by causes of death listed in 1870 but destructive newcomers isolated from the older ones by progressive medical technique were added. Deathly fears of enteric fevers, typhoid, dysentery, consumption, skin diseases, debility, cramp colic, brain fever and scores of others of the older generalized classifications were lessened considerably in succeeding decades. Parisitic infections, devitalizing pellagra, tuberculosis of many kinds and general malnutrition soon occupied important positions at the top of the list of life-destroying diseases.

Spread across the face of modern charts and pictorial maps of health reports and vital statistics was an ever-changing picture of the status of life. With cringing disgust visitors to the South watched people gathering and eating lumps of clay, and rushed away to write horror stories of what they had seen. As the influence of the land-grant colleges and their schools of agricultural and home economics began to be felt, attention was focused upon living conditions of rural people. Bête noire of the domestic scientists, pioneer state health departments and home demonstration agents was the "white diet" which took its heavy annual toll in a dozen different ways. . . . There is molasses by the thousands of barrels, salt meat by trainloads, cooking oil, flour of a dozen inferior grades and bolted meal by thousands of tons. The myriad orders told more eloquent stories of malnutrition than did the public-health laboratories with their fantastic displays of chemicals and bubbling test tubes.

Ten years after inquisitive census takers had labored indifferently in reconstruction and disorganized South Carolina to make sense of their fragmentary reports, E. P. Mobley of Fairfield County wrote a sordid answer to several of the causes of the state's 7,380 deaths. In an old-style handwriting in which the tail of the first of double *S's* came below the line, he asked that one of his tenants be supplied "a gallon of molasses, 12 lbs Bacon one Bushel of meal on his Liean 10cts worth Tobacco." This is a random order; from 1865 to 1920 an incalculable number of such missives reached the country stores, and the reaction from the monotonous and harmful diet which they asked for was mirrored in the lengthening rows of vital statistics.

In the midst of the formidable phalanx of diseases which swept thousands of southerners into the arms of their fathers is a catchall classification entitled "debility." Behind the deaths from this cause, however, are the exceedingly human stories of shriveled and worn bodies which withered away more from living too long and too hard than from the blight of a specific disease. Like an ancient and stubby shovel sweep which had been dragged through too many long furrows, the force of life in these individuals was gradually blunted and worn away. Palsied hands fluttered and dropped uselessly at sides and quivering arm muscles gave up the struggle to lift them again. Outwardly debility was the only cause of death and so it was explained in vital statistics. Surprisingly the list of deaths from debility was long; life with its many treacherous hazards and ineffective diet spared a large number of persons to enjoy a peaceful and leisurely old age of chewing tobacco and dipping snuff on porches and under shade trees.

There were actually few customers for coffins in the rural South prior to 1910. Death like birth was pretty much a homemade affair, and because of its eternal element of misfortune the burden was spread out to as many people as possible. Neighbors contributed to the financing of the costs of materials, and making coffins was almost always a labor of charity. . . .

Fixtures were bought from stores and carpenter-farmers spent hours shaping oblong, hexagon or curved-end boxes into caskets. The ends of death were served with the most careful workmanship possible. Hour after hour hot water was poured over pine, walnut and oak boards, and triangular slits were cut halfway through to facilitate the bending. The monotonous pounding of the bending hammer was heard on many a sultry southern night. Blinking lanterns lighted the activities of the cabinetmakers as they moved around from one detail to another. . . . Long steel tacks were set in place. Heavy screws with ornamental heads decorated with classical designs of cypress and garlands marked the bends and joints. There were other nails in the shape of crosses which held the lining in place, and sometimes were driven into a line of beading around the lids. When they were set in place against a background of black cloth and dark stained woods they presented a striking and dolorous appearance of funereal adornment.

Coffin hardware was sold wholesale by distributors located in the larger centers. Wholesale houses like Belknap in Louisville supplied fixtures in completely assembled bundles. There were four handles and a plate bearing the legend "At Rest," "Our Darling" or "Our Babe." Sometimes the handles bore imprints of lambs at rest against a background of Elysian fields, and the lid screws were leaden roses in a half-blown stage. For adult coffins there were various designs. There was the legend "Mother" for married women's coffins; the inevitable square, compass and "G" for the Masonic fraternity; the open Bible and letters "I.O.O.F." for the Odd Fellows; and the rugged lengths of tree trunks and axes for Woodmen of the World.

At Whitakers, North Carolina, Hearne Brothers and Company specialized in supplying stores with a large assortment of hardware. Their large illustrated catalogue was a graphic document of burial artistry for the years following the Civil War. Page after page portrayed designs of varying types of fixtures, and every one of them conveyed an intensity of sorrow. The last four or five pages of the books were devoted to tools and equipment for merchants who wished to become undertakers.

The Hearne Brothers' catalogue was of more than ordinary

interest. For the boys sitting around the stores it furnished a fearful diversion from the usual course of idle conversation. Perusing its pages was in fact a theft of a surreptitious glimpse at the face of life's greatest inevitability. These catalogues sometimes figured in folk beliefs. Many persons believed that looking at such things as coffin fixtures was flirting with death itself. Especially was this true of the weary colored customers who timidly pushed up to the store, or eased up to the porches to take a moment of ease only to have a coffin book opened in their faces. The realistic illustrations of coffins and fixtures sent half-frightened customers home to ponder such things in their subconscious minds and to awaken at night in the midst of dreams of death. The belief was strong that to dream of coffins and open graves was to be in imminent danger of a dreadful accident.

Underneath the shelves where the boxes of casket hardware and tacks were packed back out of sight in the stores were the rolls of crinkled gray, white and black lining which was sold by the yard for the better boxes. Even when cheap factory-made coffins were sold to the stores and stacked away upstairs in the storeroom, many of them were without trimmings and inevitably finishing them was a task for the late hours of the night. It was always necessary for either storekeepers or their clerks to crawl out of bed and spend an hour cutting and fitting a lining into a frail box.

Such a case was that of making a coffin to receive the weary and bedraggled body of Dora Richardson Clay Brock, formerly child bride of the aged Cassius M. Clay. Dora died in poverty in one of the shacks atop a phosphate dump at the mines of Woodford County, Kentucky. Her tragic life was at an end. Once she had known the luxuries of spendid White Hall in Madison County as the wife of its famous master, and then she had gone away to meet the trials of life among people of much lesser social stature. The years had been cruel to her, and finally in a moment of one of her bitterest down-sweeps in the winter of 1915 the end came. The wife of the proprietor of McKinivan's country store lined a coarse pine box for a coffin with unbleached muslin and placed padding and a pillow in it to give comfort to Dora's emaciated body in her last earthly adventure.

Everywhere in the South merchants tacked down their funereal black, gray and white linings with leaden cross-shaped nails, or they rolled off yards of black calico and unbleached domestic to be used in covering up faulty places in the jerry-built boxes. One of the important factors in life was unbleached domestic. It was, perhaps, the commonest of all the cotton cloths, and for this reason was the most universally used. It was symbolical of the whole process of cotton production, and throughout life it was a useful fabric. When a hard-pressed cotton farmer or a member of his family died, the body was wrapped in unbleached cloth in the ancient style of Lazarus. Thus it was that many a lifeless body enshrouded in six to ten yards of unbleached cloth was jolted away for burial in a cotton wagon through acres of cotton fields. In final judgment these postwar Jeremiahs of the Lower South will arise and stand before their Maker in the coarse unfinished raiment which was bought for them of country merchants.

Burial customs in the rural South in the postwar years were closely patterned after the spirit of the times. Funeral directors were unknown. When a person died he deserved better treatment than to fall into the hands of unctuous and patronizing professional undertakers even if he had possessed the money to pay burial costs. The corpse was "laid out" by neighbors, local carpenters and cabinetmakers made the coffin, a near-by store supplied the materials, and friends kept the wake and dug the grave. In all the thousands of hapless victims recorded in the vital statistics of the census reports before 1915, a remarkably small percentage of them were carried to their final resting places by anyone other than neighbors. The only charges ever made in death were those which found their way on to the ledgers as entries for fixtures, linings and shrouds. Between 1865 and 1915 it was not an unreasonable thing from a financial standpoint to die. Seldom did an ordinary casket cost more than five to twenty-five dollars, graves were dug by obliging friends, there was seldom a hearse, and the wake nearly always turned out to be a semisocial affair.

There was a commingling of sorrow and joviality in the "sitting up" parties of the South. For members of the deceased's family sorrow was genuine, but among the neighbors there were definitely mixed emotions. The tedium of a long weary night of sitting up with a neighbor was often broken by pranking and drinking. A dozing barefoot brother suddenly came to life with all the wrath of hell burning between his toes where cotton had been stuffed and then set on fire. At other times long vigils at the side of a corpse turned into feasts of eating and drinking, but always the wakes were neighborly affairs.

Pallbearers of the postwar years approached their tasks with a formal reverence in keeping with cold finalities of the occasion. Clad in their best clothes, with white gloves and, sometimes, mourning sashes, they were ready to extend their last gracious respects to a departed brother. White gloves were almost always necessary, and they were lent by storekeepers who kept four pairs constantly on hand to accommodate funeral parties. In instances where the gloves were thrown into graves by fraternal orders they were purchased from the stores.

Graves were dug in light clay or deep sandy loam by volunteer laborers. They were usually four to six feet deep with a narrower pit the size of the casket. Lowering a coffin into the grave was always a mechanical problem. The most common practice was to use buggy lines with buckles stripped off so that when the casket came to rest at the bottom the straps could be pulled out from one side. Then there were patent straps which hooked into a bracket on the side of the boxes and once the box rested on the bottom of the grave the straps were slackened and the brackets were released. Often stores kept these straps and lent them throughout their territory for use.

Once the casket was in place the boards were placed over the shoulders and the grave was ready to be filled. Throwing the first shovels of dirt into the box was a heartless operation. Always there was an inhumane maliciousness in the monotonous rumble of dirt over the boards. This was, without exception, the most morbid of all the experiences of human life in the South. As one shovelful of dirt after another poured down on top of a vacuous coffin, and the sound rolled back in a hollow roar, the very emptiness of most of life in the region itself was echoed in its starkest degree of depravity. The rising sound of fresh dirt over a grave was in reality the last full measure of the bitter sting of death. . . .

Death became a chapter in the ledgers and journals of daily store transactions. Tucked away in an inside cover of the Reed Brothers' ledger for 1882 was a characteristic itemized burial account. This miscellaneous order consisted of "1 Bx for Coffin, 1 yd print, 1 bx tack, 1 doz. screws, 1 # nail," and involved a cash outlay of $.90. A more formal entry inside the ledger included a goods box for a coffin, a dozen screws, a pound of six-penny nails, two yards of calico and a box of tacks. Near by at Eagleville the estate of W. T. Puchell was charged with four and a third yards of cassinet, one pair of black pants, one yard Italian cloth, one spool silk, one spool of black thread, one and a half yards of bleached domestic, a yard and a half of prints, a half dozen buttons and a pair of socks. In all the bill was $11.25 and this customer was buried in grand style.

While the carpetbaggers and scalawags were playing havoc with domestic peace in Mississippi, and the famous Kemper

County War between native sons and scalawags and carpetbaggers was in progress, E. F. Nunn and Company at Shuqulak sold James F. Lundy an order of burial goods which consisted of two yards of bleached domestic, a half yard of flannel, a pair of hose, three yards of velvet, three additional yards of domestic, a dozen coffin lags, three and a half yards of ribbon, a dozen coffin screws, and a loan of ten dollars in cash. Elsewhere in the Nunn books there are entries for similar funeral supplies.

Everywhere there was a shocking casualness in the purchase of merchandise for burial purposes, and in the commonplace everyday method of making entries in account books. Closely akin to the constant business of selling meat, meal, flour, shuck collars and plowpoints was the sale of screws, lining, shrouds and hardware for coffins. . . .

With monotonous regularity accounts appeared in ledgers telling of the sad end of neighbors. "Spring sickness" killed the babies and heavy winter weather thinned the ranks of the old folks. C. B. Summers made frequent entries in his daybook at Earls, Kentucky. For $2.97, a customer purchased "3 yds of velvet, 3 yds black domestic, 2 pa. tax, 1 doz screws, 1½ doz coffin screws, 2 lbs of nails, 3 yds coffin fringe, 1 child's wool hat." A $15.00 funeral consisted of "9 yds of aplaca, 9 yds of bleaching, 1 pr. shoes, 1 pr. gloves, 1 pr. hoes, 1 calico skirt, 2 yd. Ribbon, 155 ft. lumber, 6 yds. of velveteen, 6 yds. ribbon, 8 wood screws, 8 coffin screws, 1 paper of tax." Stores not only supplied the needs of its customers in the stringent time of death, but they likewise gave aid in other ways. "Please send by bearer—5 yards of bleach cashmere (if double width) or 8 if single, 4 yds of black silk 2 inches side—six yrds black calico—3 yrds white flannel for skirt—1 net skirt—& 1 pr. drawers (Ladies) 1 yrd suiting (white)—1 pr-low cut shoes—No 6—Signed John H. Clark and William Clark. Telephone to James Joyce send word to Beasly." Already the storekeeper knew what had happened to the Clark family and it took no prodding for him to call James Joyce, and he sent word to Beasly by the first passer-by. In fact, merchants took up where the doctors left off, and they continued to serve the needs of a family long after the doctors were gone. There was a lot of humanity in their services, even if their goods were cheap in price, gaudy in appearance and shoddy in quality.

Thus it was that the stores in death as in life were sources of supply for all human needs. For many they were the beginning and the end of things. There was a sort of complete story of life in the fact that there were long entries for furnishing supplies from month to month for a long span of years, and then without warning there appeared an entry for burial supplies. When this occurred that name disappeared from the books and a change in community personality was inescapable. There was Matthew Brown who traded for a score of years with Ike Jones at Black Hawk, Mississippi. His account became a permanent fixture in the Jones books. Its itemized listings of commonplace merchandise played hide and seek in and out among similar entries of fellow farmers. In a sprawling "post-office" hand Ike Jones extended week by week Mat's humble list of purchases. His was a perfect story of a man whose annual income was often less than a hundred dollars, and his purchases were fairly well within keeping of his income. In 1911 at cotton-planting time when Mat's services were most vitally needed a member of his family closed his account at the store by purchasing a $10 coffin and a few "little extras." Mat would be unable to finish his crop, but already he had produced his quota of cotton. In the midst of the long ruled ledger sheet Ike Jones posted in his bold hand a final entry for his faithful customer. He brought his affairs to a close in debt for two months' supplies and a cheap coffin. Unlike Elisha, this faithful country-store customer was not going forth to eternity in a chariot of fire and blaze of glory but in a cotton wagon and a humble winding sheet of unbleached domestic grown on the meager cotton acres in the Lower South.

Mat Brown's account in 1911 practically saw the end of the custom of neighborly burial, and of buying funeral supplies from the country stores. After this the business of death became far too delicate to be handled by such unskilled persons as neighbors, merchants and graceless cabinetmakers. Here was a golden opportunity for the oily professional sympathizers of the age of impersonal commercial transactions. No longer was it proper for a man to return his body to the clay in a country-store coffin lined with bleached domestic on the inside and trimmed on the outside with balls and fringe held down by leaden rose beaded tacks of the hardware store. Burial associations were organized to insure hearse funerals of stipulated prices worth more than three cotton crops, and for which individuals pay annual fees, ever hoping of cashing in on the investment before the last installment is paid. In this way death never comes unexpected as it did to Mat Brown—instead it is ever kept a live subject by periodic arrivals of notices that another "nominal" installment is due on a $300 funeral.

(from *Pills, Petticoats and Plows*)

FRONTIER AMUSEMENTS Generally the frontiersman was fond of sports. His amusements and games were not like those of the present in which so much emphasis is placed upon group participation; however, much hunting and many games and other forms of amusement were of a group nature. More often one frontiersman bragged of his personal prowess and found himself challenged by another to a test of strength or marksmanship. These contests involved footraces, wrestling, jumping, swimming, hunting, shooting at targets, casting knives or tomahawks (a game called long bullets), horseracing, and lifting logs with handsticks. Wherever men and boys assembled—at church, county court, muster drills, log-rollings and house-raisings—there were contests of some sort. The term "better man" on the frontier had neither moral nor intellectual implications. At log-rollings one man challenged another to a lift. "Grab a root and growl," was the old lifting cry. Both men maneuvered to get "the long end of the stick" and "to pull down" his opponent. To be defeated was humiliating if not slightly disgraceful, and many a self-conscious man went home from a log-rolling unhappy because he had been bested in a test of strength. . . .

Men and women participated together in many forms of frontier amusement. Some of these were highly utilitarian while others had no excuse other than amusement. Woods-clearing days, house-raisings, log-rollings ,corn-shuckings, syrup-making (often called stir-offs), apple-sulphurings, bean-stringings, hog-killings and even wakes brought people together in frolicsome moods. The common working, in which neighbors helped to perform tasks too difficult for single families, was a general custom. When a man had a new ground full of logs to roll, or a house to raise, he invited in his neighbors to help him; but he in turn was obligated to furnish an extraordinarily good dinner. Also, he held himself in readiness to return the work when there was a call for his services. If a man fell ill and was unable to plant or cultivate a crop he could depend on men in the community to assist him.

Quiltings brought men and women together in a holiday mood. One of the constant tasks of the frontier woman was that of providing warm bed clothing for her family. Handspun and woven coverlets were made from native materials, and quilts were fabricated from myriad scraps of material sewn in intricate patterns. No frontier home had a complete air of domesticity without its quilting frame suspended from the ceiling in such a manner that it could be raised and lowered at will.

Although frontier courtships were rapid affairs, the average youth found it difficult to make his first approach to a girl. Play-party games not only brought young people out to parties, but they also paired them off in couples, and since many of these games had kissing as a main objective, they were most efficient in helping courtship along. . . .

No form of amusement was more popular than the dance, especially where religious views toward such relaxation were not too strict. There were many forms of the frontier dance, but perhaps the most common was the jigging Virginia reel with its hilarious running sets. Cabins were cleared of furniture and the dance went on as long as the callers and fiddlers were sober enough to keep the sets going.

Zithers, banjoes, guitars and fiddles were popular musical instruments. In order to amplify the sound of the fiddle, "strawbeaters" tapped heavy straws or slender wood reeds up and down on fiddle bridges in rhythm with the music. All of these instruments were portable. Importation of the heavier instruments such as the harpsichord, spinet and harp had to await the opening of roads and the coming of steamboats.

Just as the ancient play-party games survived, so did the dance tunes. Musicians everywhere knew by memory such old favorites as *Sugar in the Gourd, Barbara Allen, Fair Eleanor, Sour Wood Mountain, Old Joe Clark, Fisher's Hornpipe,* and *Foggy Went A' Courtin'.* Along with these, many English and Scotch folk tunes commemorating local personalities and incidents were added to the musicians' repertoire.

Just as dancing and play-party games were forms of relaxation, so was bragging. Many frontiersmen engaged in harmless boasting and tall lying just for the fun of it. One of the most common forms of stretching the truth was by outlandish comparison. Seldom were things compared in their normal relationship; either they were made utterly ridiculous by understatement, or patently unbelievable by outrageous exaggeration. In a new country where achievements of a lasting nature were for the future, the extent of natural resources unknown, and individuals unhampered by lack of opportunity, imaginations ran wild. Bigness was generally considered a superlative virtue, and so frontiersmen colored their stories and boasts. Bragging and bantering were perhaps certain manifestations of social immaturity. Frontier humor was often expansive in nature. Much of it, because of obvious greenness, was self-incriminating; some of it was droll with a deep philosophical undertone; and some of it had no other merit than the gross perversion of word usage. Greenness on the frontier was a highly relative quality, depending largely upon whether it was the native or his more sophisticated visitor, who made the notes from which published contemporary accounts were written. But whatever form frontier humor took, the American frontiersman on the whole was good-natured. A failure to consider this sense of humor with a degree of seriousness would be a failure to comprehend one of the most human character traits of the pioneer.

(from *Frontier America*)

BETWEEN THE PLOW HANDLES OF EXPERIENCE That the New South was predominantly agrarian was substantiated abundantly in every issue of a country paper published since 1865. The editors had two major approaches to agriculture. One was to run original and exchange stories on the proper method, the art, of doing things about the farm. The other was to attack the system in use.

For more than forty years the weekly paper served as a meager extension bulletin from which farmers could learn of elementary advances in agricultural methods. Perhaps of more fundamental importance were the frequent summaries of agricultural progress in the South and the nation. Three or four times each year many papers published general crop reports for the cotton and tobacco belts. Weather conditions over the South were given as they affected production of cotton and tobacco, and estimates, of cotton especially, were published. Aside from formal reports, the activities of farmers were given in special news columns. Livestock trading on county and circuit court days was described; and often upper South papers ran columns of news about the activities of livestock traders who traveled through the cotton belt with droves of horses and mules. Fertilizer and compost recipes, such as the famous Furman formula, were given, and much editorial advice was offered farmers.

In the main, however, the tone of the country press toward agriculture was critical. The whole structure of Southern farming, according to the country papers, was based on a false premise, and it was the country weekly's responsibility to conduct a forthright publicity campaign to correct this basic error. The common method was to indict the system of staple or single-crop planting, and then to produce a steady fire of incriminating evidence against it. As prosecutors, editors played a quixotic role, thrusting their quills against impenetrable walls of ignorance, stubbornness and indifference. They were offering leadership to an opinionated, stubborn group which had no desire to be led.

No editor failed to realize that agriculture in the New South was the economic life line of the region. Ambitious young publishers unpacking type and putting old-fashioned hand presses in motion quickly discovered that their own success rested squarely on the prosperity of farmer subscribers. For over sixty years more intelligent editors kept the wasteful and ineffective system of Southern agriculture at the bar of public opinion while they worked to find a practical way to correct agrarian maladjustment.

Beginning with the decade of the eighties, editors were concerned with the question of impending agricultural panic. Why had the postwar South failed? The Old South had been a region of staple crops dependent on slave or very cheap free labor. The close of the Civil War brought little important change in the fundamental concept of agrarian economy, except in the vital field of labor. Where the source had been the Negro slave, it became the free Negro. Where field hands had been paid in keep and kind, freedmen had to be paid in cash or shares of the crop. For the first twenty years after the war a stable supply of cheap labor was possibly the most sought-after commodity in the New South. An excellent summary of conditions, made by the Gibson (Alabama) *Enterprise* in 1884, somewhat expresses the whole situation during these years. Southerners, wrote the editor, are not willing to try things on a small scale. They want big cotton mills, big industrial plants. They are not willing to be one-horse farmers, but want at least a dozen plows dragging around. The result: poor mules, poor homes, poor food, poor Negroes, and poor everything else. The editor also believed that "if he [the farmer] had sold his mule stock down to one good mule, and took his family without depending too much on trifling Negro labor and worked his farm, he would have been independent and happy. . . ."

No one was more certain of the real foundation of the farmers' troubles than the newspaper editors. To them no piece of state legislation affected directly the lives of more people in the South than the lien laws (laws which permitted farmers to mortgage unplanted crops in order to secure supplies and capital to finance production) which state after state enacted immediately after the war to permit the mortgaging of unplanted crops. This legislation received continuous discussions in the press. Country editors who lived close to the farmers who were most affected by it realized that the lien law was a snare and a delusion. They deserve commendation for seeing, with amazing perspective, the insidious effects of this law even before Reconstruction had ended. Scarcely a line appeared in a weekly paper justifying its existence, and when the rumor went around that the next general assembly of a state would try to amend the law, editors let it be known that they favored outright repeal. . . .

Everywhere the story was the same. Countless editorials advised farmers to grow food and supplies at home. The Winnsboro (South Carolina) *News and Herald* said in 1886 that it "would be astounding to people to know just what the South pays for meat and grain." In Greenwood, South Carolina, "from January 1 to May 15, 1886, 57 carloads of bacon, 9,560 bushels of meal, 2,391 barrels of flour, 445 barrels of molasses [were purchased from the outside]—no wonder times are hard!" There was not a single item on the list which could not be grown much cheaper in South Carolina. . . .

The one-crop system was not the only villain preying on Southern agriculture and keeping it impoverished. Interest rates, in fact, the whole capital system, freight rates and extraregional bonuses for supplies all co-operated to keep farm books perpetually in the red. Most farmers felt that editors knew nothing about farming. They believed that men who did not participate in actual work in the field could never understand the complex problems of agricultural production. One reason the country press had so little effect on farming methods was its inability to make most of its readers distinguish between the actual physical process of production and the equally important economics of production. . . .

Southern editors shared with their better-informed readers the belief that agriculture was fundamental in the economic and social structure of civilization. Many of them felt real reverence for farming as a calling. It was not treated as an ordinary form of human employment, but as a God-sent mode of life. Farming was above the workaday activities of the wage earner, it was a close and sacred link with all of the mysteries of nature. A favorite topic for editorializing was the virtue of the farm boy and girl. Many editors professed to believe that boys and girls who lived in villages and small towns were inferior to those reared on farms. Fresh air, good food and solid work made the rural Southerner a sturdy individual who was equipped for a life of productive work anywhere. Country boys and girls, they believed, constituted a reservoir of human resources on which the nation was dependent for staffing its businesses and professions.

When agricultural panic in 1893 tended to drive young people away from farming the editor of the Charlotte (Tennessee) *Independent* said the country boy was the hope of the nation, and a sustaining foundation of prosperity. A strong body and a healthy mind gave him stamina to withstand temptation. To the editor the freedom of country life was a character builder. It escaped the too close associations in which all of human vices thrived; the activities of the farm were too numerous and exacting to allow the mind to concentrate on vices. Along with the Tennessee editor, other publishers were continually advising rural people to remain on the farm. Those who moved to the city would only have to return and begin farming again with less than they had when they left the country. . . .

With all their discussions of farming, the country papers failed to deal realistically with the octopus of farm tenantry, one of the fundamental weaknesses of Southern agriculture. They frequently mentioned tenants, but the subject was usually lumped in with farmer owners, and both were spanked with the same editorial paddle. But there was almost complete silence on the whole economic structure of tenant farming. It seems to have been accepted as a matter of course. Perhaps the press longed for the day when its rural constituency would be a landowning one. Profound regret was expressed at the loss of land under the omnivorous system of farm credit which enslaved the owner and turned him out finally to waste his life in the yoke of share cropping or laboring for wages. There is, however, much evidence that throughout the postwar years editors led themselves to believe paradoxically that tenant farming was to a considerable extent a natural result of human shiftlessness or inability to do better. Certainly it was not until the depression of 1929 and the publication in 1938 of the National Emergency Council's report, *The Report on Economic Conditions of the South,* that the Southern country editors were jolted into anything like a realization of the full implication of tenantry to the region. . . .

Many editors rejoiced when agricultural and mechanical colleges and their associated experiment stations were founded, while others were either skeptical or bitterly opposed to them as just so much humbuggery. One discordant voice was raised in Mississippi by an editor who was quoted by the Macon *Beacon* as believing a $15,000 budget for entomological research at the Mississippi Experiment Station a flagrant waste of tax money. "O! we are great on bugology down in this part of the vineyard," he wrote, "and it is a demonstrable fact that there had never been found a bug in this latitude more expensive to the farmers and less use to the general public than the species that infest the experiment station at Starkville. . . ."

So frightening were accounts of the approach of the weevil that many a subscriber rushed to newspaper offices with harmless insects which he thought were boll weevils. Then one day a farmer came with a tiny brownish-gray bug trapped in an amber glass snuff bottle and the editor announced the weevil had arrived. "Mr. A. G. Hammill recently sent us a boll weevil from the northern portion of the county," wrote Will C. Hight of the Winston County (Mississippi) *Journal* in 1910. "Our people had as well make up their minds to accept these pests next year; they will be with us."

This was the beginning of the end of a system of agriculture, the end many editors had so long predicted. Southern farmers were faced with destruction. Too long they had worshiped at the throne of fabulous King Cotton, and in idolatry they had shrugged off editorials on diversification as the impractical space fillers of editors who needed something to write about.

Although editors had been unable in forty years to persuade farmers that they were pursuing the wrong track, the hard decade from 1900 to 1910 brought them to a realization of the fact. There was the boll weevil working its way across the cotton belt and leaving havoc in its path; the Texas fever tick came from the same direction. Finally came the disclosure of Dr. Charles Wardell Stiles, a persistent scientist, that he had discovered the presence of hookworm. Those were momentous years in which a distraught rural South took a drubbing from insects and parasites. . . .

Newspaper publishers tried valiantly to create new markets for new products and to batter down the old habits of planting cotton and tobacco. Their perennial sermons hammered away. Still the weeklies could not measure their real accomplishments with much pride. They had kept alive the germ of better farming methods and dinned basically sound principles into the reader, but the situation required stronger remedies than the press could administer. Two world wars and two progressive periods in national politics were necessary to direct Southern agriculture toward the goal which country editors had always believed was the golden mean of the balanced agrarian way of life.

(from *The Southern Country Editor*)

LAST SOCIAL BARRIERS OF THE FRONTIER Within three years after the passage of the Homestead Act, a flood of settlers moved into the great public land areas of the West. Many Union veterans went directly on to the frontier to begin life anew. In camp and battlefield bivouac, the West had beckoned to soldiers; they made plans to seek free lands in pairs or in companies as soon as the war ended. . . .

The Homestead Law was not a satisfactory piece of legislation. It was characteristic of legislation which results from public pressure. Possibly no one before 1840 gave much serious consideration to the area involved, for the Great Plains were regarded as a desert where settlement would be long delayed, if in fact it ever occurred. Provisions of the act were devised largely from landholding experience on the 98th meridian. A quarter-section of land was ample to support a family in Illinois, Iowa, or Missouri, but it was probably inadequate on most of the plains. Some of this western land required eight to thirty acres to graze a steer, while other parts grew an abundance of grass. Where field crops were to be grown, farmers had to think in terms of larger acreage than in regions with more abundant rainfall. Some idea of the inadequacy of the law is suggested by the fact that out of the 86,936 entries made for Kansas lands between 1862 and 1882 involving 11,746,949.80 acres, only 34,055 entries were registered for 4,660,734.83 acres. In Nebraska there were 64,328 original entries for 8,183,076.25 acres, and 29,140 final entries were registered for 3,566,447.29 acres.

Beyond its basic inadequacies, the Homestead Law threatened dangerous disaster to the plains. Where the native sod was broken, wind erosion drifted top soils into piles of dust and sand. The native grasses were destroyed, and the soil was exposed to the merciless winds and dehydrating sun. In 1873, Congress in a partial effort to correct its former mistake passed the Timber Culture Act. This law provided for the encouragement of timber culture on the High Plains where nature had decreed otherwise. A settler was required to plant and maintain forty acres of trees not more than twelve feet apart for ten years; if he did so he would be given the quarter-sections on which the trees were planted. Settlers already holding a homestead grant could shorten the time of final entry to three years by planting an acre of trees on their claims. A belief prevailed that the climate of the plains could be modified by the growing of trees. Even precipitation could be increased by the presence of forests.

After the passage of the new law, it was possible for a settler to establish claim to 480 acres of land under the combined terms of the Pre-emption Law, the Homestead Law, and the Timber Culture Act. By locating his claims strategically he might even gain control of a couple of sections. The three quarter sections might be located around the outer edges of sections so as to make the interior units undesirable for another settler. On March 3, 1877, Congress enlarged the possibilities for a claimant to acquire an additional section of land by passing the Desert Land Act. This provided that if an individual would irrigate his lands within three years after filing a claim he could purchase it for $800.

These laws often served to open the West to wholesale exploitation by unscrupulous claimants. Not even Congress could make trees grow in places where nature had failed to accomplish the task. For the chiseler, these laws offered just the right pretext to lay claims to large blocks of the public domain. All kinds of subterfuges were used to secure possession of land claims. . . . Rich mineral lands fell into the hands of shrewd exploiters by methods little short of public robbery. When W. A. J. Sparks became Land Commissioner in 1885, he instituted several reforms and suspended entries which he believed were fraudulent. It was not until 1891, however, that the Pre-emption, Timber Culture, and Desert Land laws were repealed. By that time the frontier had technically ceased to exist. . . .

Most early houses on the plains were either "dug-outs" or "sod houses." Dug-outs were cut into hillsides and banks. They were lighted and ventilated with improvised doors and windows. Sod houses were constructed from clumps of sod cut from the land with a special sodbusting plow. Long strips of turf twelve to fifteen inches wide were sliced loose from the ground following a rain. These long ribbons were then cut into blocks fifteen inches long and were laid into walls somewhat after the fashion of bonded brick. Crude frames were erected to hold windows and doors, and the sod was pressed firmly around them. Walls varied in height from four to ten feet. Tree forks were placed at the peaks of gable ends and in the middle to support ridge combs and the weight of roofs. Rails or poles were laid from the walls to the peaks and heavy grass or cornstalk mats were then put down to catch the leakage of dirt which filtered down from the sod roof.

Dug-outs of necessity were small, dark, and dirty. They had the virtue of being dry most of the time, they were easy to build, and were cool in hot weather, and reasonably snug in winter. On the other hand they were dusty, leaky, and were all but impossible to ventilate. Dirt was forever dropping to the floor. Animals, snakes, and birds burrowed into the walls and roofs. Occasionally a rattlesnake worked his way inside to cause panic, and sometimes tragedy. Cattle roaming about the plains would stumble onto a dug-out roof and fall through, or a traveler driving in the dark would land his team and wagon atop a caving roof before he saw it. Yet, for the minimum expenditure of less than $5.00, an industrious man could purchase the necessary materials to build his plains burrow. One further virtue of the dug-out was the fact that it was below storm level and there was little danger of disaster from this source.

Sod houses corresponded somewhat to the more commodious log houses of the earlier frontier. They were more spacious and versatile structures. In fact, they could be made almost as large as the builder chose, and they could be erected at almost any desirable spot so long as a suitable supply of sod was available nearby. Some degree of specialization of domestic functions was possible for families living in these structures. Being above ground the sod house afforded more light and ventilation than did the dug-out; at the same time rain and wind storms caused greater damage. Seldom, however, was fire a hazard. There was no way to keep a sod house from shedding dirt or leaking. Often it was necessary to prepare meals under a sheet or an opened umbrella. Hunks of wet sod fell into cooking food or beds, and not infrequently walls and roofs became water-logged and fell down.

Much of the plains frontier environment inflicted genuine hardships upon families. Many a wife went west to join her husband and discovered that she and her children would have to live like animals under the ground in a dug-out, or in a crumbling soddy. . . . Some easterners were driven almost to the point of distraction by the constant blowing of the wind. There was seldom the stillness on the plains which prevailed in heavily wooded country. . . .

Not until railroads were built across the plains and lumber could be imported from the timber-growing regions was it possible to substitute wooden frame houses for those made of sod. In the beginning even churches and courthouses were built of sod. Even then many settlers were unable to afford the cost of new houses. . . .

Vast areas of the western plains were without timber. So long as settlement remained along the streams, wood of a sort was available, but once people moved away from the valleys they left the timber line behind them. In some areas during the early rush of settlers, government and railroad lands were denuded of trees. In fact settlers considered that the railroads had all but stolen the land from the government; therefore they thought little of lifting timber from the public domain. Long cold winters in most of the plains country necessitated the maintenance of fires for extended periods. People traveled long distances in search of wood, and they used every sort of substitute. Cow and buffalo chips were gathered from the grazing lands. Large weeds, sunflower, and cornstalks were cut into fuel. Experiments were made with grass and grass-burning stoves. Corn and corn cobs were used in place of wood. Coal was too expensive for the poor homesteader to buy, and most often he was too far removed from the railroad to permit him to procure it even if he had the money. The mere act of keeping a fire going on wintry days and nights was almost a full time job for a man. Frequently houses were heavily smoked and begrimed by the fire. Some of the substitutes for wood, such as grass bats, created a smoke that often threatened members of households with suffocation.

Water was almost as scarce as wood on the arid and subhumid plains. Not only was it difficult to obtain water for ordinary domestic purposes, but the land often lacked the necessary moisture to produce crops. Orthodox crops and orthodox methods of cultivation were not sufficient for agricultural success west of the 98th meridian. There were recurring drouths in the Ohio and Mississippi valleys, but these were seldom of an extended duration. Almost never were settlers left without water. On the plains, however, it was obtainable in many instances only after the expenditure of a vast amount of labor. Wells were bored or punched in the ground to a depth sufficient to tap the natural water table. It was then hauled to the surface by the use of a long slender bucket, or by a pump. After 1870, windmills came into common use to operate pumps. This was a slow but relatively effortless method of obtaining water. Because the wind blew constantly, the mills could be kept at work. . . .

The scientific process known as dry farming has expanded since the 1850's as a result of vast experimentation. Actually it is one of the oldest agricultural practices in the history of civilization, but not on the North American continent. From the beginning of recorded history, man has struggled with aridity in extracting a living from the soil. Ancient Asiatics learned many of the secrets of tilling dry soils. For thousands of years men, like the East Indians of the Punjab and those living near the Rajasltan Desert, or along the Malabar Coast, have battled drouth year after year. Millions of sleepy camels and bullocks have tramped around deeply padded circles dragging levers of creaking Persian well wheels in efforts to lift enough water from the ground to produce meager crops. Moses and Aaron battled aridity in their long wanderings with the children of Israel. Countless generations of nomadic Arabs have drifted over the boundless middle-eastern deserts. Man long ago learned to adapt his activities and agricultural practices to conditions of the seasons.

In keeping with ancient traditions, American frontiersmen approached a new mode of life on the plains. They were forced to use all their ingenuity to survive. In certain restricted areas enough natural stream resources existed to permit irrigation. There was not enough available water, however, in all the West to irrigate the region's arid lands. Even if water had been available, capital was lacking with which to finance the construction of facilities for getting water to the land. The next best answer was the "new" agricultural practice of dry farming. Almost 700,000,000 acres of land lay within the area where dry farming had to be practiced in order to utilize available moisture. For dry farming to be feasible it was necessary to have an annual rainfall of more than ten inches. The principle of this kind of cultivation was to plow a depth of seven to ten inches just before the winter rains and snows fell. Then it was necessary to keep the top soil stirred so a fine dust mulch would form and maintain a capillary action that drew moisture up to root systems of plants. This process of cultivation necessitated a constant stirring of the soil, and in some cases crops were planted on a bi-annual system of rotation. . . .

Peculiar environmental conditions of the plains area worked an unusual hardship on the American frontiersmen. The social pattern beyond the ninety-eighth meridian, however, varied little if any from that which had prevailed along the

Ohio, Wabash, Illinois, and Wisconsin rivers. Common workings enabled neighbors to accomplish tasks which otherwise could not have been performed so efficiently or pleasantly. There was no need for logrollings, but house-raisings, common plowings, and harvesting demanded an increased amount of labor. . . .

In between harvest seasons life moved on at a monotonous pace. Families were often so badly isolated that they literally hungered for human associations. Women and children especially longed for opportunities to see other people. Not infrequently families would drive astonishing distances to attend country dances, box suppers, church meetings, or to shop at crossroads stores, or to visit in towns. Plains settlers, like those in the Ohio and Indiana backwoods, held square dances in unbelievably small shacks and sod houses. Often barefooted dancers raised such clouds of dust from earthen floors that it was necessary to sprinkle the floor to prevent suffocation. Few dances went off without a good bit of drinking, a little fighting, and a generous amount of boasting and swearing. Candy pullings and play parties also served to make plains life more pleasant. . . .

Preachers reached the plains with the first settlers. Baptist preachers were themselves settlers, and Methodist circuit riders kept up with the creaking homesteaders' wagons. Presbyterian, Episcopal, and Congregational ministers went West either to accept charges, or as missionaries. Regular church services were held first in cabins and sod houses. Occasionally ambitious women established Sunday schools and maintained combination educational and religious programs either to supplant the infrequent religious services or to take their place altogether. Periodic "bush arbor" or outdor revivals brought people together for both spiritual and social gatherings. The social aspects of these meetings at times possibly outweighed the spiritual ones. Permanent churches made their appearances and religious services became more regular. Preachers offered vast comfort to the people in their moments of misfortune and grief. Often they were almost as much in demand as were doctors and midwives. In many places on the frontier, ministers were subjected to indignities. In the lusty young towns where saloons and brothels held sway, they were regarded either as objects of ridicule or as competitors.

Drinking, gambling, fighting and lawbreaking in general marred social life in many communities. Much of the free and easy characteristic of plains border life grew out of the peculiar nature of the country. Men turned to vices as forms of amusement to break the monotony of living in isolation. They sometimes flaunted their boisterous behavior in the faces of more religiously inhibited neighbors in a sort of brazen easement of their guilty consciences. It was some of this brassy type of behavior which gave a certain amount of flavor to the "wide open" West. Not infrequently a homesteader was a temporary settler who expected to stay in a community only long enough to "prove a claim" and then move on. At the beginning the plains population had a predominance of men, and this accounts for the rugged society which first existed on this part of the frontier.

Conditions often forced settlers to resort to the practice of vigilantism in certain frontier areas. Victims of these informal law-enforcement bodies were thieves, gamblers, dissolute moral offenders, and bands of robbers. Conflict between settler and cattlemen provoked local "wars" which sometimes saw hooded companies of farmers confront their common enemy, the free-grazing trail herders, with shot guns and ropes. Rustlers brought out the regulators in force. Claim jumpers were sure to provoke the wrath of neighboring homesteaders, and often a brazen "jumper" would be sent on his way after he had infringed, legally perhaps, upon the claim of an original settler. On top of the more spectacular provocations for law enforcement were the petty breaches which landed individuals in court. Many of these were conflicts between the code of the saloon and gambling halls and the mores of a more refined society.

Western towns sprang up on the plains as population moved westward. The frontier town was in fact a bubble of the eternal optimism of the American promoter. Speculators and promoters hoped to locate a town, secure the state capital or county seat, and sell off cheap land at premium prices. One of the major sports of the period, 1865-1900, was that of trying to guess right in locating a town. Crossroads, sites of blacksmith shops, railhead camps, ends of cattle trails, stagecoach stations, country stores, and railway stops all gave promise of growing into metropolises. Many promoters undertook to force the law of town location by promoting sites on the plains that had few or no justifiable reasons for becoming population centers. Railway agents worked hard at locating towns for various selfish reasons. Politicians often took a hand at town building. . . .

The average plains town was a rather unattractive place. . . . It stood stark and naked on a treeless knoll, as raw and unadorned as a picked chicken. Its gray wood buildings lined a dusty main street, and it possessed little of architectural taste and beauty. Occasionally rickety boardwalks paralleled the street. Hitching racks ranged along the streets in front of store doors, and heaps of horse manure gave the towns something more than a nostalgic odor. In some of these frontier towns, saloons and gambling houses outnumbered stores. . . .

Those who rushed westward with hopes of claiming their share of the national domain not only had to combat aridity, and a lack of timber, but also the fierce insect scourges, dry winds, dust storms, blizzards, and prairie fires. During the years 1874–1877 the great grasshopper invasion ate almost every green thing before it in a wide strip across Kansas. The swarm of insects in 1874 first appeared as a dark cloud rising and falling in erratic swells, displaying a silvery hue as it swirled in the sun, just above the landscape. At first settlers thought it was a rain cloud, and then they discovered the grasshoppers dropping down upon their crops. Settling to the ground in clicking hordes they gave a slight impression of a vast hail storm. Within a day's time almost every green thing was consumed. Onions and turnips were eaten down into the ground. Harness was gnawed to pieces. Tool handles were nibbled so badly that they were hardly usable again. Even the boards on houses were eaten bare of their softer weather-beaten surfaces. Streams and wells were contaminated by the insects that dropped into them or by the excrement of the vast swarms. Professor John Ise has described most graphically the struggle of his father and mother to rescue a part of their corn crop from the grasshoppers. His father cut the corn while his mother dragged it into shocks, but on the second day the hoppers had devoured the remaining crop and there was nothing left to harvest.

Combatting the insect invasion caused settlers to waste energy and to suffer tremendous heartbreak and disappointment. Both state and federal governments attempted to grant relief to sufferers of the plague and to find means to destroy the insects. Experiments were undertaken to destroy both eggs and young grasshoppers before they had a chance to swarm over the land. After 1877 the ravenous swarms ceased to appear, although the grasshopper menace in a more limited way continued. The use of poison, and development of a more complete knowledge of the life cycle of the pests helped to bring them under control.

While grasshopper swarms stripped fields and grazing lands of crops and grass, dry, hot winds blew over the land withering plant life before them. Early drouths prevented seeds from sprouting, and those that came later in the season destroyed growing crops. Many a plains farmer felt the hot winds blow in his face day after day and saw his fields and pastures parched to a crisp. Water resources failed, and livestock either perished or became so weakened that it was all but worthless. Settlers left the country in droves, going east to keep from starving, sometimes driving cattle and hogs before them to pay the expenses of their retreats from failure.

Behind the searing drouths came the suffocating dust storms of summer, and the death-dealing blizzards of winter. Thunder storms of summer sometimes developed into wild blows which reached tornado proportions. In the open country the flashes of electrical storms, and the rolling dark clouds could be seen for miles away. The surging of the clouds and the long rolls of thunder created a sort of majestic horror. Dust storms boiled up in the same way. Often it seemed the whole earth was being lifted heavenward, and as the storm thundered on it deposited drifts of dust and sand against every barricade in its path. Winter blizzards swept much of the plains country with blinding ice and snow storms. A traveler caught in a plains blizzard was in real danger. He not only had the problem of withstanding the cold and exposure of the storm, but he had to think of the dangerous psychological confusion which would occur. He was in grave danger of losing his sense of direction and identification so that he might travel in circles or fail to identify familiar landmarks.

The growth of prairie grass and intense drouth of the region heightened the danger of fire. A careless traveler allowed his campfire to get out of hand, gun wadding sometimes fell afire into a clump of grass, or a tongue of lightning started fires. Huge rolls of flames leaped into billowing waves of destruction. Clouds of ominous black smoke darkened the sky, and falling ash and cinders indicated destruction on a scale dreamed of only by Dante. . . .

When these disasters swept over the land, they left death and poverty in their paths. Many settlers turned back, but many more remained and brought the country under their conquest. Those who survived were tempered in the furnace of hardship and discouragement. Though a peaceful, simple folk at heart, these settlers had to fight greedy men and corporations, the elements, and their own psychological frustrations. . . .

In the frontiersman's rush to settle the continent he brought under exploitation a territory which might well have taken a less energetic society centuries to accomplish. The American could not withstand the challenge of so large a block of public lands. Individual and corporation sought to get their share of the public domain. Both helped to create economic and social problems which radically changed concepts of the function of government. At the same time the national government was forced to reach a high state of maturity in a remarkably short interval of time.

(from *Frontier America*)

CHAPTER THREE

THE FLAVORFUL FRONTIER LIFE

KENTUCKY SOCIETY Early Kentuckians were a simple-living, conscientious people, among whom crimes received immediate punishment. Men away on campaigns were scrupulous in moral conduct. Thievery was an abomination to the frontiersman's soul and reputation. . . . Often thieves were chastised with the "Law of Moses," or forty lashes, and petty criminals were disciplined by application of the "United States Flag," or thirteen stripes. Individuals guilty of horse thievery were punished with death. This crime was a capital offense because it deprived a man of his livelihood and sometimes his means of escape from danger. Gossipy women were permitted to practice their art unmolested but with a distinct understanding that recognized gossips were not to be taken seriously. If a man doubted the veracity of another and called him a liar, a fight was a certainty if the abused man were to save his reputation. Pioneer affairs of honor were settled in various ways. Occasionally the challenged and the challenger settled their disagreements with rifles according to the code duello. Most often, however, they fought it out hand to hand, resorting to the Virginia practice of gouging. In this practice opponents took every possible advantage of each other; ears were bitten off and eyes gouged out.

The pioneer was, generally, an easily satisfied individual. Making a living was a simple process, for the pioneer and his family were perfectly satisfied with what the seasons and the rifle brought them. In matters of clothing, the men were contented if they acquired an outfit consisting of a deer skin or linsey woolsey hunting shirt, a pair of heavy cotton drawers, leather breeches, a pair of woodsman's moccasins, and a coonskin cap.

Perhaps no article of frontier clothing was more important or more interesting than the moccasins the hunters wore, for little effort and few instruments were necessary to manufacture such simple footwear. Shoemakers required only pegging awls and rolls of "whang" leather with which to bind the seams. In many respects, the moccasin was ideal for footwear, since the hunter could walk all day without cramping his feet between stiff soles and uppers. Uppers of the ordinary moccasin were long enough to be tied about the wearer's legs to keep out sticks, pebbles, and snow. Moccasins intended for winter were made with the hair side of the leather turned in to keep the feet warm, and summer moccasins, when worn in winter, were stuffed with hair or wool. In spite of the comfort of this type of boot, the pioneer's feet were the source of nine tenths of his suffering, for the disease of "scald feet" was prevalent, and often its victims were disabled for several days by tender, aching feet. . . .

Contrary to belief, the pioneers did not live in the stockades for any great length of time, but they lived in separate cabins near the forts. When an Indian raid threatened, they loaded packhorses with household goods, herded together their cattle, hogs, sheep, and chickens, and rushed into the fortification.

Western fortresses were interesting from the standpoint of structure; they doubtless constitute the frontier's architectural contribution. Usually there were several cabins enclosed in strong puncheon walls. These walls were constructed of heavy timbers, twelve or fourteen feet in length, standing on end and placed as close together as possible. These timbers were pegged to railings which, in turn, were fastened to posts planted within the enclosure. In this way the wall presented a solid front, exposing no openings through which attackers could insert pry poles or torches. The upright pieces were pegged with self-expanding pins which made them virtually impervious to external efforts at destruction.

Every fort had from one to four blockhouses, well constructed of carefully notched heavy timbers. Cracks were chinked with clay to prevent an enemy from inserting torches or shooting arrows into the rooms of the house. Blockhouses were taller than the stockade walls, and their upper stories extended from two to four feet over the wall of the fortress. This extension enabled riflemen within the house to protect the walls of the fort against a surprise rush from its attackers. Guards from these upper stories were able to watch for fires which might be started against the walls. Log sides of these guardhouses were pierced with portholes which closely resembled those of a medieval English castle. From these coigns of vantage in the taller structures, frontier riflemen broke up the sieges of Indian invaders and prevented further outrages against their homes.

Life inside the walls of the frontier forts was drab, . . . for people, cows, horses, hogs, dogs, sheep, and chickens were crowded into a small space. Human occupants were often not any too congenial, for though there were many families in the forts who were genteel in manner, there were as many others of the rough and tumble, uncouth frontier type. No provisions were made for separation of the sexes, and this led to difficulties. Sewage disposal was impossible, and fortress commons became veritable breeding places for disease. As filth and litter of the courts drained into the springs, it was not uncommon for large puddles of filthy water to collect in the depression of the yards. It was by rare good fortune that the pioneers escaped smallpox epidemics or other contagious diseases during their confinement within the fortresses. Perhaps the only redeeming feature of fort life was an abundance of fresh air and frequent sunny days. No medicines, except simple home remedies concocted from native herbs, were available. There were no physicians to administer to the frontier ailments, and lack of sanitation in the forts caused a great number of families to move out into the open country, since they preferred to stand their ground with treacherous Indian foes rather than endure the exposure and congestion of fort life.

With all the trials and tribulations characteristic of settling a new country, where both animal and human kingdoms conspired against them, the Kentucky pioneers were not without their lighter and happier moments. Distinction in social rank was the exception rather than the rule, for one man's rifle was as effective as another's, if both were good shots. . . . On the American frontier there were fewer women than men and . . . this condition naturally led to whirlwind courtships and hurried marriages. A single woman was a highly coveted prize by every bachelor, and no woman, regardless of her homeliness of appearance or state of decrepitude, was forced to remain single for any length of time. Widows hardly donned their weeds before being "spoken for."

When courtships resulted in marriage, the whole community prepared to celebrate, for frontier weddings were generally accompanied by as much ritual, pomp, and ceremony as a royal nuptial. The bridegroom's friends gathered at his father's house, and from there they proceeded to the home of the bride. The party timed itself to arrive at the scene of the wedding shortly before noon, for the wedding was allowed to interfere in no way with the customary infare following the ceremony. . . .

After the wedding ceremony, the bridal party went from the home of the bride to that of the groom, where the infare was served. A cavalcade set forth, the young males of which performed numerous antics to the amusement of their lady escorts. Often a young gallant would purposely frighten the horse of his partner to hear her scream and to give him opportunity to rush to her rescue. Occasionally, the wedding party was a victim of practical jokers who preceded it and threw obstacles in the way by cutting down trees or tying grapevines across the path. . . .

At the bridegroom's home . . . there were venison, beef, pork, and fowl. Vegetables, such as cabbage and potatoes, were present in abundance. There were biscuit and hoe-cakes, treacle (molasses), honey, sweetened corn meal mush, and milk. The "bottle" was passed freely, for the feast was a merry affair. Individuals traded witticisms; toasts were drunk to the newlyweds; jokes were told at the expense of the bridegroom; and, inevitably, prophecies of large families were made—prophecies which were soon fulfilled.

When the wedding banqueters had finished their revels at the festal board, the musicians, led always by the fiddler, struck up a merry tune for the dance, which lasted for hours. A unique dance was developed on the frontier in the well-known "square dance," and the Virginia reel was a favorite in some communities. Fiddlers confined their selections to favorite frontier "breakdown" tunes such as *Billy in the Low Ground, Fisher's Horn Pipe,* and *Barbara Allen,* tunes which still enliven dance parties of many Kentucky communities. In the midst of the evening's gaiety (about nine o'clock), a deputation of young ladies stole the bride away and put her to bed in the bridal chamber. This room was most often in the loft, which was reached by climbing a peg ladder to the hatch in the ceiling of the "big" room. When the ladies had finished their task, a group of young men stole the bridegroom away and saw that he was placed snugly beside his bride. Then the party continued until later in the evening, when the merrymakers returned to the kitchen for sustenance. In this lull the bride and bridegroom were not forgotten. A party climbed aloft with food and "Black Betty," the bottle, to minister to the hunger and thirst of the newlyweds.

Weddings were not always free of unfortunate consequences, for often there were those in the community who had been overlooked when the invitations were made. They felt that this snubbing justified revenge, and the favorite trick of the jealous ones was the shearing of tails, foretops, and manes of the wedding attendants' horses. Many were the revelers who returned home in an evil mood because some sneaking neighbor had disfigured their saddle horses.

Honeymoons were short, and bridal trips were unknown. The young couple proceeded to the business of making a home, if neither of the couple had been married before. Land was selected by the husband, often a part of his father's estate, and a site was cleared of trees and underbrush for the house which the neighbors assisted in building. Building a house of the ordinary log or rude frame type was a matter of only a few days' work; many times a log house was built in two days. When the house was finished, the young bride moved in, bringing with her, if she came of a thrifty family, a hope chest, containing some homespun clothing. She brought also a flax wheel, a cow and calf, and sometimes a brood mare. The young man supplied the land, the house, horses, hogs, chickens, and cows. Life was simple, expenses were few, and the young couple could, and seldom failed to, rear a large family. To the pioneer a large family was the symbol of domestic virtue; also, a family of several members could "roll logs," grow large crops, and better provide for themselves.

As there were no organized sports on the frontier, the chief diversions required individual prowess rather than concerted effort. . . . Frontiersmen enjoyed foot racing, wrestling (no holds barred), leap frog, kicking the hat (similar to modern soccer), fighting free-for-all, gambling, bragging, and marksmanship. Early Kentuckians were proud of their ability to shoot, and able marksmen were numerous. Frequent notices, appearing in the *Kentucky Gazette,* mentioned "squirrel shoots" in which individual riflemen killed hundreds. . . .

Sports along the river were cruder than those of the inland communities. River landings, like the one at Louisville, gave rise to a rip-roaring, notorious people, who called themselves "half horse, half alligators, tipped with snapping turtles." A man's prowess in individual contests was boasted of freely and as freely demonstrated. . . . Men worked hard, played hard, and fought hard. Justice was, to the average frontiersman, an individual matter to be speedily meted out to one's enemies.

There was in the Blue Grass, however, the beginning of a more complex type of society. Society here rapidly absorbed elements of eastern culture. The flow of immigrants to this section brought with it the Englishman's fondness for horses, which naturally led to an early introduction of horse racing. It is impossible to determine the date when horse racing began in Kentucky. Undoubtedly, the first hunters were fond of horses and horse racing; hence the beginning of the institution dates back to the first visits of the whites to the state. In 1789 the first race course was established at Lexington, and from this beginning, organized racing has become one of the three state symbols, and proud boasts—whiskey, pretty women, and fast horses.

Lexington, in the Blue Grass, was not without its gayer moments, for it was visited as early as 1797 by traveling entertainers and wax galleries. Later, a place of amusement and exhibition adjoining Coleman's Tavern was built by George Saunders. . . . There is an account of a theatrical performance held in the Fayette County courthouse as early as 1798, and in 1807 John Melish, a western traveler, spoke highly of the numerous forms of amusements in the West.

Not only did traveling theatrical companies venture into the unsettled country west of the mountains, but there came carnivals to display waxen figures portraying interesting scenes and incidents in literature and history. Washington at Valley Forge, as President, and in other scenes were favorites. Years later a wax favorite was the duel between Aaron Burr and Alexander Hamilton.

Forerunners of the circus were passing through the West as early as 1805. An entry in the Trustees' Book of Lexington records an ordinance prohibiting citizens of the town from keeping pet panthers. In the same entry the town fathers gave Thomas Arden permission to "shew his lyon" upon payment of $5.00.

No historian can estimate the amount of satisfaction and amusement afforded by the fiddle and the dulcimer in the pioneer settlements. Among Scotch, Irish, English, and, to some extent, German immigrants, this form of entertainment was most popular. These backwoodsmen amused themselves for long hours with dances and music of their own creation (based upon English and Scotch folk tunes). Lovers of folk music are deeply indebted to the frontiersmen of Kentucky for creating and preserving American folk tunes and customs. As central Kentucky became more densely settled, and as planters from the East moved into fine houses in the Blue Grass, the more polite music of the harpsichord in the drawing room forced the "breakdown" fiddlers, dulcimer players, and their folk music and songs back into the highland districts. Frontier Kentuckians found boisterous music and dancing an expression of their contacts with a hardy environment. Indian raids and other hardships would have been unbearable without this familiar form of relaxation.

With the transfer of other social institutions from Virginia, the church found its way across the mountains. It is interesting to note, however, that the denominations were slow in making their appearance in the Kentucky country. The Presbyterians were first to appear. This denomination, under the leadership of Father David Rice and two assistants, under very trying circumstances, organized Presbyterian assemblies. Following the example of the Presbyterians, the Methodist Society (so called until 1820), the Baptists, and the German Lutherans made their appearance. . . . Catholic missionaries exerted an early influence in the settlement of Kentucky. It is believed that Doctor Hart was (with the exception of Doctor Thomas Walker) the first physician to practice in the state. He and William Coomes, an Irishman, came out to the West to found a Catholic colony. Following these pioneers, a Catholic colony moved from Maryland to Kentucky in 1785. Almost the entire Catholic population of Kentucky immigrated from Saint Marys, Charles, and Prince George Counties, Maryland. This colony, which came in 1785, settled on Pottinger's Creek near the present city of Bardstown.

Protestant denominations were in the majority, and their ministers preached at large in an attempt to convert the masses to their particular faiths. By the time the state was admitted into the Union, the various Protestant ministers had become powerful community and political figures. . . .

It is not to be inferred that the pioneers were without a type of religious faith. Sons of the frontier were believers who applied a practical religious belief of foreordination to their daily lives. Nearly everyone believed that his fate was a sealed book and very philosophically accepted his hardships as God-sent. This belief is typical of people who live close to nature. Religion on the frontier was as rugged and hard as the virgin oak. A dying hunter believed that he could invoke Divine mercy as promptly with oaths as he could with pious supplications.

From 1783 to 1784 the population of Kentucky expanded from approximately 12,000 to 24,000. From October 1786 to May 1787 the Adjutant at Fort Harmar, opposite Marietta, Ohio, counted 177 flatboats with 2,700 persons aboard. In 1788 it was estimated that 10,000 persons had floated down the Ohio River. In 1790, according to the first United States Census, there were over 70,000 persons in the District of Kentucky.

A majority of the immigrants had come into the district principally from North Carolina, Virginia, Maryland, and Pennsylvania. Immigrants from North Carolina and southwestern Virginia came over the Wilderness Road, but those from Maryland and Pennsylvania came down the Ohio River. One traveler has left an account of a visit to Kentucky during the great immigration period, in which he tells of seeing the roads lined with families moving westward. He found many of the immigrants stranded by the roadside for the want of food and clothing, and in one case a family attempted to travel barefooted through the snow.

This wholesale immigration was not without due cause, for a popularization of the frontier, coupled with a scarcity of good land available to immigrants along the east coast, proved influential. In Virginia and North Carolina, Tories had been maltreated, and in most cases they were deprived of their lands and forced to move themselves and families elsewhere. Revolutionary soldiers of Virginia were unpaid, and the state used her western lands to settle these debts; this accounts for the great number of soldiers of the Revolution buried in Kentucky. Richard Henry Lee's explanation of the increase of immigrants was based on the argument that the rate of taxation in Virginia was so rigid that the average family found it difficult to live after paying its taxes. Perhaps Colonel Lee was partly right, but, after all, the basic reason for the general emigration from Virginia to the West was the decreasing fertility of Virginia's soil.

Unlike incoming settlers, eastbound travelers were unable to take advantage of the currents of the streams to transport them to their destination. Parties went overland from Kentucky to Virginia. However, many families never returned to Virginia to visit, once they moved westward. The principal travelers between the West and the East were members of the Virginia Assembly and itinerant preachers and a few private individuals who were willing to undergo the hardships of the trip. . . .

With an increase in population and an expansion of settled area, a division of the three counties of Kentucky became necessary. The first of the original trio to be divided was Jefferson County. In 1784 the eastern portion of this county formed Nelson County, and the next year Bourbon County was made from the northern portion of Fayette. In the same year (1785) Mercer and Madison Counties emerged from the northwestern portion of Lincoln.

(from *A History of Kentucky*)

FIDDLIN' "Right-hand man of the Devil was a fiddler," said the frontier preachers. The Reverend John Taylor, a shepherd of the regular Baptist faith, moved out to Kentucky from Virginia, and here he found that Moses Scott "a small man of stature" had preceded him and was a captain in the ranks of Diabolus. Brother Scott had shed his cloak of moral scruples and godliness which he had worn back in the Old Dominion as a communicant of the Presbyterian faith. He now labored in the new country with marked faithfulness for the cause of Beelzebub. Scott was known throughout his section of the West as a great fiddler, and was "fond of all amusements connected with that practice. It may generally be taken for granted," said Brother Taylor, "that . . . this Scott gloried in his native strength of intellect, and connected with his wit, capacitated him to make wickedness acceptable to men." He was indeed a sore trial to the Baptist brethren. The cause of the gospel made little headway so long as the profane Scott was able to "saw out" tunes, and more than once he had turned a Baptist "night meeting" into a rip-roaring dance-party. Even conversion to the faith did no good, because as soon as a gathering took place in the neighborhood, the Devil ordered his "airthly" captain to the front, and the preachers were left without hearers. Time and again this great fiddler led the "good" people from the altar, but Satan was not to succeed forever. By providential intercession, the abominable instrument of temptation, along with its owner's house perished in flames.

On the frontier where there were such numerous dignitaries as majors, colonels, doctors, preachers, professors, tavern-keepers, judges, sheriffs and governors, none ranked higher in popular affection than the fiddlers. From the beginning of the first settlement in the western wilderness, the fiddle took its place as an instrument necessary for entertainment. . . .

The West was not alone a land of "injun" fights, wars with Britishers, conspiracies with tricky Frenchmen, and disputes with stubborn Spaniards at New Orleans. There were lighter moments. "Yankee Doodle," in a letter to the editor of the *Spirit of the Times*, said that the frontiersmen showed their nobler points in their hunts, fish fries, barn dances, shuckings, raisings, housewarmings, infares, quiltings and in a thousand other pleasant ways. Fiddles in the hands of masters of the heel-bruising "hoe digs" were as much instruments of construction in the West as were axes which girdled trees, paddles which propelled boats, and rifles which fetched down meat and redskins. . . .

Tunes such as "Leather Britches," "Barbara Allen," "Old Joe Clark," "Fisherman's Hornpipe," "Fair Eleanor," "Skip--to-my-Lou," and hundreds of others—many of which have been forgotten—excited the boys and girls of the backwoods. There was no excuse like a square dance for a boy to do a little experimental hugging and kissing of the maidens in the neighborhood. Perhaps, by rare good fortune and malicious intent, a backwoods beau could confine his fondling activities to a single chosen one for a whole night of storming the puncheons. . . .

Fiddlers seldom hit the high mark as they did at weddings and infares. A wedding of any importance was the best excuse a frontier community ever had for dropping the lines and turning loose with all fours and forgetting its collective troubles. Fortunately several accounts of frontier nuptials have been preserved by participants in these joist-shivering debaucheries. Courtships were short, and directly to the point. The frontier swain had little or no time to go moon-gazing while holding the trembling hand of a reserved but interested female. Competition was fierce, and if he was to play a leading role in a wedding he had to speak up and get an answer with a minimum of lost motion. . . .

Housewarmings were generally more rampageous than were the cavortings on wedding nights. The floor of the "big room" was covered with a thick coat of bran which polished the puncheons, and by nine o'clock scuffing boots had worn the whole surface smooth and slick. Seldom did the merrymaking in a new house cease before the morning sun shone through the windows and doors. Unless the fiddlers were kept merrily drunk in these celebrations they were "sawed out" in relays, and the party ended. . . .

When winter days grew short and cold, women of the frontier called upon their nimble-fingered sisters to aid them in the endless task of preparing clothing and covering for numerous offspring. Pickings, cardings, knittings, cuttings and quiltings were held in order to complete quickly the chores of the household. Quilting frames suspended from the ceiling by four cords were as necessary equipment in the rooms of the frontier homes as were buckhorn rests for the family rifles, or ticking Yankee clocks. . . . At night, following these "female workings," the men gathered at the fireside, the quilting frame was hoisted to the ceiling, the cards, the wheel and the loom were shoved back, and the fiddler struck up a tune. These parties went into whirling "stomping" dances which kept up for the better part of long winter nights.

Fiddles whined merrily at barbecues and burgoo stewings. Barbecues always bore the stamp of politics. These took place during the heavy campaigning seasons for offices, or at Fourth of July celebrations. . . . Fiddlers were hired to entertain those who gathered for the purpose of being entertained and politically gulled. . . .

The fiddlin' West was a happy-go-lucky section. Numerous frolics, and a frolicsome nature, sometimes left unfavorable impressions upon serious-minded travelers who did not understand the music, and believed the square dance the work of maniacs. Such an observer was the sophisticated Fordham who wrote in his journal "a grand ball will be given tonight, to which I shall not go, as I do not choose the risk of being insulted by any vulgar Ohioans." However, this snob was impressed with the democracy of the frontier entertainments. On Christmas Day in the West he found the churchgoers attending sermons and prayers from breakfast to supper, another set cooking wild turkeys and dancing. The young men were "firing *feux de joi* almost all the preceding night." They explained that "we backwoodsmen never fire a gun loaded with *ball into* the town,– only from parts of it, out towards the woods." Fordham found a judge at the dance with his daughter, and other local dignitaries who were unconscious, as he thought, of their positions long enough to unbend and do a little fancy "cake walking" with the wild boys who were firing "*feux de joi. . . .*"

No frolic was ever complete without the fiddle or some other manly musical instrument such as the dulcimer, the banjo or the guitar. Fiddles were loaded with rattlesnake rattles. Frontiersmen claimed that the rattles from a snake added a weird, but delightful tone to a fiddle because they vibrated with the impact of the bow upon the strings. Many fiddlers never seemed to realize that the instrument on which they sawed out rasping tunes was capable of producing gentler music. They had learned to play by ear, and had never heard anything except the raucous and blaring music which they and their masters played. . . .

High public officials were not above playing the fiddle in true backwoods style, and most of them could send boisterous dancers through jigging sets in fine spirit. Judge George M. Bibb, Chief Justice of the Kentucky Court of Appeals, could rasp off any tune which had ever crossed the mountains. When N. M. Ludlow's theatrical company played at Frankfort, he and Sam Drake loafed with Judge Bibb and Humphrey Marshall. The judge would insist on Sam Drake playing the "new short tunes," and he would follow along as "second." During the winter sessions of the general assembly, Bibb would play for the legislative dances. He kept the lawmakers in a giddier whirl with his fiddle bow than he ever did with decisions from the high bench. Ludlow became very much enamored of a young Frankfort belle who was reputed to possess a fine estate, and during his company's appearance before the legislature he called upon her with serious intentions of courtship. When this adventurous caller reached the home of the young lady he was mortified to find her in the parlor with a fiddle stuck snugly under her dainty little chin playing a lusty Virginia breakdown. This sickened the theatrical caller, for like every other man on the frontier, he was convinced that the alabaster chin of a western belle should never clamp a fiddle butt. Women could play fiddles without bringing discredit to themselves if they held them well down in their arms as in the manner of an awkward young mother holding a bawling first-born, or they could perform a secondary function by beating straws. No self-respecting frontier woman could "chin" a fiddle and get along smoothly in polite society.

(from *The Rampaging Frontier*)

LIARS A Hoosier declared to a Yankee, "Why our soil is so rich—why, you never seed anything so tarnal rich in you life;

why, how d'ye suppose we make our candles, ha? We dip them in mud puddles." Making certain that he did not understate the virtues of Indiana bottom land, the native continued, "Well, old Yankee, I'll just tell you all about it. If a farmer in our country plants his ground in corn and takes first-rate care of it, he'll get a hundred bushels to the acre, if he takes middlin' care of it he'll get seventy-five bushels to the acre, and if he don't plant at all he'll get fifty. The beets grow so large that it takes three yokes of oxen to pull up a full-sized one, and it leaves a hole so large that I once knew a family of five children who all tumbled into one before it got filled up, and the earth caved in upon them and they perished. . . ."

Travelers through the West marveled at the tall talk of the natives, and some of them took their verbal jousting seriously. Even so accurate a scientist as was John J. Audubon sometimes talked in extraordinarily tall terms. He claimed that he had seen a rattlesnake jumping from limb to limb in a treetop in pursuit of a gray squirrel. In discussing certain aspects of wild life in western America before British scientists he was denounced as a highly imaginative creature whose word was of no value. "Sir," said one of the scientific Britons, "this is really too much even for us Englishmen to swallow, whose gullets are known to be the largest, the widest, and the most elastic in the world. This perhaps was a true statement regarding the Englishman's gullibility, but among the journals left by the Anglo-tourists there is a remarkable absence of the expansive story.

It remained for Americans like Flint and Baird to discover and record the charming essence of American exaggeration. Baird published what is doubtless the most understanding explanation of the elastic quality of accounts of actual situations. "The people," said he, "of the West live amidst the elements of greatness. The lofty mountains on each side of the valley, the extensive inland seas on the north, the immense forests and prairies, and mighty rivers"—all had an important bearing upon the western conversation. This traveler explained that "these external influences are not important of themselves, except to excite the imagination and to supply striking and appropriate similes, metaphors and language of wonder."

George D. Prentice of the Louisville *Journal* was a first-rate promoter of tall literature of the West. One of his best contributions was the famous story of John Champion's hogs. Prentice said that in the very early days many hogs were driven from Madison and other counties to the hill county of Estill in Kentucky. The people of Estill became much wrought up over the injustice being done them by their neighboring hog raisers and swore vengeance on the trespassers. The offended citizens of "bloody" Estill recalled that hogs had a great fear of bears and that if one of the varmints came near a drove of hogs the "porkers" left the woods immediately. Champion had a razorback sow which had mothered generation upon generation of longsnouted tushers, and she had made so many "mast" hunting trips to Estill that she had every cup oak tree located by memory. This hoary old female assumed the role of matriarch over the drove. She was caught up by the scheming and offended citizens of the neighborhood and sewn into a bear's skin. Prentice, in the style of a gloating native, said, "I tolled them up, and caught a good runner, and sewed her up in a bear's skin and turned her loose, when she ran after the rest, they flew from the supposed bear. The last that was seen of them was at Bassett's Creek, near forty miles from my house, only two being alive—one running from his fellow sewed in a bear's skin, and she was trying to catch the other—the rest were found dead in the road, having literally run themselves to death."

Animal activities formed the basis for an excellent frontier tale. The antics of the common gray squirrel are subjects for dozens of yarns. One of these is as old as the famous Long-Horned Elk story. In a mountain community a colony of gray squirrels became particularly pestiferous in their raiding of a cornfield. They were ingenious creatures, however, because they had learned that only one side of the river was safe. Unfortunately for them the cornfield was not on the safe side and in order to harvest their share of the crop they had to use considerable strategy in crossing the river. The owner of the cornfield said; "I once had a hundred-acre river-bottom farm as fine as a crow ever flew over. One year I raised an enormous crop of corn. After the corn had ripened, I noticed on the side adjoining the river that a large quantity had disappeared. So I concluded to watch and see who was stealing my corn. I concealed myself the following morning, early, in a small thicket that bordered the river. I had not been there long before I saw a number of objects start from the opposite bank. For a time I could not discover what they were, but as they came closer, I discovered they were squirrels—about a hundred of them—each seated on a shingle and propelling it with his tail. When they reached the bank they left their shingles in a little cove and went out in the field. Presently, each one returned with an ear of corn, and, mounting his shingle propelled it to the opposite side of the river. The next day, in company with a dozen expert wood choppers, we cut down every hollow tree on the side where the squirrels landed, and found four hundred barrels of corn, besides killing many of the squirrels, indeed we lived on squirrels for several weeks." This story belongs absolutely to the Ohio Valley frontier, but it has never been localized. Some versions have the squirrels crossing back and forth over the Ohio River from Kentucky to Indiana.

The modern age rang down the curtain on the tall story of the frontier, but the old age passed as it had endured—with vigor, imagination and downright cussedness.

(from *The Rampaging Frontier*)

WHERE THE LION ROARETH AND THE WANG-DOODLE MOURNETH FOR HIS FIRST-BORN A wrathful God kept vigilant watch over the western frontier. He was a God of tremendous force, who, in the highly descriptive words of one of his backwoods servants "toted thunder in his fist, and flung lightning from his fingers." These claims of divine power were not made, however, until the beginning of the nineteenth century. The earliest frontiersmen were too busily engaged with immediate worldly matters to "fall down before a wrathful God."

Settlers at Boonesboro in 1775 held a religious meeting, and later Baptists, of a dozen strains, Presbyterians, Catholics and Methodists swarmed over the mountains to evangelize a sinful western population. But the early frontier was not truly worshipful. It was not, on the other hand, godless for it did have a deep religious feeling, a feeling which was buried beneath a covering of determined individualism. Frontiersmen appealed to God, but their appeals were direct, in their own words, and on their own terms. Once the back country was free from Indian attacks, and Westerners saw their way clear to permanent settlement, their thoughts turned to more organized Christianity.

In 1800 the spirit of the Lord began to make itself manifest upon the frontier. Beginning in Kentucky, this wave of riotous religious revivals poured over the West with an increasing fury. At Russellville, and later at Cane Ridge, in Bourbon County, there was an outpouring of the spirit which outdid anything the frontier had ever seen. Hundreds of poor wretches fell in their tracks as though they had been fired upon by a legion of crack militiamen. The Lord indeed "toted thunder in his fist, and flung lightning from his fingers." The noise of these meetings was likened to the roar of the cataclysmic Niagara. "The vast sea of human beings seemed to be agitated as if by a storm," said one observer. "I counted seven ministers, all preaching at one time, some on stumps, others in wagons, and one, the Reverend William Burke, now of Cincinnati, was standing on a tree which had fallen and lodged against another. . . ."

Cane Ridge and its associated outpourings were the beginnings of the camp meeting in the West. From this great outpouring of the spirit, native converts flocked over the frontier to spread the gospel wholesale. Zealous preachers disavowed their former modes of life, and preached long sermons on the horrible examples of sinfulness which they had seen. One of these militant servants said of his conversion that while he was at Cane Ridge he became excited, but there "being a tavern a mile off, I concluded to go and get some brandy, and see if it would not strengthen my nerves. When I arrived I was disgusted with the sight that met my eyes. Here I saw about a hundred men engaged in drunken revelry, playing cards, trading horses, quarreling and fighting. After a time I got to the bar, and took a dram and left, feeling that I was as near hell as I wished to be, either in this world or the one to come." He became so excited and frightened that he got on his horse and started for home, but at the Blue Licks he was stricken down by the Lord, and not until he decided to become a Methodist circuit rider was his peace of mind restored.

Frontier preachers, for the most part, were curious individuals indeed. Many were "unlarnt" for they had been called to the service from between the handles of the plow or from other manual labor. They drifted through the West mounted on underfed nags, with their battered saddlebags thrown across the seat of worn saddles. In these bags they carried the trinity of the circuit: Bibles, hymnbooks and copies of *Paradise Lost*. It was not a serene heaven which these roving evangelists held out as a reward to their listeners, but rather it was a matter of avoiding eternal destruction in a sulphurous hell. John Milton's highly imaginative lines describing an infernal pit stimulated the faculties of the backwoods parsons and they drew with lusty strokes pictures of destruction which were awful to behold. They led their flocks away from hell, and seldom if ever to an attractive heaven. Celestial rewards for worldly righteousness were only incidental in the whole exhorting process. . . .

Ringing sermons peppered with flowery, but misused words,

and violent word pictures of helpless and tormented souls pouring into the scorching maws of hell fetched the mourners in droves. Smoke, fiery tongues of flame, and sulphurous smells swirled through the camp meetings like typhoons through coast cities of the Far East. Few self-conscious sinners could withstand the rampant persuasiveness of these "hell-fire" sermons. A preacher who could not bellow like a scrub bull in a canebrake during cocklebur season had little success in the pulpit. Many congregations demanded long-winded and noisy ministers. One board of stewards warned a minister, after he had used notes for his sermon, that "we don't want you—no 'Piscopalians here—no Prispatarians nother."

Denominational fights were often substituted for the theme of eternal perdition. Hardshell Baptists avowed that their faith was the only route to celestial happiness in the afterlife. "My text is this:" said an orthodox foot washer, "'On this rock will I build my church, an' the gates of hell shall not prevail against hit.' Now I'm goin' ter speak the truth terday no matter who hit hits. Ef they's ary man in this aujience thet don't agree with me, thet's his lookout, an' not mine. The question fur us to answer 'bout this tex' is this: Whut church war hit thet the Lord founded? Whut church is hit thet the gates of hell hain't agoin' ter prevail against? I'm agoin' ter answer thet question; an' I'll tell yer whut church hit is; hit's the Ole Hardshell Baptist Church; thet's whut it is." These "New Lights" of the cretaceous variety condemned every other faith to eternal destruction because they attempted to "go it dry. . . . "

Methodist and Baptist brethren sat up and argued by the hour about the saving grace of their respective faiths. The Methodists accused the Baptists of being "forty-gallon" Christians, while the Baptists chided the Wesleyan faith for its fear of water. Bascom, Axley, Mason, Finley, Cartwright, and, earlier, Asbury, challenged the free-will brethren to open debates. Some of these hoary servants even invaded meetings of opposing sects and took the ministers to task before their congregations on points of theology. Hard shells became numerous in the West, and from time to time they were called "New Lights," but it is doubtful if their doctrines were either new or enlightening. Like many of those vigilant champions of the Methodist cause they had a perfect disdain for "book larnin'" and depended upon the Lord to meet them at the pulpit with a sermon. . . .

Backwoods sermons were clumsy at best, and they generally took a practical turn. The ministers were keen judges of their audiences. Some of them started the services by making a whole series of announcements which had nothing to do with their sermons. A Hoosier divine announced from the sacred precincts of the pulpit that a neighbor "living down the lower end of Sugar Holler, would like to hear if anybody in this here settlement has heern or seed a stray crittur of hissin, as his hoss-beast, a three-year-ol' black gelding, come next spring, with a switch tail, but kinda eat off by his other colt, slipt his bridle on Hickry Ridge last big meetin', and he ain't heern or seen nothin' of him sense." This opened a general discussion and a brother allowed, "The crittur didn't come over here, as he'd been heern on or seed by some of us—but if anybody hears or sees sich a stray we'll put him up, and let neighbor Bushwack (evidently a made name) know about it."

Preachers of the back country had a way of sizing up their auditors and leading them one by one to a general conclusion by using their individual interests as illustrations. Brother Merry, seeing that he was about to lose his hearers asked in a loud tone, "My friends and neighbors don't you all shoot the rifle in this settlement?" He then fired away with a long discourse on shooting matches as a moral stigma upon the community. Spying a jug sitting in the audience he began another tirade by assailing the vices of drinking and swearing.

Before he had finished he stepped on every toe in the house. "You all know," said the overwrought parson, "how as we are going through a clearing we sometimes see a heap of ashes at an old log heap—and at first it all seems cold and dead, but when we stir it about with a piece of brush, or the end of a ramrod, up flashes sparks, and smoke, too, comes out. Well 'tis exactly so with our natural hearts. They conceal a thing like a shooting match, or when we get angry, or are determined to have money or a quarter section of land at all hazards." This was the final straw, and the native sons gave in rather than be pounded to death for the next six hours by a masterful orator who hit close home every time he introduced a new subject of attack.

If preachers took an informal attitude toward their duties as shepherds of wilderness sheep, the flock was even more informal. Homes were thrown open for gatherings, and the preachers accepted such accommodations as they found. Sometimes they were forced to pile up for the night with a dozen snoring fellow communicants in the same room. To add to the discomfort of the situation there were good sisters jammed in among the flock to give rise to suspicion. The preachers were shown the courtesy of being allowed to sleep on the bed, but to the man who occupied the middle there was ample reason to doubt the genuineness of the backwoods gesture of hospitality. Cord beds sagged, and it took all the fortitude of a strict ministerial disciplining to keep a brother in the good graces of his flock. . . .

Perhaps the most difficult part of preaching on the frontier was coming in contact with and dealing with drunken bullies who tried to break up meetings. Confusion was the rule in many of the meetings, and when this occurred, especially in the class meetings of the Methodist faith, outsiders became excited and caused trouble. Brother Mason said that in one of his class meetings a devout convert shouted, "Oh, there's a better time a coming, hallelujah!" This sounded off the charge, and in a few moments the room was a bedlam of shouting, screaming, jerking, crying and laughing Methodists. This uproar excited the dogs under the floor and they began barking and fighting, sounds of which could be heard for a mile. The "barbarians" in the community who were without the pale of the sect began to wonder just what went on in one of these services. Especially was it a matter of wonderment to husbands whose wives showed a fondness for attendance upon these thunderous upheavals. One deserted husband decided that the time had come when he should know in detail why his wife found these meetings so fascinating. He appeared before the door and demanded of the keeper that he be admitted, although he was not "a jiner." The doorkeeper refused to admit him unless he promised to become a communicant in the faith. "Well," snorted the excited benedict, "I won't jine your meetin', for I believe you're a set of howlin' hypocrites you won't do nohow; and you're enemies to the country and to our dimocratic government. Meetins' ought to be free anyhow. See here, friend, ain't you going to let me in?" "Can't do it; it's agin' the rules," pleaded the doorkeeper. The intruder declared that his wife was in there and that he was coming in if he had to trample on the dead body of the stubborn doorkeeper. These words set the two at each other and they fell into the midst of the shouting congregation in a bloody fist fight. Women jumped through the windows, old men rushed out the door, and strong-armed brethren tussled with the invader. Outsiders rushed in and took a free hand in the fight, and in short order the whole room was wrecked and the floor smeared with the blood of the fathers of the neighborhood.

Camp meetings were among the most attractive community affairs in many sections of the West. People came from miles around and stretched tents or built cabins and lived on the grounds for two weeks' to a month's time. A complete community was organized with the "tabernacle" as the center.

Here attendants combined gossiping, horse trading, courting and frolicking with shouting and "getting religion. . . ."

Camp meetings not only attracted the devout, but likewise the scoffers. Pastors occasionally had to take a hand in "roaching" disturbers. Peter Cartwright did not hesitate to take the erring brethren to physical task when they invaded his meetings. . . .

There were gradations of preachers. Those who could only get up steam and lay the groundwork for the "power" preachers were called *eight o'clocks,* but those gospel titans who could open up the horrors of hell, and display the wonders of heaven were reserved for the eleven-o'clock period. The *eleven o'clocks* were the ones who could paint the most horrible examples of human failures which the mind of man could conceive. One of these "Sampsons of the eleventh hour" pictured to a congregation a sinful and wayward man of the community returning to his home, and just as he started in the door the Lord struck him down. In a semi-conscious state he shouted, "Oh hell! hell! hell!" he then withered away while his religious brethren prayed over him, and then the light appeared. As he beheld the promised land within the "gates" he jumped to his feet and shouted in a strong voice, "Glory, glory, glory!" In a few moments this hardened sinner had been within both the gates of hell and heaven. Such illustrations were certain to bring a flock of mourners crowding to the bench. Sometimes, however, it brought some queer specimens to their feet and they frightened away those on the road to salvation. . . .

The West produced scores of preachers who took the gospel to the doors of the frontiersmen, and among this number there are many who stand out today in the history of American churches. None is more famous than Peter Cartwright who started his preaching career in western Kentucky and later moved into Illinois. He was a man of determination and daring. He asked no odds of anybody. If he found it necessary to take the situation in hand he never hesitated. On one occasion it was said that General Andrew Jackson entered the church where Brother Cartwright was holding forth with his usual vigor, and a cautious brother nudged him and whispered that Old Hickory had just come in "now be careful what you say." This just excited the circuit rider that much more. He astonished his hearers by shouting, "Who cares for General Jackson? He'll go to hell as quick as anybody, if he don't repent!" This boldness pleased Jackson and he was reputed to have said, "Sir, give me twenty thousand such men, and I'll whip the whole world, including the Devil. . . ."

There were more enterprising and sporting clergymen on the frontier than those preachers who used homely terms to catch the attention of backwoods listeners. As civilization moved deeper into the western country it became less attentive to spiritual matters than affairs of the world. The Reverend Blaney appreciating this fact fetched the sinners in when he advertised "The Reverend Mr. Blaney will preach next Sunday in Dempsey's Grove, at ten A.M., and at four o'clock P.M., Providence permitting. Between services, the preacher will run his sorrel mare, Julia, against any nag that can be trotted out in this region, for a purse of five hundred dollars!

"This had the desired effect. People flocked from all quarters, and the anxiety to see the singular preacher was even greater than the excitement following the challenge. He preached an elegant sermon in the morning, and after dinner he brought out his mare for the race. The purse was made up by five or six planters, and an opposing nag was produced. The preacher rode his little sorrel and won the day, amid deafening shouts, screams and yells of the delighted people. The congregation all remained for the afternoon service, and at its close, more than two hundred joined the church; some from the excitement, some from motives of sincerity, and some from the novelty of the thing, and some because the preacher—in the unrefined language of the country—was 'a damned good fellow!' " . . .

S. P. Avery has preserved the classic sermon which follows. Avery did not identify the source of this rousing exhortation, but it is expressive of the preaching of the West. Perhaps a sermon very similar to this one might be heard at any of the many Holiness meetings held in the backwoods today.

Where the Lion Roareth . . .

I am an unlarnt Hardshell Baptist preacher of whom you've no doubt hearn afore, and I now appear here to expound the scriptures and pint out the narrow way which leads from a vain world to the streets of Jaroosalem; and my tex' which I shall choose for the occasion is in the leds of the Bible, somewhar between Second Chronicills and the last chapter of Timothytitus; and when you find it, you'll find it in these words: "And they shall gnaw a file, and flee unto the mountains of Hepsidam, whar the lion roareth and the wang-doodle mourneth for his first-born."

Now, my brethering, as I have before told you, I am an oneddicated man, and know nothing about grammar talk and collidge high-falutin, but I am a plane unlarnt preacher of the Gospil, what's been foreordaned and called to prepare a pervarse generashun for the day of wrath—ah! "For they shall gnaw a file, and flee unto the mountains of Hepsidam, whar the lion roareth and the wang-doodle mourneth for his first-born—ah!"

My beloved brethering, the tex' says they shall gnaw a file. It does not say they may, but shall. Now, there is more than one kind of file. There's the hand-saw file, the rat-tail file, the single file, the double file and profile; but the kind spoken of here isn't one of them kind nayther, bekaws it's a figger of speech, and means going it alone and getting ukered, "for they shall gnaw a file, and flee unto the mountains of Hepsidam, whar the lion roareth and the wang-doodle mourneth for its first-born—ah!"

And now there be some here with fine close on thar backs, brass rings on thar fingers, and lard on thar har, what goes it while they're yung; and thar be others here what, as long as thar constitooshins and forty-cent whisky last, goes it blind. Thar be sisters here what, when they gets sixteen years old, bust thar tiller-ropes and goes it with a rush. But I say, my dear brethering, take care you don't find, when Gabriel blows his last trump, your hands played out, and you've got ukered—ah! "For they shall gnaw a file, an flee unto the mountains of Hepsidam, whar the lion roareth and the wang-doodle mourneth for his first-born."

Now, my brethering, "they shall flee unto the mountains of Hepsidam," but thar's more dams than Hepsidam. Thar's Rotterdam, Haddam, Amsterdam, and "Don't-care-a-dam"—the last of which, my brethering, is the worst of all, and reminds me of a sirkumstance I onst knowed in the state of Illenoy. There was a man what built him a mill on the north fork of Ager Crick, and it was a good mill and ground a sight of grain; but the man what built it was a miserable sinner, and never give anything to the church; and, my dear brethering, one night there came a dreadful storm of wind and rain, and the mountains of the great deep was broke up, and the waters rushed down and swept that man's milldam to kingdom cum, and when he woke up he found that he wasn't worth a dam—ah! "For they shall gnaw a file, and flee unto the mountains of Hepsidam, whar the lion roareth and the wang-doodle mourneth for his first-born—ah!"

Now, "What the lion roareth and the wang-doodle mourneth for his first-born—ah!" This part of my tex', my beseaching brethering, is not to be taken as it says. It don't mean the howling wilderness, what John the Hardshell Baptist fed on locusts and wild asses, but it means, my brethering, the city of New Y'Orleans, the mother of harlots and hard lots, whar corn is wuth six bits a bushel one day and nary a red the nex'; whar niggers are as thick as black bugs in spiled bacon ham, and gamblers, thieves, and pickpockets goes skiting about the streets like weasels in a barnyard; whar honest men are scarcer than hen's teeth; and whar a strange woman once took in your beluved teacher, and bamboozled him out of two hundred and twenty-seven dollars in the twinkling of a sheep's tail; but she can't do it again! Hallelujah—ah! "For they shall gnaw a file, and flee unto the mountains of Hepsidam, whar the lion roareth and the wang-doodle mourneth for his first-born—ah!"

My brethering, I am the captain of that flatboat you see tied up thar, and have got aboard of her flour, bacon, taters, and as good Monongahela whisky as ever was drunk, and am mighty apt to get a big price for them all; but what, my dear brethering, would it all be wuth if I hadn't got religion? Thar's nothing like religion, my brethering; it's better nor silver or gold gimcracks; and you can no more get to heaven without it than a jay-bird can fly without a tail—ah! Thank the Lord! I'm an oneddicated man, my brethering; but I've sarched the Scripters from Dan to Beersheba, and found Zion right side up, and hardshell religion the best kind of religion—ah! 'Tis not like the Methodists, what specks to get to heaven by hollerin' hell-fire; nor like the Universalists, that get on the broad gage and goes the hull hog—ah; nor like the Yewnited Brethering, that takes each other by the slack of thar breeches and hists themselves in; nor like the Katherliks, that buys threw tickets from their priests; but it may be likened unto a man what has to cross the river—ah!—and the ferryboat was gone; so he tucked up his breeches and waded acrost—ah! "For they shall gnaw a file, and flee unto the mountains of Hepsidam, whar the lion roareth and the wang-doodle mourneth for his first-born!"

Pass the hat, Brother Flint, and let every Hardshell Baptist shell out.

(from *The Rampaging Frontier*)

THE SIGN OF THE COCKPIT There is an old pastime in the Bluegrass which has been practiced from the time the first settlement was made. Cooped up in many of the panniers which rocked back and forth from the sides of pack horses were gamecocks and hens. Old Virginia bloodstock was being brought across the mountains to entertain the Kentuckians in their moments of relaxation from the fight against the raw frontier environment. Since "cocking" is a bloody business, it made a ready appeal to the vigorous frontiersman. Likewise its gory aspects have caused it to be under a ban from certain elements in the Bluegrass. Its written history in the Kentucky River valley is exceedingly spotted. Once and awhile a traveler referred to it or a sporting magazine carried an article in the abstract about this sport. Frequently there were articles about cocking in the *Turf Register,* but these were written about procedure in breeding and training rather than as descriptive of the contemporary state of the art. Always, it seems, cocking has been an illicit consort of horse breeding and racing. In 1845 the sport was well developed in Bluegrass Kentucky. William Porter included a note in his miscellaneous column in the *Spirit of the Times.* He wrote: "Yesterday, and today were 'some' at Memphis, Tennessee. Shy and Means of Kentucky and Colonel Abingdon of Tennessee, were each to show twenty-one cocks [a main], and $100 on each fight. If 'General Jim' heels for Old Kentuck, I should like to back him for a small smile."

Today there are many cockfighters in Bluegrass Kentucky. They do not shout their identity from housetops, but within the clan this fact is well known. In the winter and early spring, the sport goes on with a boom. Down a lonesome tree-lined country lane, a highway signal lamp burns in a farm gateway. This is the sign of the cockpit, and in the community, perhaps at the top of the nearest hill, a yellow light flickers dimly through the chinked cracks of an innocent-appearing tobacco barn. The visitor pulls his automobile up in line with the others parked in a semicircle. A group of men speaking in subdued tones stands about the door. Just inside the vestibule a ticket salesman asks a dollar for admission to the pit. Once inside the door, the visitor sees before him a strange row of latticework cages extending almost up to the ceiling across one end of the barn. In a hasty glance, these clumsily constructed enclosures have somewhat an Oriental appearance. From deep in the block of cages comes a lusty crow from a long-legged cock who is ready for the fight before him. In front of the coops are tables and racks where the cocks are prepared for the pit. A sweating man works away vigorously with a sharp pocketknife, fitting collars to the stubby shanks of a rooster. Another holds the bird's feet in position to receive the gaffs. These are long slender steel instruments with needle-sharp points. The collars of the shanks are thrust down tightly over the collars of the muted natural spurs and are tied on with leather thongs. A few minutes later the cock will be placed in the ring to cut, hack, and pick at an opponent until one or both of them are dead. One of the cocks jumps up; a leg flashes past his opponent; the gaff goes home; and his victim is "rattled." A bead of telltale blood bubbles on the end of the injured cock's beak, and the referee shouts "handle your birds" to the managers. The injured cock is gathered up in the handler's arms. The handler places the bird's head in his mouth and draws off the strangling ooze of blood. Next he bites the comb and blows on its back. Again the cocks are in the ring to fight until one or the other is dead or victorious.

Around the ring, loud jovial betters shout "two on the red," "five on the black," or banter with robust badinage, reflecting upon the fighting capacities of the combatants in the ring. A wave, a nod, a wink, raised fingers make and accept bets. There is no centralized betting organization. A bet is a gentleman's obligation, and the loser is obligated to hunt up the winner and pay off.

Two cocks are released in the ring, and a wave of excitement runs through the crowd. Enthusiastic cockers crowd up to the ringside and talk in knowing professional lingo about the fight in process. Back in the crowd docile farm women nurse babes at breast and watch every hack and pick made by the blood-thirsty gamecocks. A bird is down; his wings and legs give one ghastly shudder and then quiver to a dead stop. He is dead; a gaff has touched a vital spot. But before the opposing cock can claim the victory, he has to hack or pick at the dead bird once within twenty minutes or the fight is a draw.

Cockfighting has given rise to a strange lingo. A "dunghill" fowl is a coward who flies the pit and runs from a fight. His doom is sealed because his owner wrings his neck in disgust. A "huckster" is a sharp chicken trader, dealing usually in mongrel stock. Then there are the descriptive fighting qualities of cocks. They are "game," "close hitters," "bloody heelers," "ready fighters" with "good mouths," and are "quick to come to point." For months before a cock is pitted in combat he goes through an intricate series of maneuvers. He is "flirted," or tossed into the air, to develop his wings. He is held by his thighs and "fluttered" to strengthen his legs and wings. Before a fight the cocks are "dried out" by careful rationing of water; and when the season is over they are "put on the walks" to run wild in natural surroundings. Under a year of age, cocks are stags. They are in the height of fighting form if they live to be three; and at four they are ready for retirement. Cocks are fought in "hacks" or in single fights, in "mains" of fifteen to twenty-one cocks of one owner pitted against a similar number of another. They are fought in tournaments and derbies on terms agreed to between owners.

Cockfighting is sometimes called the poor man's sport in the

Bluegrass, but actually many of its most ardent patrons are wealthy people. The clan is tightlipped where the sport is in danger of being prohibited. It is quite possible that hundreds of people have lived long lives in the Bluegrass without ever having heard of the cockpits in the region or having seen a cockfight. Yet along a country road a game cock flies across the road ahead of a speeding automobile, and a flock of timid hens take cover from the approaching machine under the tall grass in the ditch. Sometimes it has occurred that an enthusiastic cocker's family has not even known of his interest. An old-time fighter in the Bluegrass stood with one foot on the side of the ring and laughed heartily at the mess his wife got into with their preacher. She had cooked one of his gamecocks for dinner, but it had been rubbed with oil of peppermint, and the meat was ruined. It struck the old-timer as high comedy to see the preacher being offered gamecock for dinner.

This silent sport, hidden away behind the beckoning highway signal flare and the chinked walls of a tobacco barn with its improvised amphitheater about the pits, goes on with vigorous support. To stir up the Humane Society and the women's clubs would be bad business. Yet the Bluegrass Kentuckian of today has not undergone a tremendous change from the day when the cantankerous English travelers in the region spent much of their time reading the vigorous announcements of sport-to-be from the handbills tacked to tavern walls.

(from *The Kentucky*)

TOLLGATE RIDERS Roads [in Kentucky] were poor, and users felt they could scarcely get their wagons and teams from Glensborough to Lawrenceburg, for instance, without being robbed by the tollkeepers. Money was scarce . . . in 1890 . . .

There was an old custom, which was really a bit of common law, that a man going to mill in some communities could pass the "gates" free. Anderson County farmers begin riding to

Lawrenceburg astride bags of bran. But even this was no answer to the oppression of grasping companies. Too, it did something to Kentucky pride to sit astride a bag of bran and know that it was a lie done up in cotton twill. Why not tear down the gates and be done with hypocrisy? What was the matter with the legislature? The days of Jacksonian frowning upon public internal improvement were past. The people needed and were going to have free roads. They wanted to drive out the annoying gates and gatekeepers and go to market like decent free men. Tollkeepers themselves aroused animosity, for many of them had come into their jobs because of their earlier connection with the roads. For the most part they were rock pounding "turnpike" Irish who had been elevated to the position of toll collectors. . . . Kentuckians had always been independent, proud people and if they were stimulated to action they generally got what they wanted. Farmers of Washington and Anderson counties were no exception to the rule. They had made up their minds that the gates were coming down, and the best way to bring them down permanently was to intimidate the gatekeepers.

Armed and masked men rode out of Washington County early in April, 1897, and forced frightened gatekeepers to chop their pikes (poles) into pieces. Keepers were warned not to bar the roads again, and if the pikes were restored there would be urgent need for buggy whips tapered off with rawhide crackers, warm buckets of tar, and goose-feather pillows.

Vigorous resistance to the toll roads spread like wildfire. While enraged Washington County yeomen destroyed gates and issued dire warnings to shivering Irish tollkeepers, Anderson County raiders stormed against the lordly keepers of the pikes. They masked their faces, mounted themselves on their best horses, and galloped up to gatehouses cursing the attendants. They forced shivering Irishmen to crawl out of bed, come out on brisk April nights, and to destroy the gates under the drawn guns of their tormentors. County officials were as badly frightened as were the benighted toll collectors. When men rode with their faces masked, sheriffs and constables were at a loss to know how to stop the marauders. . . . Once the raids had begun, gates were destroyed over a wide area. In Mercer County people were likewise agitated over the shameless profiteering of the road companies. They were served poor roads in return for high tolls. Now was the time to strike! On the night of April 4, 1897, night riders raided the Cornishville gatehouse. The gatekeeper was the grizzled Irishman Cal Atkinson, who attempted to defend his besieged family with his shotgun. The raiders were too numerous for the stubborn Cal, and within a few moments his house was surrounded. There were raiders hammering away at both front and back doors, and when they met with resistance the mob became excited. Cries for drastic action were loud, and one trigger-happy raider emptied his shotgun into the Irishman's face. The gang rushed on and left their victim, with sight in one eye destroyed, to suffer the agony of death in the arms of a frantic wife.

News of the Cornishville raid traveled fast. Gatekeepers all over central and northern Kentucky grew panicky lest they should be the next victims. One tollkeeper's wife said that she couldn't go to sleep at night for fear the raiders would come and burn the house over their heads and shoot her husband. This same wife cried out in her anguish that "lawless men seem desirous of overturning all law and order. We do not know what minute our property will be destroyed and we live in dread every hour of the day and night. I do not know what can be done, for our relief, but it seems to me the legislature at Frankfort ought to take some action whereby the governor could legally investigate the outrages against the citizens of the commonwealth and bring them to just punishment." The assembly in 1898 did pass an anti-tollgate raider law, but the raiders had to be caught first, and on this point the law was silent. Every morning newspapers published stories of new raids; at Maysville, Georgetown, and Owingsville the raiders were busy. . . .

Owners of the roads and gates swore they would keep them open at all costs. This was an idle boast, however, for ninety-one raiders galloped across the Kentucky River and, just beyond the famous old Wernwag Bridge at Camp Nelson, made keeper Whitaker fetch out his ax and slash his pole into the customary pile of "stovewood." That same night other raiders made half-naked gatekeepers hack down several gates on the Elkhorn Creek in Scott County. Two widows were deprived of their means of livelihood, and several prominent neighbors were accused of the crime, but the court took no action. A hundred men stormed into Lancaster on the night of May 29 and destroyed four gates. They left instructions that no more toll was to be collected, and they were positive in their note scribbled on dirty, cheap school tablet paper that "they meant what they said."

Other gatekeepers were warned by letters and bunches of switches thrown on their porches that tollgates would no longer be tolerated. One ingenious agitator notified the "Toll Gate Keepers of Garrard County, Kentucky" that their days were numbered. A local detective named Welch was advised to make his estate over to an undertaker. Officials of the road were threatened with whippings, and a raid over the whole county was promised. Positive and picturesque notes asserted:

NOTICE TO GATEKEEPER

> We ast you not to collect no more tole, you must
> Not collect one cent if you do we are Going to Destroy
> your House with fire are Denamite So you must Not
> collect No more tole at all. We don't want to do this but
> we want a Free Road are agoing to have it, if we have
> to kill and burn up everything. Collect no more tole
> we mean what we say, so Fair warning to you.

A distraught people was on the warpath, and frequent raids seemed to indicate that the irate authors of the threatening notes did mean what they said. A fellow raider wrote the hard-boiled workhouse supervisor, Thomas Durr, of Mercer County, a pointed note: "Thomas Durr and William Schuman: We don't want no more toll collected. If you collect anymore will hang you we will wait on you in ten days. If you do not quit collecting toll, then hang"—TOLLGATE RAIDERS.

Durr, however, was a stubborn Irishman and refused to surrender his lucrative post to the raiders, thus making a second warning necessary. This time the appeal was even more direct and specific: "To the Honorable Thomas Durr: We don't want no more toll collected here. If you do (*sic*) look out for your neck, the board must take heed to this warning"—MERCER COUNTY REGULATORS.

These were ominous warnings, warnings that even Thomas Durr could understand. He was reasonably certain that he would be killed if he didn't give up his job as toll collector. Directors of the road were less frightened than Thomas Durr and they hired two tramp printers, Dick White and Jim Saunders, of Lexington to keep watch over the gate. Raiders had destroyed the gatehouse, so a whiskey barrel was planted on each side of the road and a pole rested across the heads. The bold printers consented only to collect toll in the daylight.

At Harrodsburg the grand jury failed to make headway in its indictments. Prospective witnesses fled the county and the state, and refused to be brought back. No one would admit that he knew who the raiders were; in fact, members of the grand jury might have been raiders for all the court knew. Crafty county officials refused to pay guards for their services at the gates, and men were unwilling to stand guard and take chances of being injured without pay. Courts became useless instruments of protection; even some lawyers and judges believed the anti-tollgate raiders' law, passed by a frantic legislature, might be declared unconstitutional.

Active leadership in Kentucky faltered in those drab years 1880-1908. It failed largely because a baggy-pants political control throttled everything that even smelled of progress, and because this was the age in which the lost generation born in the Civil War came to maturity. A wave of conservatism and fear swept the state. Kentuckians shied away from taxation, on the one hand, and were ignorant of the advantages of good roads, on the other. Nevertheless, a faint impulse of progress stirred, and some people responded blindly to demands for better roads.

A better way to serve the people and to restore peace would be for the state to buy the tollgates and make the roads free. Permit a man to go to town with his wagon load of corn, or drive his buggy courting, or ride his horse where he pleased. Snatch the Kentucky highways free from the shrewd, scheming rascals who held the people in slavery to the pike poll and gatehouse. The county should buy the roads from the private companies, and where they could not buy them, build competing roads that would break the oppressors. For instance, the county could buy, at a reasonable price, the roads of old Billy Baldwin, "the turnpike king," from Maysville, or build "shun-pikes" and bankrupt him. County officials, like legislators, were slow to see the point, but before another year of raiding passed the roads in much of Kentucky were freed.

Like most militant and highhanded direct reforms, the misguided messengers of progress before the tollgates never stopped to think through their demands for free and better roads. This would mean new taxes and new political manipulations and self-seeking. A public roads authority functioning under the domination of courthouse rings produced luscious political plums, but slender results on the roads themselves. Thus it was, in a moment of violence, that Kentucky was directed along a new path of progress clogged by the usual political shackles.

(from *Kentucky: Land of Contrast*)

THE PEN OF THE COUNTRY EDITOR Every Southern paper reflected the personality of its editor. The term "personal journalism" was most accurately used when applied to the weekly press. Here the editor virtually was the paper. He formulated the policy of his paper, wrote editorials and news stories, edited locals, knew his readers personally, set type, ran the press, mailed the papers and smoothed over the ruffled feelings of irate subscribers. It was he who made financial arrangements for the publication of the paper, and it was his back that went bare if it was not a success. It was hard for the subscribers to think of the paper apart from the personality of its publisher. In a vast majority of cases it was not so much a matter of finding out what the Winston County (Mississippi) *Journal*, the Woodford (Kentucky) *Sun*, or the Sparta (Georgia) *Ishmaelite* said on an issue as it was to know what Will C. Hight, Dan Bowmar and Sidney Lewis thought. Mister Will, Mister Dan and Mister Sidney were important people in their communities.

To the editors their papers were vital things. They regarded every issue to come as a son after an unbroken sequence of daughters. Files might be preserved in rolls of tattered paper stuffed atop cabinets or packed away in the basement to catch soot and ashes next to the furnace, but the next issue was always a thing of promise. It came from the press a bright, fresh sheet smelling of green ink and was sent on its way to assure everyday Southerners that they were somebody. Their names were in print—and printer's ink gave them a coveted dignity. The editor's political and personal views were expressed in both editorial and news items. They provided the common man with a pattern by which he could think about politics and political personalities. They gave him an insight into social and economic problems which affected his daily life. It made little difference whether the country paper was ultimately shredded into bits by children with scissors, pasted on cabin walls as decoration and insulation or put to a humbler and less gracious end; it was respected for its services.

Though an active Southern press existed in 1865, never did

the profession of editor seem more appealing than in the latter quarter of the nineteenth century. Publishing ranked along with storekeeping and mill management as desirable professions in the New South. Perhaps no other calling offered so much prestige and community honor in so short a time as did editorship. An ambitious young man possessing a common-school education, some gumption, imagination, business ability and mechanical sense could establish himself as a solid figure in a remarkably brief time. Many country editors lacked high-school educations, and few had been to college. Their writing frequently reflected hard common sense, but little grammar and cultivated style and only a sketchy knowledge of spelling and sentence structure.

Launching a weekly paper was a proud moment in an editor's life. When enough news was gathered to assemble at least two pages of print, the new editor saluted his prospective subscribers. He usually assured them that his paper would be safe politically, that it would boost its community, seek to attract desirable immigrants into the county, encourage local progress and attempt to correct certain faults of governmental administration. Important as these advance promises were, the selection of a suitable slogan for the masthead was perhaps just as essential. The new paper had to sail under a proud slogan. Many sentiments could be expressed—among them, "A Friend of Every Man, Woman and Child Who Toils for a Living"; "To Tell the Truth, Obey the Law, and Make Money"; "Talk for Home, Work for Home and Fight for Home"; and "Hew to the Line, Let the Chips Fall Where They May."

Just as no extensive amount of education was necessary in the editing of a weekly, so also only a limited amount of mechanical training and equipment was needed. It was possible to compose and print a paper in a remarkably small building space. A single room was frequently adequate housing. . . .

Once an editor acquired materials and established a paper, he assumed certain responsibilities. First, he had to protect his good name if his subscribers were to respect it. He inherited from his ante-bellum forebears an extremely delicate sense of honor, and it was not at all unusual for him to become involved in fist fights with subscribers and fellow editors. . . .

Much editorial battling resulted from a rural and frontier sensitiveness, but some of it was due to the clumsy, blunt expression and tactlessness of many half-educated editors, who were unable to campaign for an idea without writing personal attacks on opponents. They pitched headlong into battle, shouting bold and defiant words which invited trouble. Although there were, of course, editors who engaged in good-natured arguments with neighboring publishers just for the sake of enlivening their columns, such urbanity was rare.

Readers were at least as bad as the editors. People today can hardly realize how sensitive the old-time subscriber was. News stories and notices which seem perfectly innocuous now touched off emotional storms when they first appeared. If an editor confused a name, or located a tenant farmer on the wrong place, he was told to correct the error. Many a disgruntled reader stalked into the office and canceled his order for the paper on the spot. Occasionally an unreasonable subscriber demanded that the editor finish out his subscription period by sending a roll of blank paper each week.

When a paper was safely started and the new editor had time to feel at home with it, he gave serious attention to the objectives of the local region. The editor became the official community puffer and booster. His town and county were usually supreme in promise if not in progress. The land was fertile, the climate healthy and pleasant, churches were numerous and business on Main Street was booming, or would boom with some publicity.

This last note brought the editor around to the vital subject of advertising. Before a mercantile establishment could succeed it had to advertise its business, and only local newspapers offered this service. Here editors faced a difficult task. They had to destroy the provincial attitude that all the prospective customers needed to know was that stores existed—and this they knew already. Village-minded merchants believed there was no need to advertise staple merchandise. In consequence, literally thousands of stories were published to illustrate the benefit of advertising. . . .

Both advertising and subscription rates were low. In the nineteenth century space averaged about twenty cents a column-inch, and thirty-five to forty cents for a double-column spread. Legal notices were fifteen cents a line, obituaries five cents a line and all other notices ten cents. Page advertisements were sold at thirty to one hundred dollars a page. These advertisements, however, were negotiated for on a special arrangement between the advertiser and the editor. It is doubtful that many papers had what is known to modern journalism as a "rate card." It would be practically impossible by a space analysis to arrive at anything like an accurate estimate of what advertising income the average country weekly received. Both the amount and the rate of advertising varied according to the size of the towns in which the papers were published and the spirit of rivalry which existed among merchants. Usually, before 1900, ads of foreign merchandise far outmeasured those of home products. Many small-town stores never bought an inch of advertising space.

It was this failure of merchants and business and professional men to support their local papers that caused friction between editors and their communities. Each week a paper was called on to publicize not merely the community but individual citizens as well. In provincial neighborhoods where social intercourse was either limited in scope or was stratified by a contradictory and emotional caste system, the editorial task was complicated. Any individual's success was measured somewhat by the amount of personal publicity which appeared in the paper. Publicity seekers were continually pestering editors for more, whether they deserved it or not. One ingenious publisher developed a scale of prices for delicate personal-vanity services. For bragging in public about a successful local citizen who was in fact as lazy as an army mule, $2.75; referring to a deceased neighbor as a man mourned by the whole community when actually only the poker players missed him, $20; writing delicately of a "gallivanting female" as an estimable lady whom it was a pleasure to meet, when it was a known fact that every merchant in town had rather see the devil (horns, tail and all) coming into his store than she, $10; calling an ordinary pulpit pounder an eminent divine, $60; and sending a hardened sinner off to the pearly gates with poetry, $5. Yet, aggravating as it was, this vanity factor helped make the country paper a popular institution.

Most editors accepted the responsibility of exposing frauds. Just as circus people uttered the famous cry "hey, Rube" when they were in danger, so the editors printed the warning phrase, "Pass Him Around!" Unfair and fraudulent advertisers were "passed around" through the exchanges; counterfeiters, board-bill jumpers, fake salesmen, labor agents, bogus preachers, quack doctors, kerosene safety salesmen and questionable itinerant females felt the sting of widespread editorial warnings. . . .

The editor was not only the plumed knight driving out the cheating knaves who preyed on his people but also the critic rebuking the slovenly ways of the local people. He was ready to rap knuckles for shiftlessness as well as vice. . . .

Editors generally worked with small staffs. They ranged from one man to a crew of half a dozen. Tramp printers were both numerous and unpredictable. They appeared from nowhere and disappeared when they felt like it. There was a tacit understanding that every publisher would give them either work or a small sum of money. They expected to have the shops left open for them to sleep in at night. Sometimes these "birds of flight" remained only long enough to get out an issue of the paper, and sometimes they stayed for several months. . . .

Besides the typesetter there were the devil, the pressman and the inevitable handyman. It is ironical that the army of brawny Negroes who pulled the levers of old hand presses or turned the cranks on cylinder presses, folded papers and made each issue possible were illiterate almost to a man. Devils learned the art as well as the bad habits of the tramp printers. They were general apprentices, expected to master both the mechanical and editorial sides of publishing, and were often sons following in their fathers' footsteps. Thus before schools of journalism were dreamed of, country shops were schooling their own people. Many editors now publishing Southern weeklies came up through an apprenticeship in their own shops.

The shops themselves were interesting. . . . Often there was simply a crude pine table which groaned under its load of newspapers, with just barely enough cleared space on one corner to put a half sheet of note paper. Along the walls stood at least one ramshackle cast-off cabinet crammed with odd books, pieces of equipment and dog-eared files. There was the inevitable stool, which symbolized the ivory tower from which the editor viewed the world. Papers were stacked everywhere, and every pigeonhole and crack bulged with files. Walls were lined with handbills, calendars, maps; and file hooks gave way under their burdens of notes and bills. There was a stove, and always a filthy wash pan and slick, greasy towel. To all this confusion was added the rather pleasing smell of printer's ink.

Just as the country store was a favorite loafing place, the country newspaper office was a gathering place for villagers. The editor of the Marietta (Georgia) *Journal* listed ten plagues of the newspaper office, which were loafing bores, poets, cranks, rats, cockroaches, typographical errors, exchange files, book canvassers, delinquent subscribers and the man who knows better than the editor how to run the paper.

Among the plagues perhaps the greatest were the poets. They blossomed at all seasons of the year. Spring, summer, fall and winter, the muse was active. There were poets of incurable love and of perpetual sorrow. A few sentimental souls turned to the classics for inspiration, while others preferred the more romantic periods of chivalry. Lycurgus Barrett of the Hartford *Herald* found that he had lost the manuscript of an original poem entitled "The Tattooed Knight." "The verses," he said, "abounded in pointed satire and overwhelming humor, were exceedingly Hudibrastic in spirit." The Dickson County (Tennessee) *Press* spurred the poets on to the fray in a long editorial on the spirit of spring by saying that this was the season for the local Shakespeares to sound their lutes. "Write only on one side of your paper, send the manuscript to us at once, by special messenger, as the mails are too untrustworthy to entrust such a document with, and upon receipt of it we'll—chuck it into the waste basket." W. P. Walton of the *Interior Journal* dealt literature in Lincoln County, Kentucky, an irretrievable blow. In his schedule of advertising rates he served notice that a charge of one dollar per word, payable in gold before the poem was written, would be made for poetry.

Another of the Marietta *Journal's* plagued taxed the patience of all editors. This was the delinquent subscriber. . . . Often subscriptions made up the smallest part of a paper's earnings but sometimes they provided the margin between profit and bankruptcy. Patrons were indifferent about paying the editor and cash was difficult to collect. Always the local publisher appeared hard pressed for money and he used much of his own advertising space to scold delinquents. He begged for fire and stovewood, meat, potatoes, grain or anything else which could be sold or eaten. Often a subscriber paid over produce worth far more than the subscription price for the paper.

Publishing a weekly was never a lucrative profession. An editor could usually get a respectable living but little cash. It was said that when somebody tried to rob editor Willingham of the Georgia *Free Press* in 1881 he was much flattered by the compliment. The Marietta *Journal* thought "the fellow was evidently a stranger, or he would have never attempted to rob a newspaper man. We have heard of people robbing graves, but he who would attempt to rob a Georgia editor at once establishes his claim to a front room in the new insane asylum no matter where it is built."

The poor income placed a severe economic strain upon Southern publishers. Most of them seem to have been family men, and their broods demanded a reasonable amount of support. This situation forced many into other businesses as sidelines, or into politics. . . .

Southern editors could take much pride in their accomplishments. Many of them speeded up industrialization in their communities. They fought for improved farming conditions, better roads and schools and a happier way of life. They passionately advocated the building of railroads and were down to welcome the first trains with genuine happiness. They recorded a vivid story of counties growing out of the woods and muddy-road isolation. Their papers were unofficial invitations to immigrants to move in and make themselves at home. They communicated the views of local constituencies to public officials and offered personal criticism with genuine courage. Constantly they warred with inefficient employees of the postal system before the advent of the rural free delivery—which they accepted as an interesting experiment. As the Schley County (Georgia) *News* said in 1898, "If the balance in the treasury is large enough each year let us have free delivery—but if it will require additional taxation in any form, let the scheme die in its infancy."

In every other field of human endeavor the country editor was an influence. He was rightfully accused at times of operating a free press for the benefit of the syndicates and their medicine company patrons, but . . . usually he was free of every kind of pressure except that of neighborliness.

(from *The Southern Country Editor*)

PART II. THE FRONTIER OF SOCIAL CHANGE

CHAPTER FOUR

SOUTHERN BURDENS

THE SOUTHERN MIND IN THRALLDOM The influence of superstition and common folk belief upon the Southern mind is great when measured over a period of five decades. It is difficult to estimate the influence of the newspaper in fostering beliefs of all sort. Much preposterous material was certainly disseminated by the press. The formal editorial attitude was of little actual consequence so long as the papers continued to offer this sort of story. Inadequately schooled readers lacked the discernment to distinguish truth from legend. To them the printed word was gospel, and they were not equipped to detect facetiousness or subtlety in it.

. . . The rural mind was not a rational one. Collectively it gave evidence of not having the capacity to follow through in its process of reasoning. It accepted the idea that man functions in the universe under the direct power of a series of supernatural controls. It is true that this concept is of ancient origin, but perhaps it was never more pronounced in a civilized society than in the New South. Progressiveness was always in conflict with established local order, and outside influences had to filter slowly through the social structure. Many new ideas had their origin in Europe or at least outside the region, and both sources were suspect in the South. To effect material change in local custom and usage required tolerance, courage and well-directed energy, none of which was sufficiently prevalent generally to make appreciable departures from old ways of life. . . .

Out of the great mass of folk material published in the country papers it becomes clear that a powerful guiding force in the rural Southerner's life was his stern evangelical religious faith. Fundamentally it was presumed that his religious ideals were based upon the gentle and humane teachings of the New Testament, but history as recorded in the papers eloquently refutes this. It is to be seriously doubted whether an appreciable number of literal-minded Southerners read their Bibles understandingly beyond the authoritarian Book of Job. God, as reflected in much of the weekly press, was a highly personal and jealous master. He observed and judged each individual act upon its merits. For sixty years after the Civil War this seems to have been the only system of accounting which most agrarian Southerners could understand. It was the stern God of Abraham, Isaac, Jacob, Moses and Job who kept vigilant watch. The slightest personal default was marked against the transgressor. Thus it was that revival singers everywhere cherished the ancient hymn "Give Me That Old Time Religion."

Of all the sins man can commit, blasphemy was regarded as one of the worst. It received much publicity in the country weeklies, and according to some editors it was immediately punishable. The Princeton (Kentucky) *Banner* told of an old man who complained of dry weather. He cursed the Lord because of the drought and was instantly struck dumb. At Marietta, Georgia, said the *Journal,* a young man sat astride his horse chatting with his companions. He too was embittered by the drought and criticized God. As he did so, lightning played around him in a menacing fashion. Frost came early in Shelby County, Kentucky, said the Oglethorpe (Georgia) *Echo,* and John Cotton was much agitated. He swore bitterly until he was suddenly struck dumb. In Oglethorpe County "a pious good man" bought a pen of shucks from a profane neighbor. Before he could move them a cyclone blew away the sinful neighbor's property but the shuck pen remained unharmed. . . .

It was a simple transition in the folk mind from punishment

of individuals guilty of capital sins to predictions of the destruction of the whole human race. Calamity howlers told country editors that the world would end on certain dates. In 1874 Cyrus Holmes of Illinois created a sensation in Georgia by predicting the world's end in 1878. He was a "Second Adventist" who was sure that hell was in the middle of the earth for he had seen it. Cyrus claimed he understood thoroughly the Book of Revelation, and that it was revealed to him that Abraham, Isaac, and Jacob represented the human organization. Isaac portrayed the mind, Jacob the soul, and Abraham the body. Samuel P. Quins of the Athens (Tennessee) *Post* regretted that Brother Holmes could not move the date of destruction up four years and save him from having to get out the paper.

Prediction of the Second Advent in 1878 was merely a beginning of this type of story in country papers. By 1882 calamitous prophets were certain that the world would not endure through the year. Scriptural passages were cited to prove the point, and Lycurgus Barrett of the Hartford (Kentucky) *Herald* said resurrection robes were being added to his list of subscription prizes. The Covington (Georgia) *Enterprise* reported the people of Cedar Shoals were excited over a curious spider web spun across Beaver Dam Creek. It was filled with strange symbols and letters, and people came from miles around to see it for they believed it an evil thing. This same kind of folk prediction of calamity was transferred to the erratic markings which appeared on eggs. Occasionally some frightened subscriber rushed into a country newspaper office with an egg bearing a crude "W" which he was convinced foretold war. The same superstition applied to the "seven-year" locusts which roared out one stage of their septennial metamorphosis with "W" on their wings.

Sometimes the earth itself created wild rumors. With people believing firmly that hell was not far underfoot, any surface disturbance of the earth was enough to throw a community into hysterics. Frequent notices of tremors left the impression that it was only a matter of time until flames would belch forth from inner chasms and consume the universe. Large cave-ins of the ground attracted crowds and spread horrendous tales that civilization would be swept away. Especially was this true in the Appalachian highland area. Predictions appeared in 1874 that a volcano would spout forth along the whole eastern mountain chain. . . .

When the earth was not misbehaving, human beings who walked upon it were exhibiting strange manifestations of unusual powers. There was an astounding amount of poltergeist material of local origin in the country papers. A long feature story of the strange powers of Little Clara Richardson of Memphis, Tennessee, appeared in the exchanges in 1871. She was a student at Brinkley College and was outwardly a normal girl, but she began to have visions. A spectral visitor told her of a secret which lay buried before the college. So specific were the apparition's instructions that a group of men began digging for the object. When they tired and stopped the ghost admonished the girl to dig for the secret herself. When she had removed a few spadefuls of dirt she reached over and picked up something and then fell to the ground in a dead faint. A medium called up the spirit who said the girl must continue to dig. For an hour the exhausted Clara labored with the spade until she unearthed a glass jar which contained a long yellow envelope, but the apparition said it would have to remain sealed for sixty days. *The Tri-Weekly Republican* of Americus, Georgia, published two accounts of this weird case. Suspense was created by the provision that so much time had to pass before the jar could be opened. Robbers appeared, however, before the time elapsed and stole the jar. Country editors no doubt knew that this type of story was utterly fantastic, but they continued to publish them as serious news stories without explanatory notes.

Somewhat more valid than the account of the Brinkley

College ghost were those of boy and girl preachers. . . . The army of boy and girl preachers whose thin little voices echoed on Southern church grounds had only their visions and their neuroticism to captivate audiences. They were not so well-endowed to entertain as were the "electric girls" publicized in the weekly newspapers. These girls were able to do astonishing things by a seemingly miraculous use of physical power. Electricity baffled most Americans of the eighties and unusual physical phenomena were at once attributed to this strange source of energy. Among the more famous Southern "electric girls" was Lula Hurst who lived in Collardtown, Polk County, Georgia. She defied physical force, laws of gravitation, logic and reason. At least three editors visited this young woman and saw her demonstrate her magical powers. A 180-pound man was unable to hold a chair to the floor when she touched it even with her fingertips. She hurled two men out of bed, tore up an umbrella, bent iron rods and broke pieces of wood without apparent physical exertion. Lula could lie perfectly still and make melodious music sound around her. She could stand on tiptoe on one foot and two men could not shove her over. . . .

Whether or not Lula Hurst had any intention of adding to the woes of her already downtrodden neighbors was unknown. On her elaborate tour through the South she was interested in relieving them of money for admission tickets to witness her public demonstrations. In Alabama she excited the weekly editors by her appearance. Several columns of Lula's activities appeared in the Eufaula *Times and News.* It was believed there, said the editor, that the Georgia girl was a strange force loose in the world. Mayor Comer of Eufaula, appearing on the stage with a boutonniere in his lapel and a diamond stud in his shirt, said he believed God was showing his omnipotence through the medium of the girl from Collardtown. Lula tossed the local gentry about the stage, broke a number of chairs, caused a supernatural orchestra to play and walked away with a nice sum of money. Elsewhere, however, she had trouble. A New York physician said she was a fraud, and the irreverent Detroit *Free Press* poked fun at her in a facetious article on woman's electrifying power.

Other magnetic females competed with the Polk County wonder. Mattie Lee Price of Murray County, Georgia, demonstrated that the tips of her fingers possessed the power to lift men off the floor. She took sticks away from strong men by laying her hands upon them and tossed them about the stage and broke chairs for the fun of it. . . .

All snakes and everything which had to do with snakes made gripping news. Every year most papers felt duty bound to publish enough material on this subject to keep interest at a good pitch. Rattlesnakes were given almost as much space as most county officials. Fantastic accounts of human accidents with snakes and of the unusual places into which the reptiles wormed their way always gave spice to locals. . . .

Snake stories were usually sinister as well as fantastic. As an example take the one published by the Wadesboro (North Carolina) *Herald* which claimed that two Negro children found a nest which they mistook for that of a quail and ate the eggs. Unfortunately these were snake eggs and the children died.

Perhaps the strangest and most incredible stories were written about the cabbage snake. In 1904, the weeklies of Tennessee, Alabama, Mississippi and Georgia told of the appearance of this remarkable, almost microscopic serpent. In Greene County, Alabama, said the Selma *Canebrake Herald,* persons reported snakes in their cabbages. These were said to be about four inches long and the size of a sewing thread. They ranged in color from green to dark brown, and were extremely difficult to see. As usual with such stories, some unnamed doctor declared these creatures were deadly poisonous. Accounts were published about an entire Negro family dying as a result of eating cabbage soup which contained the tiny reptiles. Tennessee papers said that the cabbage fields of Trousdale, Cheatham, Smith, Franklin, Coffee and Bedford counties were infested, and at Cookeville, according to the Fayette (Mississippi) *Chronicle,* Mrs. Z. T. Hinds found a small pink snake about the size of a number 40 thread. This was enough to set off rumors wherever cabbage was grown.

These irresponsible stories made people afraid to eat cabbage and the market for this vegetable was seriously affected. Grocerymen, truck farmers, vegetable brokers and the United States Government were disturbed by the falling off of sales. Immediate steps were necessary to restore public confidence. A search by Department of Agriculture officials failed to produce a single cabbage snake or to locate anyone who could make oath he had seen one. Graves of the people supposed to have died as a result of eating contaminated soup could not be found. Publication in country papers had given the story credence, and only by their publishing a denial could it be discredited.

Those superstitious Southerners who survived the cabbage snake scare were still exposed to horrors. Too many people in the South believed that live reptiles took up residence in the human body. White and black alike were victimized by this ancient folk legend. Three full columns of the Jackson (Tennessee) *Whig and Tribune* quoted a fantastic story originally published in the Murfreesboro *Record* of the extraction by Dr. J. M. Burger of a mature water moccasin from the stomach of Thankful Taylor. It was said that this girl might have picked up the snake in drinking water, or perhaps it had crawled down her throat while she was asleep. As the reptile grew it needed air, and every time it came up to breathe Thankful had fits. Dr. Burger's extraction was described in nauseating detail. To give validity to the story, the old mountebank produced three affidavits and these were published in full in the *Record.* Significantly, two of these statements were signed with cross marks. Thankful Taylor was only one of many people who appeared in country doctors' offices with live things in their systems. "Lizard leg," as one such disease was called, was said by some editors to be common.

Folk treatment of disease was of major importance in the rural South. Something has already been said of the scarcity of properly trained physicians, the lack of pure water supplies, sanitation and facilities for the care of the sick and the general ignorance of the people as to all matters of health. With this condition prevailing, country newspapers inevitably became conscientious sources for disseminating folk medicine and cures.

One of the most frightening calamities which could happen to anyone before Pasteur's discovery of a serum for rabies was to be bitten by a mad dog. Southerners liked dogs and kept them around in packs. A poor white or a Negro, even though too impoverished to own a gun, often had a pack of half-starved dogs. So long as communities swarmed with dogs there was constant threat of rabies. Editors were always on guard, and they tried to keep communities warned of danger. . . .

Newspapers reflected the folk mind at work in other scientific fields. Farm animals suffered from the strange medical aberrations of their masters. Cows lacking sufficient food in the winter were treated with regularity for hollow tail and hollow horn in the spring. Hogs were given cures which were more debilitating than the ailments they suffered. In fact, it was not until after 1920, and then through an intelligent campaign in the rural press, that much of the frontier folklore about farm animals was replaced with scientific information. One of the reasons the South had failed to produce more meat at home was the prevalence of disease among animals. Farmers lacked information on how to keep them healthy and free from disease. . . .

What should have been of concern to the realistic rural editor was the enormous economic loss which his section suffered because of superstition and folk belief. Backwardness, illiteracy and reactionary attitudes are wasteful and expensive. No thinking editor could observe the dense smoke pall hanging low over the South each spring and fail to appreciate that his community was destroying its resources. Ignorant and violent local people believed that forests were alive with snakes, varmints, insects and miasma, and the surest way to destroy these was to use fire. Spring after spring they set fire to the woods. Millions of dollars were lost annually to the section because of such twisted beliefs, perhaps more than enough money to maintain a first class medical school in the South. Hidden away in the musty files of the country papers is this weird, wasteful and virulent chapter of social life in the New South.

(from *The Southern Country Editor*)

BIG HOGS GREW IN IOWA A Georgia farmer wrote, "Our Fathers which art in Troy, Wiley & Murphy be thy names, thy kingdom of provisions come, thy will be done on my farm as it is at your store. Give us this day our daily bread. Forgive us our tresspass on your barn as we forgive those who tresspass upon ours, lead us not into temptation but deliver us from hungriness, for thine shall be the crop, the mules and the land forever and ever if we don't pay—Amen. P.S. If this is good for ten bushels of corn and three hundred pounds of bacon, fling it in the wagon."

George Bevlry, an Alabama farmer, and his neighbors were most numerous in the South's rural population. In March, 1893, he requested a merchant to "sen me six pounds of meat & one galon of lassies, [give] Jack Hern five pounds of meat fer Wilson Hern & [one gallon] lassies fer John Hern & sen me the Bil of it." It was March of the hard year of 1893, and these cotton-belt farmers were already out of home-grown meat, meal and molasses.

Back of George Bevlry's illiterate note was a significant story in domestic economy. Perhaps this was the major chapter in the history of southern storekeeping, and here the merchants exerted an influence which was to effect the very sinew and bone of the region. The whole big question of regional diet stemmed from the meat boxes and bread barrels of the storehouses and their shed rooms. Merchants converted their neighbors to an economy of getting food supplies from elsewhere. Thus the basic fare of the store became as monotonous as the prevailing system of agriculture and politics, and was a subject which provoked the wrath of editors, agrarian reformers and apostles of the New South. . . .

Perhaps it would do the dignity of the good people of Alabama no great injustice to compare the human population with the number of hogs they owned in 1870, 1880 and 1890. In the first tabulation following the war the census taker accounted for 996,884 persons and 719,757 hogs. Ten years later when figures were more accurate the ratio between people and hogs was still out of balance; there were 1,262,505 people and 1,252,462 hogs. In 1890 when the New South was developing and farmers were again on their feet, emphasis in this pork-loving state was still on cotton and people. The human population climbed to 1,513,017, and hogs were behind at 1,421,884. In most of the Confederate States during these three decades the picture was not materially different from that in Alabama. Occasionally the increase in hogs ran slightly ahead of that of human beings, but in most it dropped behind.

It was a great contradiction in economics that southern farmers liked pork and disliked hogs. There was a sentiment that "a dad-blamed hog and a dad-gummed cow were the most aggravating things that ever made tracks on a piece of cotton land." Farmers generally regarded the hog in the same unfavorable light as a Fayetteville, Alabama, merchant who declared vigorously that it was a destructive thing to have about. In a brief paragraph he wrote the hog's obituary. "A two dollar hog," he declared, "can hoist the front gate off its hinges at night, when you are asleep; root up the herbs in the garden that cost us years of trouble to get; eat all the chickens and ducks in the fowl yard; root the yard into holes; root down the side walks; fill up the ditches, enter your store, while you are engaged in waiting on a customer, turn over a barrel of molasses and let it run all over the house, damaging other goods to the amount of hundreds of dollars in less time than you can say sooey! rip up everything in their reach; and do any other thing which is too bad to be endured."

This was an attitude which prevailed in much of the South. The hog was too difficult for cotton farmers to handle. They refused to fence in productive land for pasturage or to build good fences. Usually they penned two or three half-starved hogs in a hillside pen as bare of vegetation as a marble floor, gave them a pot of kitchen slop once a day, and then wondered why the devil the brutes were always shoving the fence down and rooting up the place. . . .

A local observer, in 1872, wrote that the towns of Selma, Rome and Dalton were packed with freight. Hundreds of carloads of meat and grain products rolled in from the Northwest. Cincinnati, Louisville, Des Moines, Chicago and Indianapolis sent shipments of foodstuffs to feed the cotton growers.

Every Saturday in the stores was a day of sending out rations for the forthcoming week. Clerks kept busy about the meat boxes supplying requests for what was euphemistically called "bacon." It was an every-week occurrence for malnourished customers, sated with salt meat, to plead with meat cutters to find them pieces with streaks of lean. They knew too well the lack of variety in fat slices of Iowa meat which had only a dividing line of tissue to break its angelical whiteness. . . .

Saturday night at the stores greasy and exhausted clerks

stood between meat boxes and scales slicing off pieces of fat backs. All day they had wielded heavy butcher knives on flabby slabs of sowbelly and fat back. A timid Negro ambled up to the box and asked for eight pounds of meat, five pounds of lard or a gallon of cooking oil. A white farmer bought a side of meat and a five-gallon can of lard which he parceled out a little at a time at home.

All afternoon and night cotton wagons rattled away from the stores with their pitiful loads of rations. Hunched over a spring seat a cotton farmer jolted homeward behind a jaded pair of mules with a can of kerosene, a hunk of meat, a pail of compound lard, and dust-covered bags of flour and meal.

This was the store diet in transport. At home wives sliced off thick pieces of the Iowa meat and fried it for breakfast, boiled hunks of it for dinner and fried more of it for supper. They thickened the gravy with flour and served it and molasses as sop for corn bread and biscuit. Three times a day and fifty-two weeks a year, for many, was a long monotonous year of meat, corn bread, biscuit, gravy and molasses. Farmers complained of "burning out" on them, and some ingenious wives hit upon the idea of rolling slices of meat in cornbread and momentarily camouflaging them as fish. This was food for what the rampant editors often called "cotton tots and tobacco worms."

Life for most of the customers was of a marked degree of whiteness. There was white meat, white gravy, white bread and white shortening for the table, white supremacy at the polls and white gloves for the pall bearers at the grave side. Next to meat in demand at the stores was corn meal. Since the days of John Smith and Jamestown corn bread has been a mainstay of southern diet. There may be much room for debating the question of how near southern farmers, since early antebellum days to 1920, came to supplying their demand for corn from the home fields, but there is no room for argument about their taste for corn bread. Stores sold meal by the hundreds of thousands of dollars' worth. During 1881 it was estimated that corn from the Northwest to the South sold for $50,000,000, with perhaps an additional $25,000,000 worth over the counters as meal. . . .

Corn was ever a scarce commodity in the cotton, sugar and tobacco South. It was rarely true that the average small farmer had enough to supply his needs from the time the rats and weevils left off with their destruction of the old until the new corn was hard enough to grind. The invoice books and ledgers supply a flood of evidence of this fact. One of the major items in the books is grain for human food and feed for livestock. Many merchants maintained gristmills in connection with their stores so that they not only reaped a profit from the sale of meal, and took toll of the grinding, but gristmills were good trade getters because of the crowds they attracted. Often homeground meal was sold through the stores, because corn in the form of meal always brought a much higher price. . . .

Actually bolted meal was only one of the sources of regional malnourishment. There were many other factors in the cause of this disease, and most of them stemmed from the types of food carried on the pages of store ledgers.

A slight degree higher in the culinary-social scale was the inferior chalk-white flour from the mills over the Ohio. Flour bread was a sort of mark of food gentility. It was all right to serve corn bread with vegetables, and occasionally to offer hot corn bread to guests on other occasions if the hostess "smiled" in doing so, but biscuits were definitely company bread. Hot biscuits with the hospitable admonition to "take two and butter them while they're hot" was a great rural favorite. Southerners generally loved hot biscuits. Three times a day they wanted them, and they ranged in size from the dainty little mouthfuls cut by the fastidious tin cutters from the stores to the sprawling islands of dough cooked three and four to the pan. One southern geologist observed that biscuit spread out conversely to the nature of the topography of the country. Certainly the quality of biscuit served on southern tables varied with the social backgrounds of their makers. . . .

Flour by the barrel became the gauge by which the prices were adjudged. In times of fair economic balance a barrel of flour sold for $3.50 to $7.00. When these prices crept upward, either the economic balance was being disturbed or merchants were guilty of charging exorbitant prices. . . .

Paradoxically the grain and meat trade was a factor in making common cause between the farmers of the South and the Northwest, yet it set them against each other. Like the Southern farmers, the meat and bread producers wished to get as much as they could for what they sold and pay as little as possible for what they bought.

From Virginia to Texas food purchases were pretty much alike. Every personal account of any consequence included frequent purchases of the staples, meat, meal, molasses, flour, sugar, salt and coffee. Molasses was made in all of the southern states, and was of three grades. There was the lowly sorghum which grew throughout the region from Kentucky to the Gulf, and which was converted into thick syrup in the early fall. All during the year it was sold through the stores for thirty to fifty cents a gallon, and made a decided appeal to Negro customers. After it had been in a barrel for six months it reached a stage of mild fermentation in which a heavy white collar stood on jugs and cans, and it gave off a loud odor of cane. . . .

Aside from the staples which have been mentioned there was the steady demand for coffee. Every customer was a potential purchaser of this commodity. In most instances merchants bought coffee in the green-bean stage and dipped it out pound at a time from the large jute bags in which it was packed in Brazil. Nearly every household parched and ground its own coffee, and it was more from this custom than from the much famed magnolias that the countryside took on one of its most fragrant odors. Customarily green coffee sold all the way from a bit a pound to three pounds for a dollar, and it was as much a necessity as were tobacco, molasses and bacon.

Sugar and salt ranked with coffee in importance. Both of these commodities originated in the region. Sugar came from the Louisiana, Carolina and Georgia cane fields. Stores in the upper part of the region secured salt from the Kanawha River source, while those in the lower South secured their supply from the Jefferson Island mines in Louisiana. . . .

Not all of the store trade in food had to do with the sale of goods which were outgoing. There was a fairly rich produce trade which yielded a steady year-round profit to merchants. Housewives longing for special clothes and knickknacks saved their chickens, butter, eggs, nuts and other marketable produce and traded them off to merchants. Although much the same attitude which prevailed against the hog and the cow was applied to the chicken, there was a rather steady flow of eggs into the stores. . . .

Thus the stores became active centers of southern human welfare. There was in both their stocks and records eloquent testimony describing as accurately perhaps as a statistical table the basis of life in the region. The story of the store's food sales was often sinful and was always dramatically symbolized by a weary man shambling away from its porch weighted down with a sack of meal, a slab of meat and a bucket of molasses.

(from *Pills, Petticoats and Plows*)

THE HALT, THE LAME AND THE BILIOUS Samuel Hopkins Adams in 1904 wrote in *Collier's Weekly* a series of effective articles attacking the patent-medicine trade. He, along with the crusading Edward Bok of the *Ladies' Home Journal* and the American Medical Association, was preparing the end for "The Great American Fraud." Two years later the Pure Food and Drug Act was passed, thus ending one of the most highly imaginative periods of lying and swindling which the country has known.

Proprietary medicine makers found ready customers by the millions in the postwar South. Booming crossroads stores and villages became profitable outlets for a vast stream of tonics, pills, ointments, liniments and dry-herb mixtures which poured out of "laboratories" in the larger distributing cities.

Three years after the Civil War the manufacturers of Plantation Bitters boasted that below the Potomac they were selling five million dollars' worth of their product each year. It was a profitable business to whet the South's indifferent appetites and to prod its sluggish colons. Alcohol-laden bitters of various types were regarded as fine conditioners for the ex-Confederate system, and country merchants lined their shelves with them. This was commonplace merchandise which required little or no selling, and only a slight portion of profits went for advertising.

Manufacturers were quick to sense the changed political condition of the South. Through the columns of the *Carolina Watchman* of Salisbury the makers of Kookman's bitters advertised their medicine and their political spleen in the same box. When Hinton Rowan Helper was replaced as Republican postmaster by a more subservient rival, the medicine men gloated. "This gentleman (Helper) is not radical enough to please his party and has been removed as postmaster at Salisbury—use Kookman's Bitters."

But the bitters trade was to move on to new fields. Country-store ledgers in Mississippi tell a long story of moral crusading against the use of liquor. To drink liquors was one thing, but to take a generous "dose" of port wine or alcohol in bitters was altogether different. Some of the stores' customers became so decrepit that they were forced daily to replenish their stock of "medicine." Long before Edward Bok and the Massachusetts

Board of Health discovered the high alcoholic content of bitters, country-store customers in the South knew the secret, and not from laboratory analysis!

Gallant compounders and distributors of bitters made a brave fight to keep their ancient formulas before the public. They first played upon local political prejudices and then turned to the new age of industrial expansion for catch phrases and names with which to give their products a timeliness. In Chicago, H. E. Bucklen and Company gave their powerful medicine the name "electric." For a time it caught on and was a big money-maker. Even though the New South was in a period of economic and political prostration, it was too rich to be handed over to the unimaginative bitters trade without keen opposition. Within ten years after Appomattox, trees, barns and country stores were lined with garish ads offering peace and health to all who were in pain. It mattered not where nor what the pain was. The southern country was now free, and the "sky limit" was high. . . .

Diets of fat meat, corn bread, hot biscuits, molasses and white gravy week after week clogged the whole physical system with poisons of constipation. The skin broke out in sores. Teeth decayed from lack of care. The breath was bad. Backs gave out. The memory grew weak. Piles preyed upon most southerners like dread ghosts from the pine-hill graveyards. Appendixes ruptured in the night, and one victim after another was carted off to be impounded in the tight clay of the countryside. . . .

Mailbags, dragged down from the backs of sweating mules before crossroads stores, were crammed with bundles of dulcet messages of health. The saviors of womankind located in all parts of the country were energetic in distributing their mauve and pink advertisements. Dr. McLean in St. Louis offered strengthening cordials, volcanic oil liniment, vegetable conditioning powders, and a horrific compound labeled "tar wine lung oil." In New England that "benevolent" lady, Lydia E.

Pinkham, with a properly bloused shirtwaist and a motherly soul, created a formula which was a boon to all females and to many males. In the South she was a strong competitor for Dr. King's New Discovery and McElrees' Wine of Cardui. Jones' Mountain Herbs brought health and good cheer, and from the byways letters of praise poured in to proclaim its saving grace. Mollie Ray of Lyonsville, Alabama, found it "a first-class medicine for ailments peculiar to any sex." From Nashville, Tennessee, there came a lifesaver called Coussen's Portaline or vegetable liver powder, which quickly developed an army of highly partisan letter writers who gave out profound literary and scientific observation on the power of this conditioner. . . .

Just as southern women were beset with their "peculiar ailments" and their eternal headaches and backaches, southern gentlemen likewise were subjected to perplexing ills. Many wonderful remedies were concocted to smooth their paths. When the merchants of Baltimore co-operated in the eighties in preparation of an elaborate book containing a mercantile directory and a bit of Chesapeake Bay history as a compliment to the trade of South Carolina, they included an advertisement from John B. Hurtt and Company, distributors of various proprietary medicines. One of these was a nostrum prepared by the eminent French physician, Dr. Francis Boudalt. He had begun selling to the American public a medicine which was "endorsed by all physicians," and in 1876 the republic had awarded him a gold medal at the Centennial in Philadelphia. His was truly a medicine of great power. It cured "weakness of memory, difficulty of recalling names or dates, inaptitude for business or study, lameness, weakness, weakness in the back or loins; weakness of the organs, with deficient, feeble powers; languor, easy fatigue from mental or physical labor, loss of nervous power and general tone of the system, weakness from loss of vital fluids at the stool or during urination, involuntary vital losses at night during dreams, weak or failing powers and threatened impotence, prostration and debility from overwork or mental effort."

It seems that the postwar male was the victim of a disease for which the bushy-faced doctors invented the name "spermatorhea." Among this new school of scientists of impotence was Dr. Culverwell who offered no medicine, but a little book which he sold through the country stores. It was he, perhaps, who popularized the name for the disease. He guaranteed debilitated males that he would aid them to marriage and happiness ever afterward. Drs. Culverwell and Boudalt had their competitors, and the increase of their advertising indicated something of the spread of venereal diseases in the southern region.

A continuous stream of letters, written on cheap green-striped pieces of nickel tablet paper, poured into the "confidential medical advisers" and told intimate tales of suffering females. Women wrote vivid descriptions of either their "private ailments" or those of their daughters. The unctuous solicitations of the county paper and almanac "doctors" gave rural women hope of deliverance from their ills and loneliness. Their letters gave away their most intimate secrets and at the same time told harrowing stories of indigestion, constipation, crying spells, spots before their eyes, kidney trouble, torpid livers and complete loss of appetite. . . .

The so-called tonics were the best money-makers. So firmly was the idea of seasonal conditioning established among the rural people of the South that spring was ushered in with a round of medicine for nearly every individual. This was so true that the very name tonic symbolized a well-toned physical system. These tonics presented the greatest possibility for the highly imaginative compounders. Ability to achieve four major results was a necessary criterion of any tonic. It had to ease pain immediately, give a cheerful warming glow to the whole body, taste strongly of herbs, and move the bowels. Equally as important as the therapeutical immediacy of the medicine was a fetching name. Actually many of the tonics were manufactured by the same agency and sold to distributors who put their own names and brands upon them. This practice likewise applied to price. A wholesale house distributed a medicine with a label on it but no price mark. In their advertising they attracted customers from among the country-store merchants by telling them that they might establish a price which they thought their trade would bear. Such a medicine was Phyto-Gingerin, "the great Southern tonic." Spurlock-Neal of Nashville advertised this tonic to merchants as "a most powerful, efficient and pleasant remedy for all diseases arising from an impure state of the blood. *Nothing better for a general appetizing tonic.* Put up in 14 oz. round bottles, $4.00 a doz. No price is marked on bottle, therefore you make your own price. We are advertising PHYTO-GINGERIN extensively."

Next to the tonics for the country-store trade were the ointments. They were easily compounded and easily sold. In many communities a majority of the customers were cursed with running leg sores, which resisted all home-remedy efforts to cure them. It took powerful medicine to check these sores, and the patent ointment makers knew this fact. Patriarch of the salves was the famous Gray's Ointment, manufactured in Nashville, which antedated the Civil War. Early invoices from drug houses contained generous shipments of this salve. There was a general belief in the rural South that a strong-smelling, greasy ointment could reach deeply into the seat of pain and that it had "sure-fire" curative power.

Actually many of their preparations were little more than a mixture of petroleum jelly, cheap perfume and carbolic acid. Their curative powers amounted to nothing more than a temporary disinfecting and glazing over of stubborn ulcers. . . .

Medical service was inferior, and often completely untrained doctors solved their therapeutic riddles with a dose of morphine, laudanum or opium. These drugs brought quick relief, and frequent use of them over a period of weeks kept the patient quiet until nature could intervene and effect a cure. In cases of acute illness, ignorant doctors were quick to use the most active sedative available. So general was the use of these agents that the rural quacks themselves eased their own troubled and befuddled minds. Storekeepers kept local doctors supplied with narcotics, and an army of rural drug fiends is to be found upon the debit side of both the merchants' and ill-prepared doctors' ledgers of life's misdeeds. . . .

King of the "standards" was turpentine, a product of the tidewater pine forests. On every mantel board, be it ramshackle Negro cabin or pillared mansion, turpentine occupied a place of medicinal leadership. It was the universal medicine. Long before Louis Pasteur established his germ theory, southerners were combating infections with turpentine and pine resin. Everything from a cut finger to worms, backache, kidney trouble, sore throat, rheumatism, croup, pneumonia, toothache and earache was treated with this cheap native antiseptic. Children with smothering colds gagged at heaping spoons of sugar dampened down with it. Turpentine had three important medicinal requisites: It smelled loud, tasted bad and burned like the woods on fire. Southern kidneys paid a heavy price for its frequent use. . . .

There were scores of other medicines, such as Epsom salts, saltpeter, copperas, sulphur and bluestone, which were looked upon as staple goods. Salts was bought in large quantities and sold in smaller amounts for nominal prices. But like turpentine, these medicines were regarded as being mild and necessary to rural well-being.

Aside from the miraculous elixirs of new life and the forthright purgatives on the drug shelves, there were preparations for the more vainglorious and fastidious. Well-advanced southern male and female candidates for matrimony, conscious of their ripening years, fought valiantly, if with faulty weapons, against gray hair. Spurlock-Neal and Company offered their Spurlock's Quick Hair Dye, and as a special inducement included a free brush with each bottle. This was a precious item and caught the eye of the trade. Purchased at wholesale for $1.75 a dozen bottles, it was retailed at the merchant's economic discretion.

For those whose locks were not traced with gray, there were the pomades of a hundred different brands. One of the quickest ways to make a small fortune in the South after the Civil War was to manufacture and distribute a reasonably satisfactory hair straightener. Any pomade which could withstand with fair success the entangling influence of wet weather assured a handsome profit. The pomades removed from the head of the colored female the tight string-wound rolls of hair and gave her fluffy locks instead. Plain petroleum jelly, one of the first patent straighteners, was soon pushed into the background by more elaborate mixtures in gaudy tin cans and widemouthed bottles. Elaborate labels vividly portrayed long waving tresses of a negroid belle—or, sometimes, the long wavy hip-length crown of a fairer daughter. For twenty-five cents a rural woman, white or colored, could buy a tin of highly perfumed jelly which would give her a pliant head of hair for twenty-four hours at least. Even the southern males found the pomades a useful aid in giving their hair and mustaches a "fixed" appearance. . . .

One after the other the "medicine books" distributed through the southern country stores described the region's diseases, and then proceeded to produce testimonials to show that there were wonderful cures. One of them said in 1898 that "*mal-aria* signifies 'bad air.' It is generally understood that malaria poisons are absorbed into the system from the atmosphere. The fact is, there are always liable to be more or less unhealthy infectious conditions in the atmosphere; it is absolutely impossible to prevent malarial germs from entering the system, but it is altogether possible to prevent their doing harm after they get in." This was a statement which attracted attention. In the South "mal-aria" signified not only "bad air" but likewise untold suffering and debility. A man with malaria was willing to take a chance with any medicine which promised relief. It was a fact that there was a belief that chills and fevers came from the air. Generally people living in the South believed night air was bad for the health, but that swamp air especially was bad.

From throughout the South there came a steady stream of letters bearing glad tidings of cures. Most of these notes of cheer were boring because of their similarity. . . . In all of this literature of healing three facts stand out. The medicines advertised were for the common man. At least ninety-five percent of the testimonials originated in the tiny villages. It was the rural man and woman who took the medicine and then wrote about it. Sometimes salesmen driving through the country solicited testimonials and pictures as a part of their business. There was ever a conscious effort to discredit local doctors, and occasionally other patent medicines. On one occasion Dr. M. A. Simmons warned: "Beware of 'Black Draught'; 'Simmons Liver Medicine'; by J. H. Zeilin and Co. when sold as 'the same' as 'Dr. M. A. S. L. M.' "

This medicine business was a major reason for crusading for a Pure Food and Drug Act in the first decade of the present century. One by one the *Journal of the American Medical Association* exposed the famous doctors' humbuggery in its column "Propaganda for Reform."

Edward Bok and Samuel Hopkins Adams would have given up in despair had they appreciated fully the efficiency of the country store as a dispenser of the medicines they so heartily condemned. It was in these stores that the medicine manufacturers had their most important sources of income. They catered to people who were ignorant of proper medical care and without adequate trained medical service.

(from *Pills, Petticoats and Plows*)

THE DAY GOES BY LIKE A SHADOW ON THE HEART Closely allied with the problems of race and law enforcement was that of lynching. A lynching made sensational news, and few Southern country editors could resist giving the full details of what happened. No one knew better than they, however, the conflicting forces mob violence released. . . .

Some editors perhaps published details of lynchings in an effort to make them so horrible that public opinion would stamp out the practice. Others approved of lynchings as punishments for certain crimes, especially when it seemed to protect and further white supremacy. . . .

The country editor was always in a dilemma in respect to the whole subject. His community's moral reputation was at stake, but his readers always wanted sensational stories. There were enough lynchings and to spare. . . .

Opponents of lynching argued—often with apparent justice—that it accomplished nothing good that the courts could not do as well. Colonel W. P. Walton in the upper South was direct in his views on lynching. In 1877 he vigorously denounced mob rule. "The infernal mob business," he wrote, "showed itself this week in Fayette County. A negro hit a white man named John Denton, on the head with an ax, giving him probably a fatal wound. The negro was arrested and taken before a magistrate and held to await the result of Denton's wound. That night a mob took the negro from the officers of the law and hung him to a neighboring tree. Each man engaged in that cowardly work, is a murderer and the law should see that they do not go unpunished. There is no palliation for the deed. The negro had committed a horrible crime but he was in the hands of the law, and would certainly have gotten the full punishment for it. Mobs are always cowardly and as great breakers of the law as the criminals they propose to take into their hands to punish."

Public opinion was sometimes opposed to lynching, and this fact appeared in the weekly papers. It was difficult, however, to determine what part of the population of a county was involved in a lynching. Mobs varied in size. If the crimes which they punished were widely publicized, some of the participants were often drawn in from other communities, even from other counties. . . .

Even where mobs were opposed, they were not easy to stop. Take as an example the Mississippi mob of 500 men who broke into the Carroll County jail. Bessie McCroy, her son Belfield and daughter Ida, who were being held for the murder of Mr. and Mrs. Talliferro, were seized by the mob, taken to the edge of the town of Carrollton and hanged and their bodies riddled with bullets. While the mob was at work the Honorable W. S. Hill and Judge W. F. Stephens stood on the jail steps with their arms around the leaders begging them to desist in favor of the courts. Soon after, Governor Andrew Longino arrived on the scene and delivered a long lecture in which he condemned lynching. . . .

Sheriffs grew nervous at the first threat of a mob. To begin with, the office has always been a political plum with many opportunities for extra income. In the South it often went to a good politician rather than to an upright and courageous peace officer. As a consequence, sheriffs have not wanted to face maddened constituencies on so treacherous an issue as lynching and racial animosity. . . .

Rape in the context of racial jealousy tended to confuse issues and make a difficult problem even more difficult. Outspoken opponents of lynching recognized this cause alone as an excuse, perhaps a vindication. Z. W. Whitehead was against lynch law, yet in a half-column editorial he wrote of rape that "the absolutely certain commission of that nameless and revolting crime which crushes peace and joy forever out of a fair young life's consolation can ever deny [*sic*] starts the pulse of indignant manhood at fever heat, transforms the quiet citizen into the stern avenger, and sets the whole community in arms to rid the earth of the wretch who cumbers it—the fiend whose life is an offense against God and humanity."

If the line could have been neatly drawn between lynchings

for rape and lynching for other crimes, people might have been clearer in their minds. But the justification for the one was constantly being extended to cover the other. In point of fact there were at least two lynchings resulting from murders to every one following a rape. And lynchings for murder were in many cases just as brutal as those punishing rape. . . .

Lynchers sought vengeance, not justice. The horror of the crime for which they exacted payment, not evidence of guilt, was uppermost in the minds of a mob. Rumor passed for fact, and innocent men were executed along with the guilty. They were denied orderly trial and conviction by public officials whose identity and responsibilities were known and clearly described by law. It was easy in a moment of hysteria, to go from one category to another in the alleged crimes for which the extreme punishment was meted, until no margin was left between high crimes and personal spites which could not stand exposure in an organized court.

(from *The Southern Country Editor)*

THE NEW SOUTH: A PERSPECTIVE IN CHANGE The South is by no means unique in its history, or in its state of change and confusion. Other regions of the United States, and of the world for that matter, have experienced during the past century a social revolution which has shattered custom and tradition. Perhaps no Americans have experienced more penetrative change, however, than southerners. They started a century ago with at least two handicaps: they had to rearrange their economy and way of life, and to confront a new racial alignment in a land that had refused to believe such a thing could occur. . . .

Above all the South has been confronted with stern reality, whether in economics, race matters, or partisan politics. At no time was this more dramatically clear than at the end of the Civil War. Not only did the region have to face up to old realities of a raw expanding frontier with its mixture of problems, an economy that was being reorganized in its many phases, a social system which was rendered in twain, the losses of a war, a race problem, and a manpower shortage, but it had to find its way back into the flow of national life in a world deep in technological revolution. The future which then confronted the region was one of blurred promises and uncertain objectives. Would the way of life of the so-called Old South be restored by new approaches to old problems? Would a new philosophy of social and political matters prevail, or would efforts be made to establish the all but unstated glories of the past?

Immediately it was clear that, aside from the physical damages of four years of military strife, the great emotional paradoxes created by a changing age were even more damaging. Groping in a decade of defeat, southerners of all conditions of society sought to overcome the past through acceptance of the challenges of the future. Some of them sought to deny that a hiatus had occurred in both the romantic dream and the southern system. Slavery was wrecked on the bars of national disdain and legality; nevertheless the former slaves were a source of highly subservient labor. Heavy participation by yeomen in the war made common cause between them and the so-called aristocratic planters. Too, the Negro and his former master found workable grounds on which to proceed. Traditions of the Old South, whether of culture, social privilege, or political leadership, now became common traditions of the two major social classes. Some way the past must be projected into the future, and the tenor of southern life restored to something approximating that of earlier years. . . .

Some historians have contended . . . that there was in fact little break between the Old and New Souths. Even with the destruction of slavery, both the method of labor and the plantation economy in many areas continued much as before.

There was even continuity of the old political systems. There were areas, however, in which the chasms widened rapidly. For the first time the South was brought with full force into . . . the mainstream of American history. However much of the past the South might try to redeem or live by, it could not live apart from the times. In trying to do so the region would certainly force itself into conflicts which could not be easily resolved. The web of nationalism might have been woven in crazy and uncertain patterns, but it was thick and unyielding, and it gathered the South more firmly into its folds in each succeeding decade.

Hinton Rowan Helper had introduced the Old South to the realism of statistics, a stern fact southerners neither fully understood nor wished to accept. This nevertheless was portentous of the future. The unbalanced burden of ignorance, human incapacity, superstition, and social blight of untrained poor whites and freedmen after 1865 added extra dimensions of adversity to the New South's history. Chivalry, the spirit of noblesse oblige, classical culture, and personal refinement were all precious values and highly cherished standards, but they added little of tangible worth to a society so heavily involved in searching out new directions, or in bearing the overweening burden of negative statistics. The new national society reckoned its advances toward the future in terms of production tables, crops grown, resources exploited, miles of rails laid, in the rise of cities, the establishment of banking houses, schools and colleges founded, and in social reform. For the South all of these things were important, but of more basic significance was education. There were dual demands in this area: the conditioning of freedmen and the training of the entire white population. Actually to compare educational efforts of the ante-bellum years with those after 1865 is to associate irrelevancies. This is not to say public schools were lacking. Public schools had been organized, but had not matured.

Education was the prime need of the New South. The crusade to build schools and to improve the quality of education in the region after 1865 was carried on with the fervor of a religious revival. The mass of southern population, however, remained indifferent to regional needs in this field. . . .

There was, nevertheless, to be much more weeping at "the tombstone of John C. Calhoun" before the South began to achieve the objectives of universal education. Two world wars and a biting depression made clear the fact that it took far more than prophetic oratory to mature an educational system. Even the jubilant prophets of 1911 could not foresee how formidable comparative statistics would become in the next half-century in showing the South its low position in relation to national achievement.

The South, after the drafting of the new state constitutions, was so bound up in its effort to keep the Negro ignorant and disfranchised that it lost sight of the greater disfranchisement of the region itself in attracting and servicing industries. No matter how many southerners went to New York to confer with bankers, the poor quality of the human resource of the South still remained a great deterrent to economic expansion of the region.

In no field of vibrant human endeavor could southerners retreat into the past, even though they often dreaded to face the realities of the twentieth century. There remained only the future with its riddles; traditions and precedents had vanished in the face of national modernization. . . .

These themes have been repeated annually in the South. Whether in regional congresses, governors' conferences, or in the daily press and conversation—the impact of the inventor, the scientist, the social reformer, the courts, and expansion of mechanization of the productive processes had brought change. A century of southern history had been marked by hills and valleys of crises. An agrarian society surrendered slowly to modernization. A farm-oriented economy definitely shaped the nature of constitutional government, the cast of politics, and largely explained the incapacities of state governments to confront the industrial and social revolution of mid-century. So far in the past century as there was a "New South," it has been only since 1930 that the region could truly lay claim to "newness," and it is only since 1945 that this has been really true. . . .

Poor educational training, however, weighed down hope of genuine progress in the South. Political leadership too often failed to look beneath the surface of emotional public reaction for answers to problems. Instead they helped the region to drift into a limited pattern of thinking, of narrow sectionalism, state-rights, and a tight binding of folk culture. Attacks on the intellect by bigots in and out of state legislatures in the first decades of the century handicapped, if it did not come near destroying, the intellectual spark so necessary to maintaining and advancing colleges and universities of higher quality. It was a paradox of broad significance that at the moment when the first impacts of American technology were being felt in southern life, reaction to higher education was so stultifying. As Howard W. Odum said:

> Before Hitler's Germany, parts of the South were revivifying an emotional culture through attack upon universities and intellectual life; through religious coloring of politics and statecraft; through appeal to sectional patriotism; through intolerance of criticism and opposition; and through continuing emphasis upon racial issues, Nordic superiority and one hundred per cent Americanism.

Southern politicians often cast their shabby image against a background of change. Campaigners promised progress and improvement. They proposed to perform miracles, but within the restrictive confines of traditionalism without disturbing the status quo. When southern politicians did strike at old political establishments and won, they did so because they promised to lead government back from some self-created brink of disaster. Modern southern political history since 1890 has been written largely within the framework of class and race conflicts, localisms, personalities, economic limitations, and political chicanery.

Noticeably lacking were crusades by southern politicians, or by the people themselves, to liberalize state constitutions, to revise antiquated state statutes, to finance the operation of vastly improved educational systems, or to reconstruct the industrial system of the South. In far too many instances the southern bloc in Congress has been highly conservative if not outright negative in its reactions to more liberal national measures. Instead of strengthening the South's leadership position in the nation as a positive force which would place the region in an effective position of national influence, this bloc has often maintained a position of flight from sectional reality.

A certain test of how positive southerners wished to reconstruct their region after 1877 as a vibrant economic and political force was to be found in constitutional revisions. It is doubtful that any of the new state documents contained as fundamental parts of their organization any philosophy that could be termed progressive in the context of modern industrial America. Quite the contrary, southern constitutions reflected not a progressive redirecting of the states toward a happier and more effective future, but rather to a series of conflicts involving the position of the races and the classes in southern society. They reflected more precisely an actual fear of the future. Specifically, there was fear of taxation and adequate appropriations to do more than sustain public institutions at the lowest possible level of operation. In a region where the per capita income was consistently not only in the lowest quarter of the nation, but dangerously below the national average, there was powerful resistance to agencies that fostered change. In discriminating against the Negro, delegates to the constitutional conventions contributed materially to handicapping further a major part of the South's white human resource.

Regional literature has been a fairly dependable measure of people and the maturity of their culture. Few if any of the regions of the United States have been written about so voluminously as the modern South. . . . In a great majority of these is recorded a history of crisis. Southern authors have often contributed precise descriptions of contemporary problems. Even more fundamentally they have understood the underlying forces of humanity and the times which shaped both the southern personality and the conditions of regional society.

The intensive search by everybody who has sought mature answers to regional questions has largely been directed toward the central forces which have shaped the South's history. Unhappily, much of the story of the past century has of necessity been written against a background of defeatism and limited accomplishments. . . . This has been true largely because transitions and changes have come hard for the southern people. These have often involved renunciations of traditions and folk loyalties which have had qualities of intimate personal bonds. If the land could have been settled from the start in the traditional way of the American frontier, it might have been true that the vastness of nature and southern geography would have shaped the personality of the region and conditioned its society by altogether different patterns. Slavery, and subsequently the race problem, was crisis enough, but secession, civil war, political conflicts, an inefficient regional economy, and a literal fundamentalist religion marked a century of change. The New South was born of crises at the end of the Civil War, and was christened in a long and bitter period of reconstruction. . . .

Two issues of these earlier years were of white-Negro relationships and power, and the foundations of a new southern economy. Unhappily settlement of the first problem was fraught with so much emotional confusion that no certain chart to the future could be drafted. No fact, however, was more important than that of making a positive clarification of its aims and objectives to Americans generally, to European critics, to social crusaders, and to politicians within and outside the region. On the surface the idealistic vision of the freed Negro to the poorly informed outsider was that of a semi-educated yeoman adapting himself quickly to conditions of Americans in urban society and to those of the West.

In the view of the ex-slaveholder the Negro was to be suspended between a condition of slavery and peonage; certainly he was not visualized as a responsible privileged person. Even more threatening to the Negro's welfare was the fact that he would quickly become a pawn of conflicting political interests. In the minds of southerners, the Negro was too backward culturally to permit him to enjoy immediately the privileges of a freedman; these were to come at an unspecified future time. As southerners looked to the past in efforts to relate themselves to the new age in America, they looked to the future for either amelioration or adjudication of the race problem. One thing they knew for certain, race conflicts had to be allayed, and they knew in this resolution they would suffer traumatic breaks with the past. . . .

It can be seriously questioned whether the agricultural problems in the century after the Civil War could have been solved by any single formula. Prices, marketing, competition, the arrival of the boll weevil, mechanization of farming, and internal and external social forces all bore on the plight of the farmer. The thrust of agriculture after 1920 lay not in the mere improvement of the farming techniques so much as in the recognition that drastic revisions of economic procedures were necessary. For the first time in its history, southern agriculture was beginning to be co-ordinated with the wide-range potentialities of the land resource on the one hand, and with the expanding American and international industrial systems on the other. Once the South became industrially involved, the question of basic agricultural production ceased really to be central.

The so-called crisis of lack of capitalization was not really a primary issue within itself. . . . There were resources aplenty in the South to tempt capital into the region, and so they did, but their exploitation required capable human talents in the forms of technicians and daring industrial leadership. It was true that tobacco was manufactured in the region, and, from 1870 on, an increasing amount of raw cotton was processed. Forests were converted into lumber, and coal and iron were dug from the ground. Petroleum products increased both in supply and demand. Water power was first used to produce direct power and then to generate electrical current, and in time utilization of this source of energy brought a southern industrial revolution. There were, however, two major handicaps; unprocessed products were shipped away from the region to yield bigger returns for non-southern processors, and too many southerners looked to outside management to organize and bring industries to their region. In this way they could hardly escape an intra-national colonialism which subordinated both people and resources to the bidding of outside capitalism and management.

It was in the field of resources management and exploitation that the South experienced a break with traditionalism. It is an astounding fact that the South as a distinct region survived so long in a nation where the basic standards of progress depended largely upon the uprooting of established institutions at least once every generation. The secret lay partly in southern geography. There is no doubt that the geography of the South went far to shape its economy and society. First there was spaciousness of land surface where soils were of fairly even quality, and which sustained for many generations a population of remarkable homogeneity; otherwise, it is doubtful whether a southern society could have survived.

In this spaciousness there existed a surplus of fairly good quality virgin land which permitted a wastefulness of soil on the one hand, and the failure to develop an intelligent land-use policy on the other. . . .

Tragically, the modern South in struggling to balance its economy between agriculture and industry sought to do so by exploiting its resources of timber, minerals, fresh water, climate, and soil in a wasteful age in American history. In spite of the fact that traditionally the region was bound in the net of a "single crop" it had the resources to develop one of the most intensely diversified economies on the continent. This fact, not politics and the Negro, was ultimately to be the most serious threat to the established traditions of the Old South.

The paradox of the economic South was that most southern leaders believed that industrialization ultimately would help the region stabilize and expand its economy, yet they feared industrialization. They thought it would destroy their way of life. It would be impossible to estimate the amount of energy expended in orating, writing, and conferring on the subject. . . . Agriculture may have been the standby of the nineteenth century, but to the new planners it was industry that promised to keep the economic sun shining and the rivers flowing in the latter twentieth century.

Extremely conservative groups wished to resist the expansion of industry on the grounds that southern culture would be left baseless, and the people of the region would become either hirelings of the machines or money grubbers. Industrialism was a northern importation which further threatened the southern tradition. . . .

It is possible that the area of greatest need for revision of the Southern system was in the field of government itself. The efforts by state constitutional conventions at the turn of the century to change the forms of government made the Negro, rather than southern economic and industrial progress, their central theme. These bodies were far more concerned in establishing white supremacy than in preparing the southern population for changes which many prophets were saying loudly would come to the South. In 1904 the Reverend Edgar Gardiner Murphy took a penetrating look at southern political issues, and at the leaders in the crusade to revise the southern state constitutions and institute "white supremacy." He regarded the loud outcries of the conventions, not so much appeals to protect white men's domination of politics as attempts "to arouse the white vote." In his view,

> "Negro domination" as a force of party control, as a weapon of political constraint, is fast losing its authority. Great masses of people are beginning to "know better." Its passing, as a party cry, will help both the Democracy and the South. The sooner the Democratic party comes to understand that, if it would hold the allegiance of the masses of our southern states, it must represent, not a futile programme of negation, animosity, and alarm, but a policy of simple ideals and constructive suggestions—a course which has given the party its historic position in our life—the better it will be both for the party and for the South. The South can then divide, and can make its division turn upon thought, fact, conviction. Every party and every section demands, in the interest of its broadest welfare, that there shall work within the regions, its traditions, and its ideas, the searching, sifting, divisive, regenerating forces of *truth upon its merits.* If this is not the privilege of the South, and if the masses of our people—through wanton provocation of the North, or through the failure of our own party leadership—are to be still possessed by the old benumbing and baffling error, then we shall have, as we have had in part already, a form of negro domination which we have least suspected. The soldier of old who bound his wretched captive to his wrist bound more than the wretched captive. If his slave was bound to him, he was hardly less in bondage to his slave. If the supreme apprehension of the South is to be the apprehension of negro domination, if our intensest effort, our characteristic and prevailing policies, our deepest

> social faiths, are to look no further than the negro, or to be even busied with the crude fiction of negro power, and ever-clouded by the outgrown demand for the negro's bondage, then at either end of this clanking chain, there is a life bound.

How prophetic was the Alabama minister! Howard Odum in *Southern Regions* presented in statistical tables the results of this southern policy. Later Benjamin U. Ratchford and Calvin B. Hoover in their survey of southern policies *(Economic Resources and Policies of the South)* discussed again the influence of government and governmental policies on the economic expansion of the South. Businessmen in states where racial conflicts and violence resulted after 1954 were quick to see that the old policies would leave them in ruin. In Arkansas, Alabama, and Mississippi especially, the results of violent racial upheavals had unfortunate economic results.

Historically, racial conflict and crises in this field existed continually. The shadow of Negro revolt from the bondages of the postwar South, from agricultural peonage, from political ostracism, from illiteracy, and from economic discrimination created so great a fear in much of the region as to cause white men even to condone murder by lynching, by armed attack, by ambush, and by miscarriage of justice in the courtrooms. The sordid crime of lynching alone was a stain far more ghastly than the lawlessness of frontier vigilantism. Its bestiality, hatred, shamelessness, and human depravity besmirched the honor of the South before 1930. As the course of history in the late nineteenth and the twentieth century has unravelled, the past was rapidly undone by social progress. The dominant element of the southern population had become firmly committed to modernization in every field, and there remained little room for the survival of the old and negative ways of life which could not be adapted to the present. Every outburst of violent resistance to inevitable changes brought the South nearer the central national objectives. The more positive the hand of the federal government in areas of decisions, the nearer the South has moved to conform with national patterns and objectives. It was not so much that mere barriers between men of differing races were being breached as it was that the whole fabric of the southern way of life was being rewoven.

There were loud pronouncements of negativism following the decision of the United States Supreme Court, May 17, 1954, and once again regional outcries in behalf of white supremacy had their effects. Islands of racial discrimination and racial violence were created to by-pass or nullify court decisions, but the heavier circumstance of national and international reactions worked too hard against such communities. This time the political impact of broad-gauged social revolution and Negro unrest had moved well beyond the sphere of influence of a southern state constitution, and even beyond that of a cluster of states and resisting political leaders trying to formulate a bloc of power that would neutralize the change. Not only was the matter of race relations deeply involved in local and domestic affairs, but it had become an enormously complex world-wide issue. Thus the South was caught not so much in change on a national scale, which it could resist directly, as in the tangled web of a world in social revolution.

Heavy rearrangements of the locale of the southern population in the scope of less than a half-century threw the old system out of balance. The historical tempo of modern regional society was so badly disrupted by internal movement and displacement that fresh beginnings were mandatory in every field of human activity. In a nation which had to consider its position and welfare in terms of advanced social and political theories, the modern South undertook to operate on realities, which, after all, involved no less the imprecisions of theory. James McBride Dabbs said that in dealing with the central fact of modern southern history the southerner has thrown realism to the wind.

> Your Southerner [he wrote] is typically a realist. He will embrace practically anything life brings if it comes without benefit of theory; but if it comes waving a banner he is almost certain to grab his sword and, without further consideration, have at it. He's pretty short on theory, and what he is short on he's naturally suspicious of. How did he get that way?
>
> Check back on the *isms* he has feared most of all, radicalism and abolitionism. Both were concerned with the Negro. The South has feared *isms* most of all because they tended to disintegrate its own essential *ism,* the one abstraction upon which its massive, concrete life had been built. What was this abstraction? [Slavery]

The sociologists have been more successful than the historians in writing of the human element of southern life. This has been true in spite of the fact that no aspect of southern history since 1865 has been of greater importance than the region's folk culture. Southern history is basically that of many folk groups responding to traditions, customs, prejudices, and cultural limitations. The frame of reference and perspective of southerners have been formed according to how well they have broken restrictive barriers. Folk history of any people is complex, but that of the South was made even more complicated by the existence of two races, a deeply sectional social consciousness, a peculiar regional economy, and the influence of vast geographical variations and influences.

It matters little that much southern tradition is largely myth; it is the myth by which southerners have lived. Passage of time has reshaped if not shattered many myths. After all cotton was not king, and much of what southerners from the beginning of their history have said they understood about the Negro has been questioned if not refuted by anthropologists, sociologists, politicians, and judges of the federal courts. The South has had little historical continuity; the overwhelming Anglo-American population on the frontier did not exhibit all the civilizing virtues in daily living and all the ability to solve regional problems apologists have ascribed to it. This appeared to be true when this civilization was appraised in various terms: statistics of all sorts comparing it with other regions of the Union, respect for law, maintenance of a highly efficient and sustaining culture, and the production of a broadly based leadership of good quality.

The complexity of southern folk history reaches more deeply into the processes of regional decision-making. How, for instance, was progress instituted in the South in such fields as agriculture, education, industry, and race relations? A deep-seated Puritanism has kept southern religion unusually conservative. The rigidity of the folk mind has been reflected in the outlawing of the teaching of evolution in three states, belief in a literal interpretation of the Bible (both reflected in the famous Scopes evolution trial in Dayton, Tennessee, in 1925), and the subsequent support by organized religion of other threats to intellectual freedom.

In other areas folk culture was of the utmost historical significance. For three-quarters of a century the South maintained an economic system that could not be justified by any reputable economist or banker, yet many areas showed dogged resistance to change. . . .

The postwar South carried in its political and social systems germs which ultimately would destroy the older patterns of southern life. Among these were the race problem, the demands of industry as against an agrarian economy, utilization and conservation of natural and human resources, a shifting political system, increased urbanization, and the drive for universal education. It is with the evolution of these changes that historians of the modern South must primarily concern themselves. Whatever else may have played a part in the region's history during the past century these facts have remained central. They concern southern traditions on which people have patterned their folk mores and their society. All of these lay well within the main channel of national concern.

As the century has unfolded, the South has had to struggle to keep abreast of the flow of American history itself, and at the same time retain as much of the peculiarly regional personality as possible. This conflict has taken place amid political conflict and change, a drive for better economic opportunities in the region, the problems of white and black men living within an integrated society, a rearguard action by Ku Klux Klansmen, citizens' councils, and bigots of every variety, and the constant crusade to reduce functional illiteracy. The region has had to face the problems that low per capita income, deficiencies in industrial development, poor agricultural output, human inefficiency, and other shortcomings that have held them back in relation to the rest of the nation.

What follows is a history of the South's breaking away from the past, and the reshaping of a southern image that was long ago cast in the mould of traditionalism and folk culture. Whatever the new image may finally become, there have been indications since 1920 that it will be a more positive one than much of the past proved to be.

(from *The South Since Appomattox*)

CHAPTER FIVE

CHANGING PATTERNS OF RACE RELATIONS

UNCLE TOM, GOOD NIGHT Pioneering in the backwoods offered a new challenge to slavery, and the Negro proved himself an excellent frontiersman. Many a vast cleared area in central Kentucky still documents this fact. Slaves chopped down the heavy timber, helped build the cabins, planted crops, and performed a thousand and one laborious tasks which had to do with settling people on the western waters. . . .

Slavery nevertheless early became a heavy social stone about Kentucky's neck. From the beginning of settlement there were those who suffered aching consciences because of the anachronism of the system in a land where men placed such great store by individual liberty and institutional freedom. Among early conscientious objectors were the Presbyterian missionaries who came across the mountains to assure the church a role in pioneering. David Rice, a native of Hanover County, Virginia, who had followed his neighbors to their new lands, was ardent in his efforts to plant Presbyterianism in the fresh country and equally so in contending that slavery should not be allowed to flourish. So loudly was his voice raised in protest that he frightened members of the first constitutional convention into writing a rigid clause which guaranteed that slavery would exist until it was struck down by amendment to the United States Constitution.

Father Rice was not alone in his views. Other liberal Virginians came west to add their protests against slavery, among them young Henry Clay, who raised the issue in his first Kentucky speech before a Lexington debating society. This, however, was an inept mistake which the young politician never repeated.

Useful as slaves were in opening the new country to settlement, the day came early when they were not nearly so necessary. By 1820 and the time of the opening of the great southern cotton belt Kentucky slaves came to have less economic significance as laborers in the production of hemp, tobacco, and livestock. In the South cotton barons were in need of armies of labor to clear their black lands and to grow their staple. This was a profitable market for Kentucky's surplus slaves. In fact many Kentuckians moved away to become cotton farmers, took their slaves with them, and sent home for more. Between 1830 and 1860 the sale of slaves southward became as commonplace as the sale of mules, hogs, and cattle. This era of Kentucky social history was sullied by accusations of slave breeding to supply the southern trade.

Again the Kentucky conscience was guilt-burdened. Nothing seemed more repulsive to the religious Kentuckian than separation of members of families: fathers were taken from children and children from parents. London Farrell, the famous slave preacher of Lexington, acknowledged the precariousness of social relationships for his parishioners when he concluded the marriage ceremony by saying, "until death or distance do thee part." A constant threat to unruly slaves was "Behave or be sold south!"

Slaveholders undertook to make their peace with God. They left behind them wills which specified that their slaves should not be sold into the interstate slave trade. However, once the ownership of slaves was transferred, the former master no longer had legal control over where they could be sold in the future. Slave dealers owned farms as way stations on which they employed their chattels, bought in estate sales, long enough for the memories of people to grow dim and then moved them to the slave pens of New Orleans, Natchez, Memphis, and Mobile. . . .

So bitter was much of public opinion against the interstate slave trade that in 1833 the legislature passed a nonimportation law which forbade dealers to bring slaves from Maryland and Virginia for resale to the South. Perhaps no other legislative act in the history of Kentucky stirred more bitter emotions for so extended a time as did this one. It became a central issue in many political campaigns and was the source of debate in a constitutional convention. Special slave interests fought for its repeal, and moralists were equally determined to retain it. Until the adoption of the Thirteenth Amendment in 1866 the Nonimportation Law remained a bloody bone of political contention and many a Kentucky politician was defeated because of his attitude toward it.

From the outset of the abolition crusade Kentucky slaveholders bore the brunt of criticism. Because they lived along the sprawling river frontier between freedom and slavery, every traveler who came down the Ohio made insidious comparisons between people living in the fresh air of freedom of the Northwest Territory and those withering in that of slavery. Every unfortunate incident was magnified and publicized. By the time the organized abolitionists had reached the peak of their crusade against the "peculiar institution" Kentuckians knew well the sting of their opposition.

(from *Kentucky: Land of Contrast*)

THE DILEMMA Beneath the stately trees, James K. Vardaman harangued his red-necked constituents for hours. And they stood in rapt attention listening to his sonorous outpourings, nodding in approval, or growling in anger when he denounced their exploiters. Pacing the green pine plank stage mounted atop an eight-wheel log wagon, the Great White Father played the poor countryman's Hamlet. In a highly alliterative style of speaking, he swayed his audiences with the assured talent of a master tragedian. He gave his hearers both pathos and hate, never allowing them to lose sight of the Vardaman objectives of white supremacy and political triumph. He was quick in repartee and wise in the workings of the minds of farmers burdened with the perplexities of cotton economics. His issues were stated in sharp personal attacks on his enemies, real and imagined, against corporations which were as vague to his hearers as his allusions to Wall Street, and in promises of help for the common man burning to a crisp on a Mississippi hillside.

His was not a campaign of specifics anyway. Both he and his noisy supporters knew that a revolution would have to occur before either would find life easier. Vardaman could always attack the Negro with safety from the recriminations of opponents. His colorful speech was adapted to the forceful uttering of age-old clichés and bitter epithets. He knew his audience lived in fear of racial uprisings, and he could strike deep notes in his subtle references to lurking dangers.

Following in the old master's footsteps in this park came Theodore G. Bilbo to cut a host of political enemies down to size. This blue-eyed crusader in many ways played a miniature Falstaff who used self-pity and personal abuse skillfully. Planted hecklers in his audiences were in fact prompters who egged the old boy on to higher levels of attack and ridicule. . . .

Vardaman's and Bilbo's voices have been stilled, but their key issue, the race problem, still agitates the people of the South. The Supreme Court decision in 1954 touched off a wave of defensive groups in the South. Just as if the calendar had been put in reverse and the region had reverted to the period of reconstruction, the future of the southern way of life seemed hinged on a highly organized resistance to the Supreme Court and other outside attackers. Not even reconstruction itself brought about the formation of so many defensive groups. Among the twentieth-century resisters are the Federation of Constitutional Government, the Grass Roots League, Inc., the Virginia League, The Federation of Defenders of State Sovereignty and Individual Liberties, American State's Rights Association, The State's Rights Council of Georgia, Inc., The Society for the Preservation of State Government and Racial Integrity, White American, Inc., and the National Citizen's Protective Association. None, however, is so powerful as the White Citizens Council, or Citizens Council, which operates in several southern states.

The first Citizens Council was organized in Indianola, Mississippi, in 1954. A preliminary meeting was held on July 11, when fourteen men of the delta country met to discuss the South's educational future in the light of the recent Supreme Court decision. . . .

The Citizens Council movement began in the delta blackbelt. Since this section was first settled, the land has been devoted intensively to the growing of cotton. Here large numbers of slaves were concentrated. After the Civil War, the freedman remained as a tenant farmer, and, indeed, there was a remarkable kinship between the master of slave days and the bossman after the war. In few other places in the United States have paternalism and its peculiar human controls been so vital to the social lives of people. To understand this fact is to appreciate the tremendous shock of the Supreme Court decision. . . .

The Citizens Council organizations spread rapidly in several southern states. Early organizational meetings were secret, even organizers were sometimes unknown to early members. There prevailed a philosophy of keeping the Negro confused and guessing. As the Councils became more numerous and better established, they operated openly. . . .

In areas where the Council or kindred body is active, it would be political suicide for a candidate or public official to voice a contrary opinion. The Council prospectus says that one of the organization's objectives is screening candidates for office to see that none goes far who holds an independent point of view. If none of the things mentioned above could be charged against the Council, it could still be called to account for the tragic destruction of inter-racial communication in the South. There is in the organized point of view a self-defeating spirit of reaction, the tarnishing of a fine regional reputation for liberality and fair play, an irrational approach to the solution of complex and highly sensitive social problems, and a lowering of respect for constituted government. . . .

Organization of the Citizens Council resulted in two immediate reactions. The press, North and South, carried numerous news stories and editorial comments about the organization. Whatever denial the organizers made, a segment of the press regarded the Council as closely akin to the Ku Klux Klan. At the same time there was a rash of organizations advocating eternal segregation and castigating the Supreme Court. The Ku Klux Klan in its various revised forms was among them. Almost every organization published a prospectus stating its philosophy and attacking the enemies of the southern way of life. . . .

While his white neighbors were organizing to circumvent court decisions and civil rights legislation, the Negro was diligent. Since 1900 he has organized the Negro Alliance, the National Council of Negro Women, the National Negro Youth Congress, the Southern Negro Youth Congress, the Urban League, the Congress of Racial Equality, and the National Association for the Advancement of Colored People. The latter organization has exerted the greatest influence on relations in the South. . . .

At the national level the NAACP has been active in lobbying in Congress against discriminatory federal legislation. It has undoubtedly influenced major executive decisions where the Negro was concerned. The real strength of the organization, however, has been its ability to maintain able legal counsel and to take its grievances to the courts. In this way it has avoided radical and emotional crusades and has consistently gained its objectives by the orderly processes of court decisions. . . .

While organizations were producing arguments and literature designed to scare southern people into active opposition to the Negro crusaders and the Supreme Court, southerners in Congress in 1956 produced the "Congressional Manifesto." Senators John Stennis of Mississippi, Richard B. Russell of Georgia, and Samuel J. Erwin of North Carolina—three of the ablest and most intelligent men in the body—constituted a drafting committee. The final draft of the Manifesto, however, was the work of Senators Russell and J. Strom Thurmond of South Carolina. The original draft was said to have been so truculent in tone that Senators Spessard Holland and Price Daniels refused to sign it. Thus the phraseology of the document was softened.

Senator Harry Flood Byrd of Virginia was active in gaining support for the declaration. Seventy-seven congressmen and nineteen senators from eleven southern states signed the statement. The majority leader of the Senate, Lyndon B. Johnson, and the Speaker of the House, Sam Rayburn, were not asked to sign. Senators from the border states of Tennessee and Kentucky refused to sign, as did the entire House membership from Kentucky. Senator Estes Kefauver of Tennessee, then a presidential hopeful, refused to endorse the statement on the grounds that "the Supreme Court must be the final authority on constitutional questions. Its decision now is the law of the land and must be followed." In his opinion, chaos and confusion could only result from flaunting a ruling of the Court.

In the minds of the Manifesto's draftsmen, the Supreme Court had deserted the principles of the Constitution and had "substituted naked power for established law." Judges of the

Court had abused their judicial powers and had "substituted their personal political and social ideas for the established law of the land." It said the principle of separate-but-equal facilities for the two races had become a part of the lives of the people, and now in rejecting it, the Court had "planted hatred and suspicion where there had been heretofore friendship and understanding." The signers expressed reliance on the fundamental law of the land, decried the Supreme Court's encroachment on state's rights, and commended the states which proposed to "resist forced integration by any lawful means." They proposed to resist judicial usurpation of power and to use "all lawful means to bring a reversal of this decision which is contrary to the Constitution, and to prevent the use of force in its implementation." Southerners were admonished not to be provoked into committing disorderly or lawless acts by agitators and troublemakers.

The Manifesto had no official sanction in Congress. It was presented as a resolution and there it rested. Like so much of this type of material which either gets before the Congress or into the *Congressional Record,* the Southern Manifesto appealed to the folks back home. No doubt it confirmed the opinions of people in eleven states that the Supreme Court had ignored the Constitution and that unidentified agitators were responsible for rising tension. It also raised hopes that somewhere, somehow, someone would find a legal loophole through which the Court's decision might be either circumvented or reversed. Historians at some future date may have a better perspective from which to view the personalities and the activities which brought the Manifesto into existence. Certainly there is evidence already in sight that tremendous political pressures were exerted on southern members of Congress to sign it, whether they conscientiously believed in its principles or not. In another respect the Manifesto outlined the sensitive points in the basic emotional and legalistic dispute with the Court.

Implicit in the Congressional statement was the turmoil occurring in the state legislatures. It would not be possible for an objective historian to read this document in light of the charged atmosphere of the times, and especially in light of subsequent actions by many southerners in the great debate in the United States Senate over civil rights, without arriving at the conclusion that the Old South is passing. This would seem to be true even in the face of vigorous senatorial debate. . . .

Legislators in the Lower South have searched for means to circumvent the Court decision. Scores of bills have reached the enrolling stage, and enormous amounts of energy, time, and money have been spent to interpose the will of the states against that of the Federal Government. In 1957, the Georgia General Assembly adopted resolutions seeking impeachment of the justices of the Supreme Court. Impeachment was asked on sixteen counts, the heart of which was giving aid and comfort to enemies of the United States by subverting the Constitution. . . .

There is, however, a body of moderate-minded people, who, though emotionally not in accord with the decision, wish to see the country's laws obeyed. But the group is largely inarticulate, for fear of economic and social reprisals and because, by and large, it has never enjoyed personal controversy. Moderates have spoken out, however, and much of what they have said has angered the extremists. . . .

Despite the enormous noise and reaction which gained so much publicity, there are moderates throughout the South. Several newspapers in the region have adopted realistic points of view. Among these are the Atlanta *Constitution,* and Louisville *Courier-Journal,* the Charlotte *Observer,* the Arkansas *Gazette,* the Raleigh *News and Observer,* and the Greenville *Delta Democrat-Times.* Editorials on racial and civil rights which have appeared in the *Courier-Journal* have been written by Weldon James, a South Carolinian. During the Little Rock school crisis, Harry Ashmore continually appealed for reason in the Arkansas *Gazette*.

Most outspoken in the lower South are Ralph McGill of the Atlanta *Constitution* and Jonathan Daniels of the *News and Observer*. They have exhibited enormous courage in both their editorials and their public speeches. Neither Daniels nor McGill has advocated an immediate end to the old southern way of life. As a matter of fact, both of them are regional sentimentalists, but they plead for a realistic and active approach to the South's racial problems, and have actively opposed extremist actions.

In the political field many southerners have demonstrated courage and a sense of reality in dealing with the South's problems. Several governors and members of congressional delegations have come to accept the Court's decision as a mandate and have instituted steps to conform. None, however, has displayed greater statesmanship than former Governor Leroy Collins of Florida. He is both highly literate and articulate. In his inaugural address in 1957 he told his listeners that they should first of all be honest in recognizing the realities of the South's position. Failure to do so would damage the moral welfare of their state. The decisions of the Supreme Court, he said, "are the law of the land. And this nation's strengths are bottomed upon the basic premise that ours is a land of law." He expressed belief that his people could find solutions for their problems, "if the white citizens face up to the fact that the Negro does not now have equal opportunities; that he is morally and legally entitled to progress more rapidly, and that a full good-faith effort should be made forthwith to help him move forward in the improvement of all his standards."

Three years later, Governor Collins addressed students at Princeton University. On this occasion he took a broad look at the modern South. The days of economic colonialism of the South were ended, and the region was faced with the challenge of accepting its new position "as a part of the challenge of accepting its part of the main stream of national life, and the responsibilities that go with it." The region, he said, would grow in economic strength, but it had to grow in moral strength and dedication to the nation's goals. "If the South should wrap itself in a Confederate blanket," he said, "and consume itself in racial furor, it would surely miss its greatest opportunity for channeling into a wonderful future the products of change now taking place. And the South must face up to the further fact that it would also bury itself for decades to come." He believed that no longer should "advocates of racial and economic reaction—the very ones against whom we in the South have to struggle on a local and state level for every inch of progress we have made—be allowed to speak for the South, simply because they have made the loudest noise."

(from *The Emerging South*)

IN THE TOILS OF INEQUITY Historically, the South has struggled with the challenge of educating the Negro. The development of a bi-racial system of education when reconstruction was ended only compounded regional problems. Though provisions were made for Negro schools, the vast majority of southerners were not conditioned to regard them with favor. Prior to 1865 the slave states forbade by law the education of Negroes. Even today this is a latent factor in some of the thinking about education of Negroes. There has prevailed the attitude that the field of activity for the Negro was largely physical, and to give him a classical education bordered on the ridiculous to many white southerners.

Further, to white southerners who bore the rigors of reconstruction, all public education was tainted with abolitionism and carpetbagging. The time was far off in the future when Negroes would be ready for education in the proper sense. Until then, they should only serve their basic physical needs. They had to learn to adapt themselves to the complexities and subtleties of modern civilization—so ran the white-southern argument. . . .

Negro education in the last three-quarters of a century has progressed largely to the extent that white and Negro leadership have received public support and outside interests have given supplementary support. In 1882, John F. Slater established the Slater Fund of $100,000 to support Negro education in the South. Twenty-three years later, Anna T. Jeannes of Philadelphia gave the General Education Fund $200,000 for the same purpose. Caroline Phelps Stokes willed the residue of her fortune in 1911 for Negro education. The next year Julius Rosenwald, head of the great Sears, Roebuck mail-order house, contributed $25,000 to be divided between Tuskegee Institute and neighboring Negro schools in Macon County, Alabama. In time this fund was enlarged greatly, and in 1930, the five-hundredth Negro school, built in part with Rosenwald money, was dedicated.

Today it is an open question what effect these vital private funds have had upon Negro education. In the early 1940's, for instance, Governor Eugene Talmadge of Georgia criticized the foundations in terms which were reminiscent of the attitude of earlier Georgians toward abolition. In many instances public management of southern education left responsibility for training the Negro largely to outside interests. . . .

In 1942, the Carnegie Foundation financed an intensive study of the race situation in the United States. As a matter of course, much of the burden of this study concerned the South. Gunnar Myrdal, the noted Swedish sociologist, was invited to direct the study. He came to America presumably free of any regional prejudices in the field of race relations. It is doubtful that he had more than an academic knowledge of the complex racial relationships in the United States. The two-volume study which resulted was the work of many people, and by the severest appraisal it is a provocative study. A distinguished southern historian said it is "the most complete study of American race relations." *An American Dilemma* has its weaknesses, which both author and collaborators acknowledged. It was meant largely to stimulate more specialized studies in areas closed to a general work. Two major conclusions of the book are that the race problem is national in scope and that the Negro problem in America is in fact a white man's problem.

In rendering their famous school decision in 1954, Supreme Court justices gave evidence that they had read the Myrdal volumes in search for a historical foundation for their opinion. Footnote 11 of the decision cited psychological and sociological studies. Immediately upon publication of the 1954 decision, extremists, some of whom had made a partial exploration of the field of sociology between the covers of Theodore Bilbo's *Take Your Choice,* attacked the Myrdal book for its supposed socialistic and even communistic implications. Leaving aside such unbalanced views Myrdal's work has much to offer the conservative southerner, as well as everyone else in America. It is an excellent source for understanding the Negro's place in American society, and it offers an effective analysis of the dilemma in which the nation as a whole has found itself in dealing with its race problem. The bibliography in this work leads far into the hinterlands of monographic and local studies of the Negro, studies which make serious efforts to help the South gain an appreciation of the nature of its central social and historical theme. . . .

An objective reading of the Supreme Court's decision reveals a sense on the part of that body of the inequities which have existed between the races in the field of education since 1870. Not even the most aroused southerner can view the South's social history through the objective lenses of statistics without becoming aware of this fact. . . .

The depression and World War II brought the Negro into a new set of relationships with his traditional background. The depression sent him to town and to areas outside the South to search for employment. Already the old agrarian system of the South was breaking down. In many instances, much of the race problem was largely drained away from the communities. What the depression left undone, the movement away from the farm is helping to finish. Few incidents in southern history have had such deep-seated effect upon the region's social life. Southern racial paternalism was largely destroyed. Only the lumber and pulpwood industries have maintained so close a control over laborers as the farm. Away from the farm the southern Negro has to live off his wages, earned in many instances in the employ of an impersonal corporation or company which supplies no "furnish" and has no other casual credit system. The breaking down of the old easy-going but ruinous relationships of the southern farm has come close to making meaningless clichés of much of what the southern white man thought and said about the Negro.

Living in town with the social problems accompanying his new form of life, the formerly rural Negro found more adequate communication with members of his own race. Often a higher cultural level accounted for changing attitudes and new forms of Negro aggressiveness. There is no way of knowing at the moment the full impact of World War II upon white-Negro relationships in the South. There was a revival of the fears which prevailed in World War I when the Interracial Commission was formed, that the Negro soldier would come back from the war an emancipated individual, and that he would set to work to destroy the traditional pattern of Negro-white relationships. Larger numbers of Negroes experienced combat service than ever before in American military history.

The young Negro in the postwar South found himself, like his white neighbor, in a changed personal relationship with his country. He faced new challenges which demanded personal courage and sacrifice, and a need for a more extended technical knowledge of things about him. Again, he was indoctrinated in the American democratic tradition in the various army training programs which placed major emphasis upon the American political system and way of life. This was really the basic objective of the war itself. There is no accurate measurement of what happened to the Negro's thinking during the war period. One indication was his changed approach to his educational problems. He sought remedy to the obvious inequities through both state and federal courts.

Before the war had ended, a group of moderately minded southern Negro leaders met in Durham, North Carolina, to draft a statement of principles by which their race could make social progress in the South. Their statement, prepared in 1942, bore the descriptive title, "A Basis for Inter-racial Cooperation and Development in the South." They said a new consideration of Negro education was mandatory if harmonious relations between the races were to prevail. This statement of principles asked first for equalization of educational opportunities which would eliminate the inequities revealed in some of the statistics cited above. They sought recognition of the fact that there was definite need for graduate and professional training on terms specified in the Lloyd Gaines case. This case in many ways was one of the most significant that led to the Brown *v.* Topeka decision. In 1938 Lloyd Gaines, a young Negro, brought suit seeking admission to the Law School of the University of Missouri. The state offered to pay his tuition to an outside school, or to establish a special law school for Negroes. He pleaded that offer of tuition to go outside Missouri was unacceptable, and that a "separate but equal" law school would not be equivalent to the work offered and prestige of the University of Missouri Law School. The Court held that opportunities available outside the state in no way satisfied the needs of a citizen within a state. "Manifestly," it said, "the obligation of the state to give the protection of equal laws can be performed only where its laws operate, that is, within its own jurisdiction."

In October 1942 the Durham statement was placed before a joint white-Negro conference in Atlanta. This group was told that the southern Negro was making an appeal frankly for educational equality, carrying out in fact the principles set forth in Plessy *v.* Ferguson. The Atlanta Conference made a clear response to the Durham Principles. "Their statement," said a conference resolution, "is so frank and courageous, so free from any suggestion of threat and ultimatum, and at the same time shows such good will, that we gladly agree to co-operate." Southern Negro leadership was commended for placing emphasis in their statement on racial discrimination in the administration of our laws. The Atlanta delegates said they were sensitive to the charge and admitted that it was essentially just. In a strong statement the Atlanta delegates observed that, "No southerner can logically dispute the fact that the Negro, as an American citizen, is entitled to his civil rights and economic opportunities."

In a subsequent meeting in Richmond, Negro and white leaders again came together in a joint conference. The group produced a forthright resolution in which they said, "In America, and particularly in the South, we face problems of readjustments to meet the demands of present and post-war conditions with reference to the Negro and the future development of a great region of the Nation. This, exclusive of the war, is the greatest crisis of the South and the Nation." The resolution took cognizance of the fact that the Negro was shifting cultural levels and that the postwar years would be a time when there would be great need for understanding and encouragement from his white neighbors. It was in this meeting that Dr. Gordon B. Hancock, Negro minister and sociologist, warned that the South could not afford to allow outside forces to extract from it certain gains. He pleaded with the conference to support southern Negro leadership then or otherwise the crusade for Negro rights would be directed from New York.

The Atlanta Covenant or Continuing Committee undertook to carry out the intent of the three conferences. The Southern Regional Council was formed and it undertook to bring about the necessary reforms that not only would retain the center of Negro leadership in Atlanta and the South but would begin a sane program of education. But charges of "nigger loving," and even Communism, scared away timid white support. The political demagogues unfairly distorted the work of both the Commission on Interracial Co-operation and the Southern Regional Council. The thwarting of this moderate Negro plea for equal opportunities was a costly error to the South's educational advancement. The South's refusal to meet the moderate challenges offered in the Durham Manifesto and to promote tolerant and objective purposes of the Southern Regional Council removed virtually the last chance for the principles of Plessy *v.* Ferguson to be applied to southern education.

By 1940 it was clearly evident to informed southerners that at last the issue of segregated schools would be taken to the courts. Already cases involving colleges and universities had either been decided or were before the courts. Extremists who had been opposed to any education for Negroes in years past now talked of trying to improve colored schools. By talking about "equal" opportunities sixty years later, they hoped they could still re-enforce the Plessy-Ferguson doctrine.

When four state-school cases reached the Supreme Court of the United States, docketed as Brown *v.* the Topeka School Board, there opened a new era of white-Negro relations in the South. Suits against the Virginia and South Carolina counties were based on lack of equal physical facilities and on the fact that segregation of the school system violated the Negro citizen's rights under the Fourteenth Amendment. This case brought squarely before the Court for the first time the issue of the constitutionality of the segregated public-school system. Again the South was being confronted by its age-old nemesis, the Fourteenth Amendment.

May 17, 1954, the Supreme Court through Chief Justice Earl Warren delivered its unanimous decision that segregation of children in schools on a racial basis in the defendant towns and counties was unconstitutional. In all but the Delaware case, a three-judge district court had subsequently denied the plantiffs' relief under the separate-but-equal doctrine of Plessy *v.* Ferguson. Argument was first heard in 1952 before the Supreme Court and again in 1954. Central contentions of the argument were conditions surrounding the formulation and adoption of the Fourteenth Amendment and its subsequent history. This was especially true as it applied to educational development in nineteenth- and twentieth-century America. The Court reviewed briefly the progress of public education in the United States, in the South, and in the field of Negro education. Reviewing the feeble state of Negro education in 1868, the Court said, "Today in contrast, many Negroes have achieved outstanding success in the arts and sciences as well as in the business and professional world." Progress in American education had been phenomenal since the adoption of the Fourteenth Amendment. It was more complex in its organization and curriculum.

Reviewing court action in the field of education, the Court took cognizance of all the cases from Roberts *v.* City of Boston, to Sweatt *v.* Painter. Unlike conditions governing the latter case, it acknowledged the fact that rapid progress had been made in the field of equalization in the tangible areas, as well as in curriculum and teacher training and qualification, but, said the Court, "We must consider public education in the light of its full development and its present place in American life throughout the nation. Only in this way can it be determined if segregation in public schools deprives the plaintiffs of the equal protection of the laws." Although this particular sentence has often been quoted, it received less analytical attention than other parts of the decision. Here the Court led the two southern counties onto the boggiest ground. Any casual examination of statistical tables showed the region at a disadvantage with other areas, and the Negro at a disadvantage with the white student.

The Court then reviewed American educational history, taking into consideration the expansion of the system, its academic progress, and the advent of compulsory attendance of children in school under the laws of the various states. It likewise considered the importance of education in modern life. In the Kansas case the circuit judge had already analyzed the general psychological effects of segregation on the school-age child. Concluding its decision, the Supreme Court said, "Whatever may have been the extent of psychological knowledge at the time of Plessy *vs.* Ferguson, this finding is amply supported by modern authority. Any language in Plessy *vs.* Ferguson contrary to this finding is rejected." And so the separate-but-equal doctrine for the races of the South was overruled judicially.

The Court realized that it had taken a momentous step in reordering the social life of the nation, and especially the South. It had snatched out in a single grasp deeply rooted social customs and mores. Before the principles laid down in its decision could be applied, enormous adjustments would have to be made. The case was restored to the docket, and the Attorney General of the United States and the attorney generals of the several states were invited to file briefs before October 1, 1954, as friends of the Court, for rearguments of points four and five. These dealt with the questions of how best to implement the desegregation of schools in keeping with peculiar local conditions. In May 1955 the Court ordered the defendant counties to begin making reasonable progress toward desegregating their public schools. . . .

In the field of education it has wrought many changes and has also brought about an enormous statutory structure which surrounds the educational process with legal technicalities. The seventeen states and the District of Columbia have made varying responses to the mandate to desegregate their schools. The border states of Delaware, Maryland, Kentucky, Missouri, and Oklahoma have proceeded with some rapidity to carry out the Court's order. So has the District of Columbia. In January 1960 there were 6973 school districts in the seventeen states; of these 747 were desegregated. Out of a Negro enrollment of 3,039,135, or 23.5 per cent of the southern public school population, 522,719 pupils were enrolled in desegregated situations. Aside from the border states, integration has been occurring on at least a token basis in the Old South states. Arkansas, Florida, Tennessee, Texas, Virginia, and North Carolina have desegregated schools. At the college level out of 195 formerly all white institutions of higher learning in these states, 124 were integrated.

Kentucky, as a border state, in many respects comes closest to representing a southern point of view. It is linked to the South by its folk origins, sentiments, social philosophy, and economic interests. A majority of its people might not have voluntarily chosen to integrate their public schools. Nevertheless integration has progressed in that state without incident, except for a brief furore in Clay, Sturgis, and Henderson. A private school was opened in Graves County, but its doors were closed within a year. After careful planning and preparation under the leadership of Dr. Omer Carmichael, Louisville not only desegregated its school system but it retained many of its Negro teachers. In Lexington token desegregation occurred without incident, and elsewhere in Kentucky the story was much the same.

Thus far integration of southern schools has not resulted in the unhappy incidents which segregationists have predicted. Wherever school boards, superintendents, and teachers have been allowed to reorganize their schools, changes have occurred without friction. Whether or not the Negro is better off sociologically and psychologically in desegregated schools is a matter which only time and mature study can determine. This much is certain: the Negro in the desegregated school shares with his white neighbor the fortunes of local education. If they are poor, both races suffer in like degree; if they are good, the two races enjoy equal opportunities to get an education.

(from *The Emerging South*)

THE CHALLENGE OF NEGRO EDUCATION After the Civil War southerners faced serious challenge in regard to Negro education. . . . If the white southerner was severely handicapped by lack of educational background, the Negro was by contrast hopelessly ignorant, and had been kept that way by statute law prior to 1865 which forbade his education. In his newfound freedom the Negro was entrusted with social, economic, and political responsibilities of which he could not conceive. . . .

The quality of Negro education at all levels became more more than an academic question to be deplored by statisticians and forgotten by southerners in general. Negro educational history down to 1950 must be considered as a separate strand from the educational history of the region in general.

Ideologically the development of common schools in the South made little distinction between the basic needs of white and Negro. This, however, was not actually true, as was reflected by the intensive discussion of Negro educational needs in the various southern educational conferences. Newly freed Negroes looked upon education as symbolizing both their physical and intellectual freedom. For many ex-slaves it had the deep spiritual meaning of enabling them to read the scriptures. For the Negro as well, one of the key ways in which he could enjoy the democratic way of life and participate in it was through education. And after the Civil War the American people made a commitment to the Negro to provide him with an education. It is significant that, though Negro schools founded during reconstruction were exceedingly poor in quality, and though a deep animosity existed in many places against educating the Negro at all, no southern state repudiated its commitments to support such schools.

The creation of Hampton Normal and Agricultural Institute in Virginia represented a major advance in Negro education. It was founded in 1861 by Mary S. Peake as a school for Negroes. Five years later General Samuel C. Armstrong was placed in charge of Negro contrabands, and in 1870 he became principal of the school. . . . Between 1868 and 1893 General Armstrong converted the struggling little Hampton Institute into an effective southern educational institution. In 1893 Hollis Burke Frissell became principal and continued the work of General Armstrong. . . .

Hampton Institute was only one attempt at improving the southern Negro's lot by education. The founding of Tuskegee Institute in Macon County, Alabama, in 1881 resulted from General Armstrong's training program. Tuskegee was located in the heart of the Alabama black belt where the Negroes made up 50 to 75 per cent of the population, but where they had made little progress toward improving their condition. There was great need for a school where the simplest rudiments of knowledge could be taught, and where free Negroes could gain practical training for simple work tasks. . . .

When Booker T. Washington arrived, Tuskegee had made only the barest beginnings as a primitive elementary school. The Alabama legislature appropriated $2000. Washington operated Tuskegee by the doctrine that the Negro must first develop the talents and opportunities he had. He preached the dignity of labor and counseled him to exercise patience until he had disciplined himself to assume responsibilities in a more advanced society. The central task of Tuskegee Institute was the conditioning of ignorant country Negroes to accept organized institutional training so they could perform ordinary tasks efficiently, develop the skills in several crafts, and produce enough teachers to begin to meet the southern Negro's educational needs. In emphasizing these themes, Booker T. Washington, more than anyone else of his race, helped to keep alive the hopes of his people at a time when they dropped almost to the vanishing point. . . .

In Kentucky, Berea College had offered co-racial education down to 1904, when the general assembly of that state enacted the famous Day law forbidding it. Berea, like Hampton and Tuskegee, provided student labor opportunities in lieu of money payments. It placed almost as much emphasis on vocational as upon literary training, and its work with Negroes was largely at the elementary level. Elsewhere after the closing of the Freedman's Bureau, the major effort to support Negro education was made by various private and missionary groups. By 1869, there were 178 private schools with enrollments of 40,000 students, 1600 teachers, and owning $7,500,000 worth of property.

Between 1869 and 1926 the Negro colleges made remarkable progress. By 1926 there were twenty-one publicly owned Negro colleges in the United States, most of which were in the South, and enrollment had risen to 35,662 students. Since 1945 Negro enrollment in formerly all-white colleges and universities has increased with each new annual registration.

(from *The South Since Appomattox*)

THE CENTRAL THEME If a modern Olmsted, Tocqueville, or Archer traveled through the present South he would hear observations southerners were making a century ago, and he doubtless would hear the same social philosophy given expression. Even in this period of transition from agriculture to industry, and from a predominantly rural society to an expanding urbanism, the Negro remains a central theme of southern life. When the modern southerner speaks so vehemently about maintaining the southern way of life, he is not talking about old economic or regional folk patterns, for these have almost vanished; he has in mind one specific subject—racial relations.

In another way the Negro influence in the South has made itself felt. In the last decade and a half not one session of a legislature in the ex-slave states has failed to give the Negro serious attention. In fact, so much attention has been given this subject that many times lawmakers have overlooked other vital legislation. Even special sessions of legislatures have been called to consider the subject. No one will ever know how much committee meetings, interstate conferences, and the communication of all sorts of political groups have cost the South in dollars and cents. If this were spent in combating tuberculosis it would go far to eradicate the disease.

In a less formal way the Negro theme has colored casual conversations. One can scarcely spend an evening in the South without hearing it discussed. Less well-informed persons inject it into conversations in the form of anxious questions. They reveal both their fears and their prejudices in these questions. Some discussions reflect lack of confidence in a large part of the southern population itself to maintain racial integrity. Newspapers, regional periodicals, religious and educational publications, books, pamphlets, and broadsides all reflect the deep concern of the South with the place of the Negro in regional society. . . .

Changes wrought by World War II were of tremendous importance to the postwar South. Not only was the Negro called upon to do his part at home and in the armed forces, and not only was he told that he was a full beneficiary of the advantages of a democratic society in which he lived, but he was helped by the emotional racist campaign of Nazism, which the American government was actively combating. Parallel to this was the rising world resistance to colonialism unleashed by the war. This anti-colonial movement was directed not only against imperialism but against discrimination against minorities; indeed, the two were equated by the newly emergent powers. It has been the United States Government, not the South or a single state, which has had to answer these charges when they have been leveled against either the South or the nation as a whole. In answering these charges of discrimination and colonialism the Government has incurred the wrath of southern extremists as well as the gibes of the new nations which raised the issues. Thus the South finds itself suddenly caught in an international net which it had not known existed.

For the southern Negro the changing world situation has had deep implications. For the first time his position as a minority person has been emphasized, and he has found powerful world support from other minority groups, who have asked many embarrassing questions of a nation trying desperately hard to maintain a foreign policy which professes a point of view favorable to the protection of minority rights. Thus the cause of the southern Negro suddenly becomes a national issue involving the delicate balance of the United States before a free world.

On the local domestic scene one of the most confusing of all issues was the "place" of the Negro in southern society. His position in the regional social system was poorly defined from the beginning, but, as years passed, it became a more highly restrictive one. This was especially true as Jim Crow laws and folk customs forced him into a perpetual condition of retreat. Modern social relocation of the Negro in the South has helped shatter the old folk pattern, a fact which has done great violence to the old ways of life. . . .

Since 1945 there has been a systematic effort to lower discriminatory barriers in areas where Jim Crow laws bound the Negro's freedom of social action in the older South. The first important area in which this has been done is at the polls. Negro leadership knows full well that its toughest fight is to gain full and accepted rights to participate freely in politics in the South. . . .

The Negro remembers the bitter struggle over his voting franchise in those grim days of the subsequent Populist crusade. He knows intimately what Theodore G. Bilbo meant in Mississippi, in the first round in the courts over white primaries, when he said that if the circuit clerks of Mississippi did not know how to keep the Negroes from registering then he could show them. On the other hand southern politicians were not oblivious to the fact that admission of Negroes to the polls would bring their careers to abrupt ends. Doubtless the whole approach to the voters in the campaign in the South would be diametrically changed if the Negro voted. . . .

Sometime in the future the Negro, after a massive amount of civil rights legislation, commission investigation, platform writing by the two parties, and court action, will finally remove barriers to his voting. However, he has a tremendous handicap to overcome. First, the mass of southern Negroes must be educated at least to the extent that they can pass a moderate high school test in citizenship. It will not be sufficient defense for the Negro to point out that literally thousands of white voters fall far below the standards set for Negro voters, but it is he who is faced with the fight to gain the right to vote. One of the most difficult issues is the educational requirements for registration. There may be no objection to setting an educational requirement at a level in keeping with national educational attainment of the mass of the population, but if it is used for discriminatory purposes then it is being prostituted.

Before the Negro in general reaches the stage where he can exert an appreciable influence at the polls, he will have to generate enough interest among his people to get large numbers of them to undergo the exasperations of registering and then of appearing at the polls to cast their votes. The Negro not only shares the southern white man's apathy toward voting, but he suffers from an ingrained fear of white retribution toward "smart" Negroes who insist on voting. . . .

In erecting barriers to the Negro's registering and voting, extremist southerners are possibly doing more than any other Americans to hasten the day when he will vote. This was implicit in Governor John Battle's plea with the Alabama registration officials in December 1959 to deliver the Macon County voter records. For while public opinion in the nation might be somewhat reluctant to push desegregation of the public school system faster than wise and lasting adjustments can be made, hardly anyone outside the South would look favorably upon the attempt to keep free Americans away from the polls, no matter what their social or educational background. Repeatedly this argument was made in the civil rights debate in the United States Senate. . . .

Participation in the political affairs of the South is possibly one of the most important goals which the Negro might hope to achieve. His achievement of this goal, however, makes greater demands on him educationally than is made of the white man. He has to erase as many of the old prejudices against him as possible in the shortest time. The idea has persisted for generations, aided by a defective educational system, that he is incapable of making political decisions. Education is after all the only means by which he may hope to achieve his free political rights, or to compete in the race for industrial jobs in the South. . . .

The southern Negro's economic condition has changed radically. He, in fact, has often to demonstrate a greater competence than a white applicant for a job in order to overcome racial prejudice against him. Thus education suddenly has become his fundamental means of moving from the old economic system into the new. Again the Negro's crusade for better opportunities has the support of a general world struggle to control men's minds. His cause is helped by the near panic at this point for advancing American educational efforts at all levels, and by the fact that national safety itself is involved in educational progress of all the American people. So for the southern Negro the equality of educational opportunity has far more meaning than the mere matter of social desegregation. It carries with it a heavier responsibility, and demands greater effort of him than of past generations of his race. He has to wipe away by achievement the fixed notion that he is incapable of meeting the challenge of the white man's society. . . .

In this era of change, with emotions running so high, it is difficult to assess with any degree of accuracy the full impact of the race issue on the region's future. Two facts, however, seem to stand out beyond reasonable challenge. The Negro has as secure a place in the history of the South as does the white man, and he is in the South to stay. It is true, of course, that large numbers of Negroes migrate annually to other sections of the country, but this does not mean that they are deserting the South as a race.

Southern cultural history bears the deep stamp of both slave and free Negro. Sectional economics have been largely conditioned by Negro labor, and regional humor and folk culture have been enriched by the imaginative language and customs of the Negro. Religious reactions have reflected the fact that the Negro too has a soul worthy of salvation. The physical organization of the early churches took this fact into consideration. In fact the whole moral code of the South was long ago shaped to include the Negro, if for no other reason than that of preserving law and order. In a more fundamental way southern white and Negro lives have developed a common interest, and the two races have a common regional sentimentality.

Many white southerners have long assumed that they have an inborn understanding of the Negro. It is a novel thing indeed that many white men are quick to declare that they understand the Negro, while it is a rare occasion when a Negro will boast that he understands the white man. In fact the Negro's precise knowledge of his white neighbors is perhaps many folds greater than is white understanding of the Negro. . . .

Failure of free and full communication between whites and Negroes has become a deep social tragedy in the South. . . . By long tradition southern whites have generally remained away from Negro assemblies. Once slave and master shared a common communion in churches, but after the Civil War this ceased to be true. It is true that Negroes have stood on the outskirts of political gatherings and listened to political orations. They even gathered on the fringes of the Bilbo audiences to hear him excoriate their race in the bitterest of language. Even so, there has been much to Thomas Nelson Page's contention that close friendships prevailed between southern whites and individual Negroes. Long years of peaceful associations at work and in community relationships document this fact. . . .

Nevertheless the deep underlying fear between the two races must be overcome. Few rural southerners over fifty years of age have not heard in their youth rumors that a race riot was imminent. Country newspapers of half a century ago carried hints of the prevailing anxieties in various communities over this fact. The pro-segregationist literature of the present also contains a tone of fear of the Negro. Possibly no negative fact between the two races is so thoroughly established as the white man's fear of the Negro sexual lust. Based upon strict objective facts of history, the fear should be the other way around, but no clearly defined and dependable notion seems to prevail either privately or in print as to how the Negro man might feel toward the white man's violation of the Negro woman. . . .

Fears of race riots have largely disappeared over the years. When the last of the bitterest of the old political race-baiters like James K. Vardaman, Ben Tillman, and Thomas E. Watson passed on, much of this lurking fear was dissipated. It passed out with the halting of lynching, and with periodic threats of the passage of federal anti-lynching legislation. The explanation of this changing phase of southern social history no doubt lies more closely in the fact that the South is speaking less and less with its frontier voice and has seen great changes in its basic economic structure.

In the present South, the age-old fears are expressed differently. The charge that compliance with the 1954 Supreme Court decision would bring about a commingling and mongrelization of the races has a background in the old fears that resulted in frequent lynchings. Historically large numbers of white men have not been able to trust themselves in the presence of Negro women, and they appear to be certain that intimate and casual relationships in the classroom will rip away the racial barrier. Roy Wilkins, speaking for the NAACP on the television program "Meet the Press" in 1958, answered a question about mongrelization by saying that the presence of so large a number of mulattoes in American society indicates that concern over the mongrelization issue is fully two centuries too late.

If the southern white man has an inborn fear of the Negro, he also has deep suspicion of the intentions of northerners. . . . Geographically the southerner has difficulty in locating the North. In his mind its centers are New York, Detroit, Chicago, and maybe Los Angeles. But it may be any place where criticism of the South originates. It might even be in Memphis, if such were the case. Possibly there is no physical line, but it is to be located more specifically in terms of emotions, social attitudes, and political reactions. It is the point where often blind prejudices shade off into a doctrinaire certainty of a single solution to the problems of the South. . . .

The South cannot exist happily, if at all, without the nation, and the nation in turn is dependent upon the South. Somewhere calm and responsible leadership must prevail to solve the larger issues of the race problem. The South can ill afford to continue to waste its emotional energies and further expend its precious resources in the negative approaches used since 1954 without suffering irreparable damages. Extremists on both sides of the issue have yet to offer solutions to racial confusions. The solution lies almost solely in the area of the repeated and implied promises that the South can find the answers to its problems. The finding of these answers, however, places a heavy and positive responsibility upon both social and political leadership to take a careful look at the region's needs and then attempt to bring about solutions in the best of faith and by the sanest possible legislation. The challenge is even greater to everyday citizens, churchmen, newspaper editors, educators, and businessmen. Solutions, however, cannot be accomplished in an atomsphere of bitter denunciation, denial of the law, threatened economic and social boycott and retribution, or dynamitings and other forms of violence.

The negative approach to solving the South's racial issues has the pressure of history against it. On the positive side there is enough calm leadership and dignity in the South to face the current social issues without flinching. It can, of course, by patience and use of good judgment find the answers to all of the region's problems. They will not be simple answers easily arrived at, but they will set the foot of the South on the road to progress.

No one can write a prescription for solving so complex and ancient a problem as that which faces the South at the moment. It seems, however, reasonable to make some general assumptions. Southerners are unaccustomed to gauging the complexity of the race problems—and others as well—on the basis of a full statistical consideration. As a result, they more often than not lose perspective in viewing actual conditions. For instance, it has been the experience of the border areas where schools have been desegregated that Negroes have not flocked to integrated classes in overwhelming numbers. Actually little more than token registrations have occurred. Too, there is a sobering lesson in the fact that these desegregated schools, including Norfolk, Virginia, have been free of unhappy incidents. Where traditionally white universities and colleges have opened their classrooms to Negroes, remarkably small numbers have registered. The more accurate gauge is to be found in the enrollment of Negro colleges, and there is at present no indication that a reduction has or will occur at any time in the foreseeable future. Again, in the political area, the Negro has neither broken nor altered the political behavior pattern of a community where he has exercised his freedom to vote. There has been little if any bloc voting. Sometimes one would conclude from the arguments of the extremists that the Negro has a capacity for leadership and change which the white man does not possess. By the sheer matter of statistics the Negro, except in certain intensely colored areas of the old blackbelt, can hardly alter the political picture in the dire way predicted by the prophets of doom.

The South's economic and social life has been developed around the two races. Both have made major contributions to the region, and a calm and objective evaluation of these contributions offers a key to future peaceful relationships. To attempt to write off or belittle Negro contributions to southern culture would be akin to disowning the contributions of large segments of the white race itself. Here is a broad common ground for the two races to base a positive and mutual respect for the accomplishments of each other.

(from *The Emerging South)*

CHAPTER SIX

INDUSTRIALIZATION AND MODERNIZATION

THE BURDEN GROWS LIGHTER Southerners are not what they used to be. Pick one out at random and he is stronger and more virile than his grandfather was. By modern American military standards of physical, mental, and moral fitness, however, more than half of the Johnny Rebs who shelled the woods at Shiloh, Chancellorsville, and Gettysburg, or stood with Pemberton at Vicksburg, might have been kept at home as 4F's. No one can say just how much pellagra and hookworm helped to sustain the Union. . . . Malaria fought on both sides. . . .

Whenever southern land touched blue water, there was ever-present danger of yellow fever; malarial infection was almost a certainty. Mosquitoes responsible for yellow fever entered the region from the Caribbean and the Gulf of Mexico. They brought waves of death. "Yellow Jack" traveled as far upstream as Kentucky, and up the coast to Baltimore. Mobile, New Orleans, Savannah, Jacksonville, and Galveston frequently became sinkholes of death. Every summer season brought its dark threat of crisis. Even Memphis in the 1870s and '80s experienced yellow fever scourges which frightened away both human beings and industry. Railroads felt the shock of disease in loss of freight and passengers. . . .

Persons who survived yellow and typhoid fevers in many areas still had excellent chances to become infested with hookworm. The nameless Dutchmen who landed the first cargo of slaves in Virginia brought the South a bitter health problem. As the white population expanded, the incidence of hookworm became greater. Barefooted and carefree men of nature defecated on the ground, giving the bloodthirsty killer in their bowels the air and soil necessary to complete its life cycle. Pale, emaciated, tobacco-stained dirt-eaters became stock characters of the natural southern scene. Wherever warm weather and moist soils hatched hookworm, there were poor whites. So definitely a part of the population were they that historians, and even some sociologists, have discussed them as a mysterious genus that existed and multiplied especially to plague the South, or to sustain the ego of cotton snobs. These shambling human wrecks became standard southern folk characters in the first half of the nineteenth century, sometimes, it seemed, for the special benefit of amazed foreign travelers. . . .

Those hard years, 1865-1910, saw great layers of southern population fall victims to the troublous regional ailments. People died largely of something else, but hookworm made their weakened systems more susceptible to other diseases. Nevertheless there was hookworm disease; ignorant doctors were unable to diagnose it. A complacent and long-suffering people reconciled their physical condition to the will of God and the illnesses of childhood. Poverty, ill-health, and economic backwardness were crosses which most southerners seemed born to carry.

In the first decade of the twentieth century, Walter Hines Page, the North Carolina gadfly, conducted an editorial and oratorical campaign in behalf of the New Yorker, Dr. Charles Wardell Stiles. As a biologist of long experience and precise training, Dr. Stiles had served the Bureau of Animal Husbandry of the Department of Agriculture with unusual professional fidelity. He had discovered that animals from the South carried hookworms in their intestines. From a study of parasitology he learned that Angelo Dupion had discovered hookworm in the entrails of workers who died while constructing the St. Gotthard Tunnel between Italy and Switzerland. He also knew that much of the southern population exhibited symptoms similar to those of the European victims; this meant that they too must be infected.

Since 1896 Dr. Stiles hammered away at the hookworm theory without getting anyone to listen to him seriously. Fortunately for southerners this was just the kind of an idea which set Walter Hines Page going. He needed ideas of this sort to use in his intermittent campaigns against southern ills. In the 1880s he had stirred lethargic Raleigh slightly out of its routine habits by attacking the Confederate myth in his noisy *State Chronicle*. But Raleigh was hardly ripe for a siege of tradition-smashing, and, although Page raised a lot of sand, he received little cash. Now in 1910 he was headed south with the double-barreled charge of illiteracy and hookworm infection.

Dr. Stiles's contention that southerners had hookworm was insulting to the South. Southern manhood was virile; if a hookworm could live through all that corn whiskey, said facetious commentators, then nothing would kill it. Southerners were just resting temporarily after a hard war. Page was an upstart, and Dr. Stiles was a Yankee mountebank.

Turnip greens, grits, sweet 'taters, sorghum molasses, catfish, and sow belly were treatment enough for even the worst case of laziness. . . . The facts remained that approximately 53.6 per cent of the people in some selected areas of Georgia were infected with hookworm, and one person out of thirty-five in particularly heavily infested zones was dying of exhaustion. Thousands of southerners were left suspended in a foggy and witless state of retarded animation.

Once news of the hookworm theory got abroad, cartoonists joined southern legislators in a field day at the expense of the Rockefeller Foundation and Dr. Stiles, and such garrulous wits as Irvin Cobb ridiculed both Dr. Stiles and his southern victims in the *New York Evening World*. The urbane Page fell victim to these wild shots of journalists who showed more wit than social tolerance and understanding.

Treatment was simple—so simple that even the most dense hookworm victim could pursue it. However, it was a sight easier to cram a dose of salts and thymol down his gullet than to put shoes on his feet and lead him into a sanitary privy to answer the call of nature—that, too, would have been a violation of an established southern tradition.

The battle against hookworm had to be won at legislative, editorial, and philanthropic levels. Page sought Rockefeller Foundation aid, but first he had to convince Dr. Frederick T. Gates and Dr. Simon Flexner of the devastation wrought by hookworm. Even these scientists were skeptical at first, but they were soon convinced. The Commission for Exterminating Hookworm was created on October 29, 1909, with a million dollars in its till. A year later, workers began a survey of Richmond County, Virginia. At the end of the five-year period for which the Commission was created over a million children were examined, and an incidence of infection of 30 per cent was found. Intelligence and physical tests were far more revealing and disturbing. Beyond a doubt large numbers of southerners were being sapped of their vitality by this insidious parasite.

Finding hookworm in many areas of the South dramatized further need for organized health services. If a microscopic worm could cause so much demonstrable havoc among the people, so could other diseases. Local health departments were organized, and existing state organizations were given more support. The region below the Potomac became health conscious, if not thoroughly active in combating diseases. . . .

In another way southerners have changed. Death comes to them in about the same form as to other Americans upon an adjusted age basis. Heart disease heads the list of causes of death, and is followed by cancer, pneumonia, accidents, tuberculosis, nephritis, congenital malformations, and senility.

In Florida, cirrhosis of the liver is a greater threat than malaria, hookworm, and pellagra combined.

In a broad field of economic expansion improved health conditions ensure the fact that southern businesses today are less subject to absenteeism than was true in the past. And one of the reasons why southern communities can advertise so vigorously that their people are willing workers is because of the region's major health advances.

(from *The Emerging South*)

ON THE FACE OF THE LAND The revolution on the southern farm just described is only a part of the changing pattern of southern rural life. Stereotypes and local traditions notwithstanding, a central characteristic of the South's social organization has been a lack of cohesion in its community structure. From the opening of the nineteenth century to the advent of the Tennessee Valley Authority, the regional community pattern was static. The old-fashioned double-log house symbolized the spread of civilization westward. Subsequent oblong bungalows, with their impending porches, reflected the complacency of a postwar era. Barns and outbuildings cluttered southern homesteads, and public buildings added little sense of form and order.

Physical qualities of homes and farm buildings, however, were not necessarily a proper gauge to the South's social and cultural impulses. By 1930, the region had finally outgrown its frontier background, and, later the development of improved schools and roads and the introduction of electrical power had elevated the southern cultural perspective.

The old way of southern community life contained a germ of defeatism. Frustration was a fruit of civil war and reconstruction, of the failures of staple agriculture, and of sinful waste of the soil. A homogeneous population brought to the frontier South a complacent sense of social responsibilities which deterred progress. Thus it was that twentieth-century southerners found themselves existing largely in a rural vacuum. . . .

Homes, soils, and human character had been deeply eroded by the end of the first quarter of this century. The dreary conditions endured by numbers of southern people became the substance of critical appraisal of the South. Faulkner's novels have involved much of this social fabric. Concurrently, scholars and critics are searching for the mainsprings of this author's materials. Oftentimes they fail to see in much of the more recent economic background of his home country some of the answers. Eroded hillsides, depleted land, and wasted resources go far to document the Faulkner material. . . .

Novelists were not alone in analyzing the rural South. Others attempted realistic appraisals of the region's failures. A constant stream of articles, pamphlets, and books describing the crisis came from the presses. A slight pamphlet entitled *The South, The Nation's Number One Economic Problem,* published by the Federal Government (1934), had an appreciable effect in shaping regional attitudes toward prevailing conditions. That same year the President's Committee on Farm Tenantry published a searching analysis of the condition of agrarian society in the South. It was a grim diagnosis. It left no doubt that people, land, agricultural system, human character, and credit methods had failed. In text and statistical table this report evaluated the erosion of sharecropping and tenancy. Farm Security Administration photographers caught the South in an extreme condition of social paralysis. No observant traveler had ever recorded so precise a description of many southern conditions.

Graphically, the Committee on Farm Tenantry revealed the cause of social failure. Insecure tenure had deleterious effects upon both land and living standards. Sub-marginal economy destroyed the affection and respect for buildings, land, and institutions. Communities were caught in a catapulting downward spiral of economic opportunity. More optimistically, the Committee expressed a belief that security of land tenure promoted the building of better homes and the preservation of the lands. "Stability," it said, "increases the family's interest in community activities and makes it possible for the children to remain in school. Secure tenure does not produce large speculative profits, but greatly increases the opportunity for a steady income to owner-operator, tenant, and landlord." . . .

In 1935 vast areas of the rural South were reduced to shabbiness. Farmsteads were cluttered and run-down, reflecting a deep-set state of poverty. Rusting implements and vehicles were scattered about in disarray of abandonment. Barns, outhouses, fences, and grounds sagged under the weight of sun and time. Even country churches stood on careening foundations atop ground that receded with the wash of recurring wet seasons. Agricultural backwardness, if not complete failure, was stamped upon homesteads as indelibly as the thrust of the hills and the slash of the streams. . . .

Rural southerners' lack of any aesthetic taste showed on the land. Both white and Negro were devoid of a sense of orderliness and beauty. Where the white man failed to maintain an attractive house, the Negro lived in an abode that was much shabbier. Unpainted boarded houses and big rambling natural pine structures were more characteristic of many parts of the South than pillared mansions. . . .

Architecture after all, however modest or impressive, was only a symbol of the quality of social life. The way of life of the people was more revealing. It cannot be overemphasized that much southern yeoman culture down to 1920 was still the culture of the American frontier. The age of a community had little to do with fundamental social and domestic advances. Old coastal and delta blackbelt regions alike were often areas of inferior homes, and there were disorganized communities without social leadership. Southern politicians were either oblivious to conditions about them or preferred not to face realities. Demagogues were able either to turn their heads to social failures or to blame someone far removed from the South for local troubles. They rationalized community failures so as to block understanding and progress.

The Tennessee Valley Authority introduced the largest program of uprooting an established pattern of indigenous society in American history. Not only were hundreds of families removed from farms and ancestral homesteads, which dated from the beginning of the famous Watauga settlements in the eighteenth century, but so were whole towns and communities. Even cemeteries were moved out of reach of flood waters. Churches and schools climbed to higher grounds. Old community lines were broken, and for some of the region social organization was begun anew.

When the TVA started, many communities in the scope of the valley were almost as primitive as they were in the opening days of the frontier. . . . The first manifestation of the new era was the improved quality of homes. New houses took the place of the old ones. They were more efficiently planned, with provisions for the conveniences which cheap power would make available. No longer were country people willing to build houses without painting them. Farmers in search of land had opportunities to wander over considerable territory in locating new homes. Almost immediately they became more receptive to new ideas of farming. Agricultural test plots in the Valley made concrete and understandable arguments for change. Farmers were more willing to listen to advice about soil types, community advantages, new types of farming, and land uses. Their lives had been disrupted, and they no longer had to fight the inertia of the fixed traditions and mores of their old surroundings. They were now out to get the most for their money, and they were highly receptive to the advice of farm experts who could predict the future capabilities of the soil.

Possibly of greater importance was the fact that the rural electrification management regarded the isolated farm home as its chief customer. Under the old system of extending electrical services, this type of customer was considered more trouble than he was worth. Availability of electric power was an enormous motivating factor in the redirection of southern community life. Labor-saving devices were in reach of large numbers of people for the first time. The drudgery of farm work was lightened. Farm houses now had available to them the conveniences of houses in towns. Turning on the lights in a rural home for the first time was akin to spiritual rebirth. The first burst of bright light revealed the shabby surroundings to many rural southerners in a manner that was impossible for them to see without electricity. Dingy walls, drab furnishings, and a general lack of inspiration in their surroundings were disclosed. Lights in these shabby homes created the greatest incongruity in southern country life: it seemed sacrilegious to maintain such run-down surroundings in their presence. Almost immediately new furnishings and equipment, and even new homes, were in demand.

Availability of electricity brought more than bright lights. Farm incomes had to be increased to buy radios, washing machines, mechanical refrigerators, pressure water pumps, electric ranges, and, later, television sets and deep-freezers. Financial drains were staggering as compared with those of the past. Almost immediately the barriers of isolation which kept the farmers in ignorance of world happenings were wiped away. Too, they had made accessible to them sources of advanced agricultural information which came at strategic moments to help them make changes in the old ways of farming. If they were to meet the rising costs of the new conveniences which became all but indispensable after electricity was made available, they had to turn to a more efficient system of farming. Thousands of householders were thrust into modernity faster than their ancient homes could be readied for change. Porches were lined with washing machines and refrigerators as though these conveniences symbolized a better social status. A man with a washing machine and a refrigerator, even if they were on his front porch, was at least keeping step with the times, and was announcing to the world that he was willing to meet both the challenge of the future and the installment collector.

Along with improved roads and better communication, electricity helped change the southern rural personality, Countrymen became good customers for labor-saving machines, vast tonnages of fertilizers, annual supplies of pedigreed field seeds, more and better clothes, and mechanized farm equipment. The new way of farm life had made them customers worthy of being courted by businessmen. . . .

Community improvement programs have attempted to comprehend all the needs of the rural South. Beautifying and modernizing the home ranks as a prime objective. Homesteads were restored, houses painted, outhouses improved, lawns landscaped, and trees and flower gardens planted. Early improvements seemed small in the face of obvious needs. To outsiders they hardly seemed improvements at all. It was so simple to relocate mailboxes, to place them on uniform posts, and to print clearly the names of owners on the side of boxes. The naming and posting of local roads might not seem a vital change, but to a backward community it was a forward step. So was the improvement of farm entry-ways. To remove the accumulation of rusting farm implements from sight broke a long-standing southern tradition. These were little things, but they reversed a custom for many southern countrymen.

A bigger task was the human problem of bringing people together and planning for community betterment. Extension service workers and city promoters of community projects were greatly tempted to push people faster than they were ready to go. The path of rural southern improvement was a narrow one indeed. Churches represented an all but impenetrable barrier. Some ministers objected to community programs because they brought people together outside the churches. Often these ministers were not qualified to assume community leadership, and their denominational attitudes sometimes destroyed general confidence in their capacity to do so. Yet ministers struggled to make themselves central community figures. One of the first challenges in a community improvement program was to organize it without becoming beholden to the local church organizations. . . .

Community leadership has been able to hasten acceptance of new ideas by farmers. Where there has been will enough to maintain a well-organized community, there has been intelligence enough to accept advanced farming methods. . . .

Pressures of various sorts have brought about vast improvements in rural roads. Country voters still have strong influence in the state house; politicians have not yet discovered the wane of an agricultural voting population. As a result, rural roads have figured prominently in the scheme of legislation during the last decade and a half. Organized communities have proved powerful influences in hastening the building of farm-to-market roads. Hard-surfaced roads penetrate back country, replacing dirt roads which even the most optimistic prophet of two decades ago would not have predicted would ever be improved. A web-work of improved local roads into the heart of the rural South has been rerouted and marked. No longer is a stranger left in many places to his navigational sense to find his way. In the past quarter of a century the South has sealed in the mud on its country roads. . . .

Some of the history of the community improvement movement in the South can now be written in positive terms. Accomplishments outweigh failures. There are failures; some communities which embarked upon improvement programs have relapsed for one reason or another to their old ways. These failures are at once visible. Paint has scaled off the once proud roadside signs announcing community borders, and the countryside has taken on a look of defeat. Not all religious sectarianism has been destroyed, and thousands of people have refused to change their political behavior. Racial tensions have grown, and in some communities which have made marked physical gains they have mounted fearfully. In fact, where extremist organizations have superseded community improvement leadership, little if any fundamental and permanent change has been wrought in these important areas of human relationships. It will take far more intensive urban-industrial development and a revolution in local and national political behavior to bring this about. Extension services and utility interests have largely kept their activities clear of politics, and so long as local leaders followed their examples community development has wrought significant change in the modern way of life in the South.

It would be fallacious to say that the South has experienced a spiritual rebirth because of the influence of scattered community improvement projects. There are, however, manifestations that conditions of southern life are improved. Painted houses, attractive farmsteads, and active co-operative farm endeavors have all drawn the rural South into a tighter social organization. More important is the fact that for the first time southerners are feeling the impact of this organization at the community level. People sense a necessity for better institutional services and are more willing to accept new ideas and social counseling. This may in turn prepare the way for the readjustment of many deep-seated southern problems.

(from *The Emerging South*)

THE ROAD SOUTH A quarter of a century after Olmsted made his notes on conditions of Virginia roads, southern country editors were pleading for improved roads. Everywhere in the region roads were poor. In winter they were mud-bound, and in summer, dust-ladened. Characteristic of the difficulties encountered during the rainy season is the story told about the Ordinary of Duly County, Georgia. He had ordered an iron safe, six by ten feet, in which to preserve the county's records. This five-ton depository was shipped to Montezuma, twenty-nine miles from its final destination in Vienna. A contractor agreed to haul the big iron box for a hundred and fifty dollars, but on the way it slid off his wagon and sat mired in mud, blocking the road. The question arose about what next to do with it. A reward of a hundred dollars was offered for the best suggestion as to how to deliver the safe. Wags suggested building a railroad to it, some said it would be easier to dig a canal and float it home, others thought it might be used as a summer resort, or possibly it would be easier to move the courthouse to the safe, and one ingenious wit suggested inflating a big enough balloon to float it home by air. . . .

Until 1920 editorial scoldings were wasted on southerners. Roads cost money and labor. The South had the labor but not the money, and there were few counties indeed which proposed raising the necessary tax money to support even the most primitive roads. This was the situation in 1894 when a small group of southern leaders realized that their region could never really overcome its economic hardships until it had breached the mud barrier to efficient transportation. A highway convention met that year at Richmond, and a year later the crusade for good roads was further advanced in conventions at Atlanta and Houston.

Already the South was feeling the impulse of rising population and industrialization. Factories were in operation in many places below the Potomac, but they were so widely scattered as to be almost novelties in the land of staple crops. If southern optimists were to substantiate their remarks about the availability of nearby raw materials and the reservoirs of cheap labor, roads had to be built to permit easy transportation. Centuries earlier buffalo and Indian had scored the South with intra-regional trails. In the dawning of southern history, trader, cattle grazer, and plodding settler had padded trails into primitive roads, and so they left them. In 1900, these roads were little more efficient than they had been in 1860. They were disconnected and their surfaces unimproved. The southerner was still largely landbound. . . .

The rise of automobile traffic during the 1914–18 period hastened the construction of improved roads. . . . The automobile destroyed much of the myth of the old-style southern poor man. Afoot and on muleback his poverty was on public display. The public could see his bare feet and ragged clothes, but seated in a car, his feet were hidden from view and his rags could not be seen. New-found mobility and speed gave the southern yeoman his greatest release from the bonds of the past. In his new vehicle he found both dignity and independence. Distance no longer held him in its stifling grip, and the persistence of payments on his car blasted him loose from the ancient routine of a southern agricultural past and its uncertain year-end returns. The automobile became actually more important to the poor southerner than either medicine or dress.

By 1918 the South faced a dilemma. States debated whether or not they should issue bonds to be redeemed by direct taxes, or whether they should pay for their roads as they used them. Shortly before, Virginia rejected the idea of a general bond issue and chose to build its roads as it collected gasoline and use taxes to pay for them. North Carolinians were more venturesome and voted a staggering bond issue of $50,000,000 to survey and build a widespread system of improved public roads. . . .

While southern state highway commissions were being organized and the task of developing state-connecting road systems was still in its initial stages, Congress passed the Federal Highway Act on November 9, 1921. This legislation cleared the way for the realization of one of the major objectives of the pioneering highway conferences. Interstate roads were to be constructed with the aid of the Federal Government. This resulted in the planning of an inter-southern highway system which not only brought the South into fairly rapid communication with all its sections, but also with the rest of the country. . . .

Intersectional roads were opened in time to transport migratory southerners flocking to rising industrial centers in search of employment. The late 1920s saw this army rushing northward by car and bus from cotton and tobacco fields and from mountain farms to help produce the automobiles that would further crowd southern roads. Highways 25, 27, 31, 41, and 51 ran flush with this flood of immigrants. . . .

The automobile has brought faster change to the South since 1920 than any crusader for industry and good roads in 1894 could have foreseen. The prophesies of those crusading editors who pleaded with the people to pull themselves out of the mud were more than fulfilled. It may be that modern southern roads are not as wide as they should be, and that total mileage is more impressive than the actual quality of the roads. The main thing is that the roads are passable in every season. Since 1945 public roads have been redesigned and rebuilt. Now many of the main lines of travel are even being redirected, and, in some instances, new arterial routes of travel are being located directly from aerial photographs and from drafting boards. Not only has there been a tremendous change in the character of southern highway transportation on the ground, but these new roads have produced a change in a fundamental southern creed—namely, that the central government in each state should be given as little power as possible. Louisiana, Florida, Kentucky, Virginia, and North Carolina, for instance, have established central authority over tremendous web-works of highways which range upward from narrow back-country farm roads to primary state roads. In the past half-century this process of centralization has concentrated in the hands of state highway commissions staggering sums of money and political influence. In many southern states one of the best gauges of political behavior is to be found in the attitudes and activities of the highly centralized public-roads authority. . . .

Impressive though comparative statistics of southern highway construction are, the real significance of the new roads lies in the fields of social and economic change. Today the southern population is highly mobile. It is difficult under these conditions for a social situation to become a provincially static one. There is little possibility that such a population can be kept in a state of social self-satisfaction under these conditions. The modern highway has not only hastened the draining away from the South of hundreds of thousands of people, but it has brought about greater meaning to firsthand comparisons of local conditions with those in the rest of the country. Provincialism is less a factor in the modern South than ever before in the region's history. Conversely, the rest of the country has gained a closer look at the South.

(from *The Emerging South*)

URBANIZATION OF THE SOUTH By many standards of measurement the South since 1870 has been a vast rural island of isolated humanity. Even though the region made manful efforts to attract immigrants, little was accomplished. The European immigrant, either because he misunderstood the land and its industrial potential or because he disliked the racial and social conditions existing there, passed up the South for the great eastern and midwestern industrial cities and the agricultural states in the Northwest. As a result the southerners were left to multiply from a basic pioneer stock of British, western European, and African origins. By 1960 this pattern had scarcely been disturbed. Foreign-born in the southern states ranged from 0.1 per cent in South Carolina and Mississippi to 2.8 per cent in Texas.

The resource which did most to shape southern history in the years after 1865 was its people. During the first decade after the war, there were approximately 10,773,000 people, of whom 6,612,182 were white. A century later these numbers had expanded to 36,295,000 whites and 10,068,310 Negroes. These figures symbolize both the human facts and the comparative productive capacities of the two periods. Whether black or white this was an indigenous population which was entrusted with the social and economic fate of the South. Between 1870 and 1965 the population of the South had exhibited considerable vibrancy, often in negative form so far as southern progress was concerned. There was a tremendous amount of movement within the region, and even more away from it. . . . In 1930 of more than 28 million native-born in the South, some 24 million were born in rural districts. The rural South was already overpopulated, and 6.5 million people were forced to move elsewhere, over half out of the South entirely, the rest to southern towns and cities. T. J. Woofter, Jr., has said that the South exported about one-fourth of its natural population increase.

The quality of individuals in this horde migrating from the South was highly variable. Among the migrants were illiterates who were prompted to move away in hope they could both better their economic and social conditions. Among them also, though, went men and women who were well educated and trained and thus urgently needed in the region to assume leadership positions. Thus the South was deprived of talent it needed to improve conditions in the region and to diversify its economy. Migration took away from an already severely limited supply of trained people necessary to make the South competitive with other sections of the country.

Conversely, the migration of poor ill-educated, untrained people unfortunately went far to shape the southern image outside the region.

The heaviest migration has occurred since 1920. In the pre-depression decade, 1920–30, the Southeast lost nearly 3.5 million persons, while in the decade 1950–60 it lost over 3 million, almost half of them Negroes. States of the old blackbelt cotton regions lost Negroes more heavily, while states in the mountainous Appalachian sections lost mainly whites. . . .

Large numbers of young people between the ages of twenty and thirty-five took part in this migration. Since 1940 this drainage of human resource occurred among those with the most education—those who had completed at least the ninth grade—most of whom were bound for urban centers. In the 1940's, more than 4 million persons in this age group left the South.

The same pattern occurred within the South itself. There was great movement away from the rural areas into the cities, and here too it was those with educational background and leadership potential who tended to move. Between 1920 and 1948, the urban population of the region increased by over 9 million. In the next decade, 1950–60, nearly 3 million southerners changed counties, which indicates the increased restlessness and mobility of people within the region; this figure, however, fails to take account of the large number of families who moved within the limits of their own counties. These population statistics indicate quite conclusively that southern farm population has been shrinking at a very rapid rate during the past 50 years. Simultaneously, and especially since 1945, industrial communities and urban centers have undergone tremendous growth.

This movement of whites has produced a violent change in the region. Youth have moved from poor rural schools to those presumably of better quality in urban centers, and they have then gone into industrial and commercial services. Farmers became industrial employees, public service workers, and retail store clerks. Likewise, towns have turned into cities, with corresponding changes in their institutions and appearance. A different kind of southern urban life had existed in those small towns, many of them county seats and a few of them state capitals—Raleigh, Columbia, Montgomery, Tallahassee, Frankfort, Jackson, and Austin—and still relatively small cities. Originally the capital cities had substantial historical and economic importance, for their business was almost exclusively that of politics and providing services for state employees and officials.

The county-seat communities have been of major significance to southern life, yet it is to be doubted that many of them have contributed materially to the creation of a southern urban civilization. Almost invariably they have been farmer towns, catering to rural customers and county officials. Primarily they were market centers in which were located gins, warehouses, cotton buyers, tobacco sales floors, livestock pens, and railway depots. . . .

In some southern states like Virginia, Kentucky, and Tennessee county court day was an important institution, not necessarily because of judicial transactions, but rather as a gathering and market day. Horses, mules, cattle, dogs, poultry, and everything else that a farmer or his wife could think of to sell were brought to town to be peddled on court day. Politicians, noisy evangelizing preachers, peddlers, con men, patent-medicine quacks with their minstrel antics, women's bazaars, and petitioners all found audiences and customers among the throngs gathered for the meeting of the court or board of supervisors. Here news, rumor, and gossip were passed along. . . . It was also the place where the weekly newspaper was published, where banks operated, where doctors, lawyers, and dentists had their offices, where one departed from and returned to in traveling beyond county limits. General merchandising houses lined their main streets, and fertilizer warehouses, cotton oil mills, and produce houses, filled their alleys. Lumber and crosstie yards, ice houses, and coal yards were standard establishments, and no southern town could be progressively respectable without them. . . .

Southern urbanism was hardly true urbanism in the modern sense. The line between country town and countryside was scarcely perceptible, and only a very small portion of the population of these places fell within the more recent technical classification of rural nonfarm. The great majority of people living in southern towns had themselves moved in from the country, and had left behind numerous relatives. . . .

Unlike the old county-seat towns and villages that revolved about southern farming activity, hundreds of mill villages and towns were organized to serve special industries. After 1870, around the rising cotton mills villages developed with workers who were even more essential to the success of the mills than was the machinery itself. Actually most of these places never became truly urban communities. They were socially and economically suspended between a rural-farming community pattern of life and a specialized industrial one. Their inhabitants seldom broke sharply with their rural backgrounds, and many of them probably returned eventually to farms. . . . The earlier mill villages did differ from older farming communities in that people lived in close proximity in overcrowded housing, the company owned and controlled housing; the daily routine was dependent upon the operational schedules of the mills, and goods were sold and credit controlled by company stores. An individual southerner living in a mill village made a tremendous surrender of personal independence of the kind he knew on the farm. No longer could he set the length of his work day, be absent from work without risking loss of his job, or control the conditions under which he worked. Since members of his family usually worked in the mills too, the family's freedom of action was often restricted. The worker also found it difficult to exercise an independent judgment in public matters in many instances.

Early villages were composed of rural people who had had no previous experience in close communal living. There were problems of breaking old personal habits, especially in areas of sanitation and public health, and of invading the privacy of neighbors, or of having one's own privacy invaded. Public water sources were contaminated at the outset, little or no public provision was made for sewage disposal, and the old shackles of rural illiteracy and ineffective schooling were seldom broken by the move to a mill village. Women and children labored under unhealthy and unsafe conditions, and this constantly threatened life and peace of mind. The outbreaks of epidemic diseases threatened whole villages with disaster. Individual moral stamina was subjected to greater temptations and strains than was the case on mountain and piedmont farms. Thus a new and more relaxed social code frequently grew out of the new patterns of mill village associations. This was sufficiently true in most cases to cause the raising of social barriers between older, smug county-seat type communities and the new communities organized around the mills. . . .

Opening of coal and iron ore beds along the spine of the Appalachians brought about the organization of hundreds of villages and coal camps. The southern coal camp had all the shortcomings of the textile village, plus some of its own. Physical surroundings, despite the great beauty of the mountains, were about as ugly and repulsive as man could make them. With its eternal sulphurous smoke haze, dust, and nauseous burning slate piles coal mining destroyed every vestige of beauty and local pride. Usually villages were located on the floors of deep coves where flash floods constantly threatened life and health. Because coal seams were highly exhaustible, few mining villages were ever constructed with the thought of permanency, hence the use of the more precise term "camp." Coal-camp houses were small and flimsy, sanitary facilities were either unknown or most primitive, water supplies were constantly contaminated, parasitic infection ran high, and other diseases, especially tuberculosis, spread rapidly.

At periods during and immediately following World War I when national industrial expansion used tremendous tonnages of coal, wages were relatively high and miners lived extravagantly in what was called the silk-shirt era. Crime rates were high, and standards of moral and social behavior fell below those of older and more stable communities. Churches were poor, and were often of the highly emotional pentecostal type. Schools were . . . defective, largely because they lacked adequate housing, mature teachers, local tax support, and the deep concern of state departments of education.

As in the textile industry there came into existence some important permanent communities which either grew up about the mines or were deeply influenced by the industry. Among these were Birmingham, Bessemer, and Ensley, in Alabama; Chattanooga, Harriman, LaFollette, Jellico, and Knoxville in Tennessee; Middlesboro, Pineville, Harlan, Pikeville, Madisonville, Hazard, and Greenville in Kentucky; and Huntington and Charleston in West Virginia.

Lumbering created hundreds of villages and camps but few permanent towns as this industry moved across the great timber belt between 1870 and 1920. The southern lumber camp, like lumber camps everywhere in America, was a rowdy amoral place where inhabitants lived by the bare-knuckle code of the wilderness. Seldom did these places have a life expectancy of more than two to four years. To speak of morals or culture in a southern lumbering village, or of local pride, is like discussing social order in bedlam. . . .

During the latter half of the nineteenth century and the first two decades of this, the southern industrial village reflected more the conditions of the expanding western frontier than of rising urbanization. It is true that the removal to villages by rural southerners broke old rural ties, and hundreds of thousands of southern rural dwellers were started on the road away from farms and cities both within and without the South. The internal migration and the rise of newer types of industries dependent upon easily renewable supplies of raw material contributed materially to the growth of larger and more stable urban communities after 1940.

After 1900 the rapid growth of towns and cities began to transform the traditional agrarian South. As in every other phase of southern life the towns had widely differing histories. Predominantly the South has been a land of rural traditions stoutly protected by countrymen. A sampling of statistics is sufficient to establish this fact. In 1900 there were only fifteen southern cities with 50,000 or more population, and only three had more than 100,000—Louisville, New Orleans, and Memphis; only Louisville and New Orleans topped 100,000 in 1870. As late as 1920 there were only nine southern cities which had more than 100,000 population, with New Orleans and Louisville still at the head of the list.

The older southern city was founded and flourished for a variety of reasons. New Orleans, Houston, Galveston, Norfolk, Jacksonville, Mobile, Savannah, and Charleston were port cities which depended almost as much upon the sea for trade as upon their hinterlands. New Orleans differed somewhat from the others because it had both sea-going and river trades, which accounted for its ascendancy throughout most of the nineteenth century. River trade sustained Louisville and Memphis, enabling both places to establish region-wide supply trades. Both had excellent railroad connections, and were important agricultural markets. Staple crops such as cotton, tobacco and cattle contributed materially to the rise and growth of Richmond, Atlanta, Dallas, Fort Worth, Lexington, Durham, and Augusta. Louisville, Richmond, and Durham were early tobacco market and manufacturing centers. Lynchburg, Lexington, Kentucky, Danville, Virginia, and Winston-Salem were marketing and warehousing centers. Railroads contributed heavily to the growth of Nashville, Chattanooga, Atlanta, Louisville, Jacksonville, Dallas, Little Rock, Roanoke, and Miami. The development of mineral and petroleum products helped to expand the populations of Baton Rouge, Birmingham, Chattanooga, Dallas, Fort Worth, Houston, and Knoxville. In later years Jackson, Mississippi, was influenced by an oil strike in its commercial area. Universities contributed materially to the growth of Nashville, New Orleans, Atlanta, Durham, Knoxville, Austin, Lexington, and Baton Rouge.

Up until 1930 these main centers, despite increasing growth pressures, actually represented little if any appreciable break with restrictive southern social and economic traditions. It took a depression, two world wars, the availability of cheap electrical current in large amounts, the mechanization of agriculture, and the "go-getting" boost of state industrial commissions, chambers of commerce, and the Junior Chamber of Commerce in particular, to bring about rapid growth and internal change.

By 1960 there were some 14,461,000 housing units in the South as compared with 5,693,867 in 1920, and the quality of the southern home had increased markedly. From a surface view the southern community was vastly improved in appearance. Both country and urban homes had changed for the better, more substantial types of construction were used, and brick and stone had supplanted the cheap types of frame construction of former years. A surface view, however, hardly reflected the actual conditions within the home so far as its efficiency and comfort were concerned. By 1964 almost 98 per cent of southern homes had access to electric current, and had some kind of electrical appliances. Running water, a bathroom, and refrigeration had almost become standard equipment, to say nothing of radio and television.

The rate of urbanization in the South since 1930 is to be

measured in several ways; first, by the elementary count of farm, nonfarm, and urban populations which included people engaged in farming and living on the land, persons living on the land but not farming, and those living in towns and cities. In 1950 there were 9,712,000 farmers, 10,276,000 rural nonfarmers, and 18,505,000 urban dwellers. By 1960 the farm population dropped to 5,417,000, nonfarmers had increased to 14,376,000, and urban dwellers to 26,679,000.

A second way of counting the central portion of urban population is by listing cities with 100,000 or more population. In 1960 there were thirty-three such cities in the South. A third gauge used for more comprehensive measurement is that of the standard metropolitan statistical area, and by this system in 1960 there were sixty-four of these either in the South or spreading over into the region. A standard metropolitan statistical area is a fairly new population measurement used by the United States Census Bureau and defines a county or group of contiguous counties having at least one central city of 50,000 population. Obviously the statistics of southern population change annually with both rural nonfarm and urban groups increasing materially, while the rural farm category continues to shrink. With these shifts in population one fact in southern history is largely concluded. No longer will the southern farm serve as the important breeding ground both for a large southern urban population and for a large number of immigrants to other regions, as it has in the past. Furthermore, it seems not unreasonable to speculate that less of the southern population will leave the region as more industries are introduced, service type of employment is made available, and metropolitan areas continue to grow.

Most interesting of the new major population categories are the rural nonfarmers. These people now represent the second largest portion of the population of the South. They are largely southerners who seek nonfarm employment, but cling to a love of the open countryside and refuse to move into crowded cities. Many of them have in fact moved out of the cities in search of space and quietude. They farm on the side, and many industrial workers, working shorter industrial days, are able after work in a factory to operate mechanized farms or cattle ranges with even more success than their fathers did by full-time farming.

Six urban centers in the South have reached the status of major metropolitan areas—Atlanta, New Orleans, Memphis, Houston, Dallas, and Louisville. In October 1959 the Atlanta area proclaimed itself a metropolis with a million population. More than this, Atlanta has developed the characteristics of a true metropolitan center. It is the seat of a Federal Reserve Bank district, a transportation center for railways, highways, and airlines, and was a major branch office and branch plant city for large American businesses and industries. The federal government maintains important district offices here, and so do many publishing houses. Atlanta, however, is not purely a branch office and plant city, for several industries of national significance were founded and developed there. . . .

The southern city's most serious problem remains its Negro population. At the beginning of the reconstruction period Negroes began a rather heavy migration from plantations to some of the towns. This was especially true of such cities as Richmond, Charleston, Augusta, Savannah, Mobile, New Orleans, and Memphis. The horde of travelers and observers who viewed the South prior to 1886 to determine the effects of war and reconstruction noted this fact. It was difficult for the country migrant to find employment or to establish any kind of stable family life, but the excitement of town life drew him to it. From the beginning, segregated quarters were established into which the colored population was crowded. Housing was poor, streets were muddy and dusty paths, sanitary facilities were largely those which nature provided, disease was rampant; and tuberculosis, for instance, took a high toll of life. Crime was widespread, and there was constant friction between Negroes and law enforcement officers. These are the quarters which current civil rights crusaders have labeled ghettos.

Prior to 1950 the urban Negro was dependent upon urban services for employment, and these ranged from draymen and janitor to house maid, Pullman car porter, and waiter. Except for a few islands, like the Negro section of Durham, North Carolina, colored professional and businessmen had difficulty in establishing themselves. Doctors were dependent upon Negroes for patients, and lawyers were virtually barred from the courts, or faced enormous handicaps in the practice of law.

By 1910 the flow of Negroes to southern cities had quickened. A few statistical examples will illustrate this fact. In 1900 Atlanta had a Negro population of 35,782; in 1910, 51,978; and in 1960, 182,820. Comparable figures in other cities for these years were: Birmingham, 16,583; 61,238, and 184,725. New Orleans, 78,158; 89,672; and 234,931. Jacksonville, 16,721; 29,370, and 82,744. Smaller cities and county seat towns also gained rapidly. In the latter years approximately 2.25 million nonwhites lived in thirty-two cities with populations in excess of 100,000. This represented slightly less than a fourth of the entire southern Negro population of 10,178,308 in the South.

As the Negro moved in larger numbers into southern urban centers he brought about a significant change in his traditional relationships with his white neighbors. . . . In the cities the Negro enjoyed a certain amount of anonymity and impersonality which greatly strengthened his courage in voicing protests and making demands. A good example of this was the result of the early sit-ins which opened lunch counters and stores to all customers. The federal courts and the Interstate Commerce Commission helped him on his way with favorable decisions. A special citizens' commission in Charlotte, North Carolina, recommended full access to public accommodations, and thus alleviated much of the tension built up by the more active demands. The bus strike in Montgomery, Alabama, achieved its purpose, as did other types of protests in Atlanta, Louisville, Greensboro, and Columbia. Integration of public schools took place with greater ease in the cities than in rural communities. In Birmingham and New Orleans racial conflict was sharpest. The angriest anti-police protest occurred in Birmingham, where Negroes objected strongly to the racists' expressions and the activities of a chief of police. The Negro vote may have been an important factor in bringing about his defeat when he ran for Congress.

Two of the most serious problems confronting Negroes in the southern urban community were profitable employment and adequate housing. Negroes have faced tremendous competition for jobs from white neighbors, and they have been confined to living in less attractive . . . areas . . . and cities. They have found it difficult if not well-nigh impossible to break into the spiraling rings of suburban expansion. Both white dwellers and real estate developers have resisted their moving into new neighborhoods. Many suburban charters contain both anti-Negro and anti-Jewish clauses which though perhaps worth no more before the courts than the ink used in writing them up, nevertheless have reflected an attitude. Public-housing facilities in most cities have improved physical conditions, if not the quality of life, for both poor white and Negro in many areas. Negroes also have been able to purchase homes of good quality which have been left by white families moving into the outer rings of the cities. Between 1948 and 1953, they bought twenty-four thousand such homes in Richmond alone. No doubt this fact was repeated in every other growing southern city. Private capital has found a profitable outlet for investment in Negro urban homes of this quality. But so far there has not been any appreciable move by Negroes from the older areas immediately downtown into the newer suburban communities. Even so there were some racial resentment and incidents over Negroes' moving near the downtown areas of Knoxville, Birmingham, and Dallas.

Since 1930 southern towns and cities have undergone changes if not revolution. No aspect of city administration was adequate to solve problems created by industrial expansion and the influx of rural immigrants. Police departments were still operated largely by town justice-of-the-peace-type mayors and semirural police constables recruiting their forces most often from rural newcomers themselves. Schools were inadequate before the immigration rush began, and by 1945 were almost hopelessly overcrowded and confused. Sanitary facilities, never adequate, were now overloaded, as were welfare and public health agencies. Churches experienced growth but were not prepared to serve the emotionally exuberant newcomers. Housing was not only in short supply, much of it was twenty-five years out of date.

In the South, as in the rest of the nation, cities had begun dying at the heart as early as 1920. Main-street buildings were small, antiquated, and shabby. Homes encircling the center areas were also outmoded and decaying. Streets, once just adequate for horses, buggies, and wagons, were too narrow and winding to accommodate the rising numbers of automobiles. No longer was a public hitching rack good enough to serve the big city trade. Parking places became as much sought after as building sites. Both families and businesses began a flight from the spread of main-street blight.

Rings of new homes encircled every town and city in the modern South. Memphis, for instance, grew into bands of suburban colonies of single and split-level houses pasted on small lots, and lined up in endless rows that resembled the contours and terraces of modern farms. These housing whorls were broken occasionally by shopping centers with their plantation-sized parking lots. Chain grocery stores, variety, discount, and chain clothing and shoe stores pursued customers to their suburban lairs. Churches, schools, post offices, and branch banks did the same thing. Thus southerners' lives were forced into standard patterns that left little if any room for regional individuality.

Critics everywhere were quick to point out that the omnivorous bulldozer, monster that it was, had uprooted thousands of acres of farm and forest without much rhyme or reason. Newspapers were filled with a constant outcry over location of new roads and streets, construction of public housing units, the location and administration of business zones, and the protection of residential areas. Many persons came to regard city and public planners, traffic engineers, and zoning authorities as agents of chaos, corruption, and confusion. Where once editors unloosed their ire on the bedeviled farmer and his shortcomings, they now went after the new city devils with even greater fury.

The Redevelopment Housing Act of 1949 set off a good part of this conflict. Under the Act's provisions, cities could secure substantial loans to cure urban blight. Fifty-one cities in the South made application for such aid by 1952, and twenty-seven of these had populations under fifty thousand. . . .

The modern urban South faces new social problems as a result of its shifting population base. Juvenile delinquency and crime require new and perhaps more imaginative and drastic modes of solution. Youth separated from access to traditional rural recreational areas has to be served by carefully planned and expensive urban recreation, a fact which is still difficult for an older generation of taxpayers and public officials to understand. In 1962 the South had approximately eight murders per 100,000 population as compared with four and a half for the nation. In other categories the southern rate deviated but little from the national average, except for larceny over $50 and automobile theft. The rest of the nation led by a considerable margin in the latter crime.

It seemed clear that in urban expansion, whereby the region

had to face problems created by urban living, the South had moved more fully into the mainstream of American life than in almost any other area. But a growing monotony of city life affected the South as it did other parts of the country. A suburban community on the outer fringes of Atlanta looked no different from one near St. Louis, Milwaukee, or Chicago. Downtown sections of all these cities were filled with the same type of smoky antiquated buildings. A housewife had little or no difficulty in adapting herself to life in a new city, whether it be North or South. In the mid-twentieth century it became increasingly difficult to absorb the atmosphere of the South in its city streets, permeated as they were with gasoline and diesel-oil fumes and clogged by the everlasting five o'clock traffic jams.

(from *The South Since Appomattox*)

BY DAY A PILLAR OF CLOUD, BY NIGHT A PILLAR OF FIRE No institution in the modern South so clearly reflects conditions of regional life as the church. Though deep change is at once noticeable, there is still an underlying fact of historical continuity. In an era of change the church remains a central force in shaping social attitudes. To appraise the South without examining in considerable detail the place of organized religion would be akin to viewing a forest without singling out the trees.

In many ways the South has preached the New Testament and lived by the narrower tenets of the Old. The rich historical and personal nature of the Old Testament fitted ideally the needs of a literal-minded and agrarian people who saw reflected in its pages images of their own struggles. The wanderings and frustrations of the Hebrew people paralleled the social confusion of the South. The story of man's beginning, followed by bitter trials and tribulations, outlined broad social forms. Much of testamentary history detailed the rise of families where numerous patriarchs gained status largely by their procreative achievements. Family was man's primary responsibility, whether he be a Hebrew father wandering in the rocky wastes of Sinai Plain or a southern cotton farmer trudging a rocky hillside behind a plow. . . .

Old South influences have retained a hold upon the modern southern church. In politics and society, the rugged domination of Protestantism has helped to color regional history. Only in the last two decades have there been discernible departures from the past. An era of economic revolution, coupled with the disillusion brought by two world wars, had little influence on the fundamental structure of the southern church.

In the 1920s bigots lashed out at science and liberalism in blind fury. Unlearned and unlettered men put pressure on legislators to do their bidding or lose the powerful rural vote. In their minds, if universal education were to survive in the South it had to keep hands off religious traditions and prejudices. The positiveness of the Old Testament's account of man's origin was sufficient answer to the Darwinists. Any upstart scientist who questioned the Book of Genesis was certain to have trouble with his literal-minded neighbors. . . .

It is doubtful that a single legislator in a state which passed an anti-evolution bill really envisioned a culprit being brought to the bar of justice. Certainly no one in the Tennessee Legislature in 1924 foresaw the Scopes Trial with its resounding and embarrassing publicity. Though southern laws threatened ominous punishment in fine and imprisonment, they were little more than legislative bluster. When an offender was dragged before a judge in the Dayton courtroom in 1925 amidst a loud clatter of contending legal counsel and the shattering bombardment of sensational news stories, even legislators who had made the law were surprised.

Behind the anti-evolution bills were two significant facts which critics of the South overlooked. One of these was the pressure to promote emotional issues in order to divert legislative energies and time from curbing the activities of special interests. Railroads, for instance, knew the price of legislation which commanded them to improve some of their public services. The other fact was the rising influence of public education. It would have been impossible a decade before to have stirred up such a furor over the contradictions of science and religion, because too little science was being taught in the public schools to provoke a dispute.

The courageous stand of many southern ministers against the trumpetings of their fundamentalist colleagues was largely ignored by the sensation-hungry reporters. . . . There were intelligent leaders who cried out against the excesses of the bigoted and the spineless legislator, but their voices were drowned in a flood of publicity of the ridiculous. These rumblings of the new order in the 1920s bear sharply upon the course of recent southern religious history. Today there is still a solid foundation of extreme fundamentalism in the South, but it would be difficult to enact into law its narrow religious concepts. Many ministers and legislators are no more enlightened now than they were in the 1920s, but they lack the quiescent support of the people which they had in that period.

Modernism has changed its coat; it now comes in the guise of social and cultural reform. The burden of modern religion is that of placing man in contemporary society rather than dealing with man's obscure origin. That he exists is a tangible enough fact and his social needs and conflicts make an interest in his origin of secondary importance.

That is not to say that certain southern religious groups have ceased to fear modernism and its unemotional approach to human questions. Darwinism is as unacceptable in most places in the region today as it was in the 1890s and 1920s. But the fear that a modern social doctrine harbors a cynicism that will blight the warmly emotional individual responses which have characterized the religious experiences of the South is greater. In some undefinable way, in the minds of present-day fundamentalists the critical attitudes of the modernists have come to share the evil intent of the Communists.

Modernism has far broader implications for the southerner than mere religious ones. For two centuries the southern Protestant minister has largely refrained from participating in politics. The mundane affairs of campaigning and office-holding were left to the masses in the pews. . . . In like manner, the pulpit largely refrained from direct action in social reform. The nineteenth-century term "social gospel" contained an implication that was alien to an individualistic agrarian society. Problems and sins were personal, not social. The proscriptions of the Hebrew scriptures reckoned in terms of individual commission of sin as well as organized societies sinning. The minister in the modern South can hardly concern himself with the new social emphases of religion without concerning himself with the social, economic, and political affairs of his community.

Beyond the traditional scope of the daily problems of economic society in the South lay the two larger issues of industrial labor in a rising urban America and the race problem. Organized labor was foreign to much of the region in the 1920s, and so was the present type of rising industrialism. There were, however, the combined forces of the city and the labor union which threatened orthodoxy and Protestantism. They both sheltered the foreign immigrant who brought with him either a strong attachment for the Catholic Church or was tainted with poisonous "foreign atheism."

Industrialism has stimulated some organization of labor, and there has been a slight increase in the number of Catholics who have come to the modern South. It has brought the disintegration of older neighborhoods where established churches have long gathered their flocks. Now the ancient fold of the church is in one place and the range of the flock in another.

Many church spires which for generations have been landmarks in southern cities and towns now represent little more than the fact of change. Congregations have fled to the outer circles of expanding suburbia, and many a meeting of administrative church boards has been rocked on the breakers of impending change. . . .

As significant as the facts of physical change are the new demands being made upon the established southern churches to serve new and differently stratified social classes. The influx of industrial management personnel has brought a new and aggressive type of church member to many old congregations. This new member is often unwilling to accept pokey southern attitudes. In some instances church leadership has slipped away from the native sons to rest in the hands of the newcomers. At the same time rural migrations of poor and uneducated countrymen to the towns and cities have created demands for less socially-minded and sophisticated churches to serve their spiritual needs and to satisfy their emotional hunger. . . .

Failures of the older southern congregations to offer emotional satisfaction to the less well-educated and economically underprivileged groups in many instances caused them to lose ground with these people. Too, some of the older denominations became so concerned with social status that they moved away and left large numbers of their neighbors spiritually stranded. Ministerial salaries were increased by competition for their services, and congregations which once paid church obligations in produce were often left without preachers. . . .

It is doubtful that any other part of the nation offers so fruitful a field for the roving evangelists as does the South. These casual men of the cloth hasten over the roads in modern cars which are plastered with stern admonitions to the sinful to repent before it is too late. They drag swaying trailers loaded with tents and folding chairs to enable them to set up their tabernacles wherever the field seems ripe for the harvest.

The peripatetic revivalist and buxom female song leader have become as much a part of the southern scene as the motel and the barbecue stand. Closely allied to the itinerant evangelists are those tireless sinners who do public penance by erecting admonitory signs across the South, reminding speeding motorists, caught in hairpin curves, that they are about to face eternity with inadequate spiritual preparation.

More than a century ago several of the older southern churches pulled themselves away from national bodies rather than succumb to northern teachings against slavery. The northern religious philosophy threatened southern views, and the anti-slavery crusade condemned slaveholders for moral and spiritual wrongdoing. Clearly the will of the pew in this instance had brought the pulpit to time. Hundreds of books, pamphlets, and sermons expounded biblical justification for the course of the South. The Scriptures were combed for light and justification.

In many local congregations today there is remarkably little change in certain social attitudes from those that prevailed a century ago. Again there is fear of the northern church bodies, not alone because of their liberal racial attitudes, but because of their deviations from orthodoxy. . . .

Theologically, an appreciable part of the southern ministry is able to deal with abstract modern philosophies without upsetting either themselves or their congregations. Many of them can even discuss so abstruse a subject as existentialism without arousing much dissent. However, there are still many southern ministers who hold tenaciously to narrow sectarian concepts of human behavior and sin. They then labor diligently to maintain their notions. The stern anti-social preacher has sometimes found the going tough through two world wars and the accompanying periods of readjustment. The old rural taboos of half a century ago are shattered by pleasure-seeking, emancipated, and mobile youth. In this age of rapidly changing tastes in popular music and the lowering of barriers between the sexes, the devil becomes a most agile adversary. . . .

Industry with its tremendous social and economic impact promises further to change the southern religious pattern. Where present-day industrialism has changed community organization, the pulpit finds itself in a ticklish situation between the older employer groups and their employees. Never before have southern churches had to deal with the broad problems of industrialization and its peculiar demands for an applied religion. Greater intensification of industry in the South undoubtedly will tend to bring Protestantism and Catholicism into sharper rivalry. The Catholic Church has under way a campaign to break the Protestant grip on the sprawling and rock-ribbed cotton belt. But it has to do battle first with an aggressive and traditional religious adversary and to overcome antagonisms aroused by church policies which tolerate liberal racial attitudes. . . .

Every major church body in the South has made some pronouncement in agreement with the Supreme Court decision regarding segregation of the races in public schools. Whatever may be the feelings of individuals and local congregations on this subject, there is the knowledge that the church cannot function as a free body in a state of political anarchy. Also, as Ralph McGill of the Atlanta *Constitution* said in the weeks after the decision, the church cannot afford to come up on the wrong moral side of an issue, and observance of the civil law is a moral issue.

The Southern Baptist Convention, meeting in St. Louis in June 1954, was one of the first large religious bodies to adopt resolutions accepting the Supreme Court decision. In a five-part resolution that body was clear in its statement that race relations also involved religion and morals. It recognized the Court decision as harmonious with Christian principles of "equal justice and love for all men." The Court was commended for granting time in which to make adjustments; the people were urged to conduct themselves as Christians during the period; and there was an expression of confidence in the public-school system. Political leaders were enjoined to conduct themselves as statesmen so that "this crisis in our national history shall not be made the occasion for new and bitter prejudices." A. C. Miller wrote under the title, *Don't Blame the Supreme Court,* a leaflet to be distributed by the Christian Life Commission, a clear-cut statement of what the denomination's attitude should be: "These [race] issues must be met by Christian statesmanship on the basis of the scriptural teaching that every man is embraced in the love of God, and every man is included in the plan of God. In the light of these truths, legal segregation cannot be maintained." These are unusually strong statements coming from the major southern church body. They are in fact statements which run sharply counter to the views of the great mass of the membership of the denomination. So far, however, attempts in succeeding conventions to expunge the resolution from the minutes have been unsuccessful. So long as it remains, it stands as a powerful reminder for the southern Baptist conscience against any attempt of the church's members to thwart the laws of the nation.

In the same year of the decision of the Supreme Court, the *Church News* of the Episcopal Diocese of Mississippi discussed that church's views on the subject of the schools and segregation. Later this article was published in pamphlet form and distributed by the Department of Christian Social Relations. Equal educational opportunities are viewed as "a basic premise of Christian democracy." "There is no room for doubt in this discussion that the central issue involved in the Court's decision has to do with human beings. The great ethical principles of the New Testament proclaim the sanctity of the human personality as that which takes precedence over every other human consideration. Man, be he white or black, is made in the image of God. This is fundamental to the Biblical concept of the Fatherhood of God and the brotherhood of man. Our attitude toward the Supreme Court decision is, therefore, essentially a religious question, since it concerns what we really believe about God and his creations. It concerns what we believe ourselves to be in relation to other human beings."

In various ways the Methodist Conferences have spoken in favor of obeying the ruling of the Supreme Court. The Council of Bishops of the Methodist Church stated a positive attitude toward law and order. Earlier, in 1952, the church had adopted a broad and liberal social creed. In 1954 the Council of Bishops, meeting in Chicago, believed that "the Supreme Court recognized that such a ruling brought with it difficulties of enforcement, and therefore, made provisions for sufficient time to implement its decision. The declaration of the decision was made in the magnificent home of the Supreme Court in Washington, but the ultimate success of the ruling will be determined in the hearts of the people of the nation. Thus the church is furnished with an unequaled opportunity to provide leadership during this period in support of the principles involved in the action of the Court. We accept this responsibility, for one of the foundation stones of our faith is the belief that all men are brothers, equal in the sight of God. In that faith, we declare our support of the rulings of the Supreme Court."

On May 1, 1956, the General Conference of the Methodist Church condemned racial segregation, "by any method or practice." This decision, opening the doors of the church to full integration, was reached with a fervent display of unanimity. Delegates stood and cheered. The Reverend C. Cooper Bell of Lynchburg, Virginia, exclaimed, "God has been with us. He has worked a miracle!" Constitutional changes adopted by the General Conference, however, are a long way from getting the South Central Conference to ratify the abolition of the separate Central, or Negro, jurisdiction and its integration into the Methodist Church organization.

rural society and to serve the professions. Too few southern educators prior to 1945 had thought constructively in terms of intense urbanization, or of the possible racial integration threat to the schools. Though arguments contended for better support of schools, and every educational survey showed the South hamstrung at the bottom of the statistical tables, educational leadership worked against great odds. . . .

New conditions in the South make the old human image as out of date and antiquated as that of the Yankee abolitionist and slave baron. If the South is ultimately to realize its promise, the new leadership will have to be soundly educated. . . . If this new spokesman for the South is to be a trained scientist, the new southerner of necessity must be superior to his father in basic educational preparation in order to find profitable employment.

There is still lacking in the South sufficient native capital to finance necessary industrial expansion. The region is still largely dependent on outside capital to finance the building and equipping of new plants. In this respect the South has made its least departure from the past. Almost every conversation, speech, or report is predicated on the fact that new industry must be brought in from the outside instead of being organized at home.

The South has been highly successful in the importation of industries. Between 1956 and July 1, 1959, 4448 new industrial plants were located in the South. Most of these were organized and managed by outside corporations. In 1956, there were 3971 banks with total liabilities and assets of $38,436,100,000 in the region. Of this amount $28,227,600,000 was deposited on demand. Southern assets represented a relatively small share of the national holdings of $250,763,000,000. This means that major financial control of industry still resides largely outside the South.

In 1929 southern personal income was derived largely from farming, service employment, and the older industries of lumbering, textiles, and mining. In eleven states it averaged $363. By 1956 it had increased to $1325 as compared with a national average income of $1940. In terms of gross income, southern farmers for 1956 received $3,855,000,000, as compared with an industrial income of $33,322,000,000 and with governmental disbursements of $9,861,000,000. These figures represent three interesting facts: Farm income is dropping phenomenally behind industrial and service incomes; government disbursements in the South are of sufficient importance to regional economy that the Federal Government is able to exert enormous pressure on the region; and there is a rising urbanism which is reshaping southern approaches to regional problems.

For more than a century the old cotton South struggled mightily with a lack of capital with which to set its economic house in order. The present South hardly struggles in the same way, partly because there is a greater proportion of native capital available, and partly because of the manner in which corporate capital originates in the American capitalistic system. This fact distinguishes the present moment from others in southern history. Before 1840, millions of rural southerners had literally no set margin of economic existence beyond which they could not survive. A small farm always provided a meager survival. This is no longer true for great masses of the population. The margin of survival in the present South is now measured largely in terms of cash-wage income and availability of industrial and public employment.

Although the South lacks both basic capital and control over that which finances industrial expansion in the region, southern economic thinking generally has moved close to that in the intensely industrial regions of the country. The actual political pattern may have changed little from that of 1920, but thinking within the political framework gives evidence of aligning itself with new economic conditions. Much of the casual conversation in the region centers upon the subject of capitalizing and managing industry. Every new expansion of industrial activity takes the South farther away from its past.

Physically the South is creating new images. Bulldozers and giant earth-movers gnaw away hillsides to create new industrial sites, airfields, and roads. Workmen with plastic and metal helmets thrust up new electric generating plants, atomic energy installations, and factory buildings. They personify the new southern industrial image. It is hard, for instance, to imagine the South Carolina Industrial Commission restraining itself in an advertising section in the *New York Times* so far as not to show an ante-bellum Charleston home or parade the state's truly beautiful women in crinoline, or to ignore the Yankee menace, the NAACP, and General William T. Sherman. The new South Carolina image has not a single magnolia blossom on it; it is that of an electrical worker looking into the sky at an encircling manufacturing-company plane and shouting, "We thought you would be coming soon." It is also that of two sophisticated men who have withdrawn from the polo games at Aiken to discuss the state's industrial promise. In this advertising, South Carolina is indeed promising to depart from its past. . . .

Of more immediate concern in many parts of the South is the survival of the public-school system in the face of the threatened integration of the two races in common classrooms. It is doubtful that the forces which opened the crusade to lower the barriers of educational discrimination between the two races really foresaw that the South would be caught in one of its most strategic moments of economic transition. An increasing number of responsible southerners have emphasized the fact that the modern South cannot prosper without making a maximum effort to improve its schools. Actions to close public schools have already provoked militant pressure groups to keep them open. In May 1959, Louis B. Pendleton of Richmond, Virginia, told members of the Sumter, South Carolina,

Citizens Council, "Getting out of the public school business isn't easy to do. When the time comes in South Carolina, I trust you will be united, but do not be surprised at the so-called segregationists who suddenly become enthusiastic and active in 'Save-Our-Schools' organizations." In Little Rock, the Women's Emergency Committee for Public Schools demonstrated how effective such organizations can be. This action hardly involves the issue segregation versus integration; it is aimed at ensuring that young southerners will not be denied educational opportunity in their vital early years. When integration of Negro and white children will take place in the public schools in several southern states is at the moment beyond the guess of the most rash prophet. Governor J. Lindsay Almond, Jr., may indeed be correct in visualizing token integration as the minimum price for preserving public schools without disruption.

Whatever the outcome of the integration crisis, the fact that better education has become a necessary image for the South is important. Before the South can realize economic success, it has clearly to meet the challenge of educational maturity. . . .

This was inherent in the statement of Governor S. Ernest Vandiver of Georgia in January 1961. Faced with the stern decision of closing the University of Georgia or permitting at least token integration upon direct court order, he and his advisers made the latter choice. The *New York Times* reported him as saying to a joint session of the legislature, "The crisis is upon us. I must tell you quite frankly that a failure to resolve it will blight our state. Like a cancerous growth, it will devour progress—consuming all in its path—pitting friend against friend—demoralizing all that is good—stifling the economic growth of the state—and denying the youth of Georgia their proper educational opportunity."

Racial integration is a highly relative condition which involves far more complex economic and social situations than mere classroom associations of white and Negro children. It may be that this is actually the least significant aspect of present efforts to abolish discriminatory racial barriers. The rise of a new southern economy has in it the necessary force to destroy many traditional discriminations. A rising scale of personal income affects white and Negro alike, and the Negro with cash in hand has become a welcome customer in all kinds of stores in many southern cities. Merchants in highly competitive situations can hardly afford to drive away customers who have only to cross the street to enrich their competitors. Department stores catering to women no longer close their floors to Negro women. In other areas barriers have been lowered. As the Negro has moved to town he has entered into an entirely different relationship with his white business and professional neighbors. He now appears in the new image of a cash customer. . . .

During these years of change the southerner finds himself faced with new approaches to solving the race problems. In 1956 Montgomery, Alabama, Negroes undertook to erase racial discrimination on the city bus system by refusing to ride the buses. In a sustained period of passive resistance they underwent considerable personal hardship to accomplish their objective. This strike was widely publicized and no doubt was effective in consolidating considerable public opinion in the nation in favor of the Negro's position.

A personal protest voice raised in the Montgomery strike was that of the Reverend Martin Luther King. Preaching non-violence, he came to speak to a national audience for an appreciable segment of Negro opinion. Passive resistance was difficult to deal with because there were no overt violations of law. Nevertheless, Dr. King has often found himself involved in the general racial argument in the South and elsewhere. In October 1960 he was arrested in Atlanta for participating in a sit-down strike in a department store in violation of a Georgia anti-trespass law which forbids persons to remain on the premises of a business after they have been asked to leave.

In all the history of racial adjustment in the South few incidents have been more disturbing than the so-called "sit-in strikes." This crusade against racial discrimination at lunch counters struck at a highly vulnerable point in the pattern of racial discrimination. Department store managers welcomed Negro trade in all other departments of their stores, but maintained segregated lunch counters. The sit-in strikes were stimulated partly by the Congress of Racial Equality and partly by Negro and white college students. In March 1960, four students from the North Carolina Agricultural and Technical College, led by 18-year-old Ezell Blair sought service at the lunch counter in the F. W. Woolworth Store in Greensboro and were refused. By mid-summer stores in nine or ten southern cities had desegregated their lunch counters. In Charlotte, North Carolina, the Mayor's Friendly Relations Committee, with Dr. John R. Cunningham, President of Davidson College, as chairman, carried on long discussions with local businessmen. In July the Committee was able to announce racial bans in the stores would be removed.

Almost at the moment Dr. Cunningham and his committee were reporting agreement in Charlotte, the Platform Committee of the Democratic party was presenting to the country a civil rights plan condoning the sit-down activities. In their protests against the civil-rights proposal, southerners argued that to favor the strikes was to condone lawless invasion of private property. They did not, however, contend that entry into a store to make a purchase from a department other than a food counter was such an invasion.

In leaving the country, the southern Negro is rapidly changing his own image. First he finds himself caught in the vacuous eye of the great centrifugal force of suburbia expanding out from old town centers. The impenetrable wall of suburban communities largely confines the Negro to older submarginal areas. Here he is rapidly exchanging the old sex-hunger image of the days when lynching was rampant for that of modern day urban violence. This is a social area where he is experiencing his greatest test as a responsible citizen. He is faced with the problem of preventing the occurrence of violence under conditions which are often highly conducive to rising criminality. Under the leadership of the Reverend Martin Luther King and students of the sit-down movement, the Negro attempts to create an image of passive resistance. Beyond this the Southern Christian Leadership Conference is undertaking to stimulate the Negro to become an active and responsive citizen at the polls.

Though the new image of the southern urban-dwelling Negro has not fully revealed itself, two facts are already clearly discernible. First, he has left the South in appreciable numbers. . . . Second, emigration of the Negro population has changed two parts of the old regional-Negro image. The Negro is now largely a town-dweller, and the race problem has lost much of its old rural form. Too, it is now national in scope not regional. No longer, except in some parts of the old blackbelts, is there a predominantly Negro population in the South. The percentage gap between the races is being constantly widened. There can be little doubt but what the final decisions in lowering racial barriers will be made in the towns and cities. . . .

In a final analysis the South's adjustment to its new age lies largely in its ability to reconcile its past to the future. The temper in which this is done will determine the course of the region in the latter half of this century. . . . Moderation is an inherent part of the best of the southern tradition. It has long symbolized the South's honor and dignity. The very heart of the regional heritage is hospitality, graciousness, Christianity, and humaneness, all of these embedded in moderation. The great Jeffersonian tradition of liberalism rests upon a foundation of law and civil obedience. General Robert E. Lee further personified a spirit of moderation and dignity in the hard years following Appomattox. These are images which the South cherishes. An injury to any of these tarnishes the honor of the South itself. For this reason, if for no other, the

South cannot tolerate the Ku Klux Klan; the schoolhouse, religious community, and synagogue bombers; or any other extremist groups who stampede the region into ignoring law and order, or who create an image of violence and injustice.

The present South speaks with two voices, and these are more often than not in sharp conflict. Extremists keep up a refrain of bitter denunciation of the Supreme Court and meddlesome outside influences which would reshape the southern pattern of life. The voices of the New South pleading for industrial expansion and a reshaping of the regional economic pattern in the image of the industrial nation make themselves heard clearly above the sound and the fury of emotionalism. The conflict between these two voices increases every year, and the one which comes to predominate will largely shape the South's economic and political decisions in the future. An atmosphere of social peace and moderation offers the modern South its most positive means of competition in this age of declining agriculture.

Spokesmen for the South in the nineteenth century were eloquent in their outpourings, whether it be for expansion of slavery or expansion of industry. Henry W. Grady and his zealous contemporaries understood the necessity of balancing an agrarian economy with industry. They, however, little realized that the future would bring with it moral and social responsibilities which would reach down to the very basis of regional economic existence. At this point in the twentieth century the mature southerner tends to view the future with a fair degree of optimism. Though statistical tables still warn that the South has far to go to accomplish both social and economic security, there is reason to hope for improvement. How successful the South is in laying claim to the latter half of this century will depend in large measure on how sound its people make positive educational, economic, and moral decisions. . . .

(from *The Emerging South*)

PART III. THE FRONTIER OF HISTORICAL RESEARCH

CHAPTER SEVEN

A SCHOLAR'S APPROACH TO HISTORY

RESEARCH POSSIBILITIES IN SOUTHERN HISTORY Two committees of the Southern Historical Association have discussed problems of research in southern history. The first of these committees was appointed in 1944 to outline possibilities for a general co-operative undertaking and to survey opportunities for securing funds to promote studies in selected fields. Possibly the most definite suggestions which came from this original committee were two proposals that bibliographical studies be undertaken. The first suggestion was that a regional inventory of published sources should be made. A secondary plan was to encourage the compilation of state bibliographies. In continued discussions material objection was raised to the latter plan because it did not take into consideration the fact that southern history in its larger implications is not state-centered.

A second committee . . . met on February 14 and 15, 1947 . . . at Chapel Hill and proceeded to inventory the needs for research in various areas of the South's history. Again the need for regional and state bibliographies was stressed, but some members believed that a guide to maps, illustrations, and other details was equally desirable. It was readily agreed that bibliographies are indispensable tools and should be undertaken by capable hands. Beyond this, however, was the obvious fact that basic research itself is needed in nearly every branch of southern history. The inadequacy of research in numerous neglected areas militates somewhat against any major bibliographical undertaking.

Co-operative studies were discussed on several occasions, but the committee generally agreed that it would be . . . impossible for the Southern Historical Association to accept responsibility for supporting co-operative research. First, it is extremely difficult for a group to organize an undertaking which involves the labors of many people because it seems necessary to have enthusiastic, determined, decisive leadership to complete such projects. Enthusiasm usually wanes with the passage of time, and with the constant changing of personnel of the Association's officers there are no Simon Legrees who will heartlessly use the academic cudgel over the heads of freely promising but reluctant scholars to get the job done. There seems to be a fatal disease of procrastination among some scholars who band together to produce co-operative works.

These discussions of the Southern Historical Association's position with respect to co-operative studies obviously did not mean that no attempt would be made to encourage the organization of many group efforts. It would be happy to assist in promoting studies in southern history so long as the Association itself would not be called upon either to underwrite or to direct the projects.

When the committee . . . met . . . it faced the elementary task of making a cursory survey of the whole field of southern history with a view to locating the more serious gaps. Almost immediately it was evident that no area of southern history has received adequate treatment. Some fields, however, have been more adequately studied than others. In a thoughtful survey of any phase of our regional history the first question to arise is that of bibliography. It is not so much a matter of a simple listing of books as it is one of analyzing the fields covered by these books and evaluating their integrity of coverage. Almost any surface examination of research in southern history will reveal serious gaps. Perhaps it should be added in this connection that much published material pertaining to the region's history has been of a local and fugitive nature, and its existence is largely unknown to most scholars. Equally important is the fact that there is a rapidly growing core of materials which do much to enlarge the body of historical literature.

The committee discussed at length the areas in which much vital research is yet to be done and finally outlined nine divisions: (1) business, (2) industry, (3) religion, (4) the press, (5) social and cultural institutions, (6) urban life and urban development, (7) labor, (8) society, (9) transportation and communication. Every division was broken down into subtopics which offered encouragement to the research student and promised fuller understanding of southern history in general. No doubt all of these lists could be extended almost interminably, but some subtopics seemed to the committee to be more pertinent than others.

In presenting this report it is the hope of the committee that it will be of some value to both research historians and those who direct studies of graduate students. It was the frank opinion of the committee that no field of southern history has been sufficiently studied. Some subjects here listed have been more capably covered than others, but in every area there is golden opportunity for enlightening research and writing. It is evident that the scope of southern history is being rapidly broadened, and there are many suggestions which will lead students into the study of the New South. This, however, is not a suggestion that the older colonial and ante-bellum periods are less worthy of study.

Appraisal of the historical literature on basic southern economy reveals that the entire area of staple crops such as tobacco, cotton, rice, sugar, and grains has either been neglected or insufficiently studied. Along with these are the subjects of naval stores, truck crops, citrus fruits, livestock, and fishing. As yet no adequate study has been made of farm financing and marketing. Though marketing has possibly been one of the South's most urgent needs, the historian to a large extent has by-passed this subject for the more glamorous ones of politics and personalities. Intimately related to production and marketing are the questions of banking, capitalization, and merchandising. So significant a question as extraregional capitalism has been overlooked, yet this subject may well hold the key to the riddle of southern economics during almost the entire history of the region.

Along with the needs in agricultural and business history are those in the field of southern industry. In recent years, when an industrial revolution has been occurring in most areas of the South, industrial history has taken on a new importance. Unfortunately, the historian has not shown a marked fondness for this particular aspect of the subject. Except for tobacco and some phases of textile manufacturing, this particular field of human endeavor is almost entirely neglected. Perhaps first on the list of southern industries which cry out for historians are lumbering and mining. Since the very beginning of the region's history timber and mineral resources have been exploited, and they have made major contributions to wealth and welfare in the South. Of the extractive industries, coal, iron, gas and oil, asphalt, sulphur, aluminum, stone, and ceramic products are perhaps the most important.

Many individual manufacturing industries have long and useful histories. Of these there are the textiles, tobacco, milling, furniture, farm implements, carriage and wagon, medicine, soft drinks, leather goods, paper, plastics and wood products, athletic goods, and distilling. Every one of these businesses has accumulated large volumes of records, and every one of them has contributed materially to the revolution of southern life. In recent decades the processing of southern products has grown into big business, but little or nothing is known of the historical background of this activity.

Perhaps no phase of human relationships has been more

influential in southern life than the church. At the same time little is known in a general way about this institution. Perhaps outstanding of all the church-related subjects would be that of southern morals. This field would include attitudes toward slavery, dueling, dancing, drinking, general entertainment, reform movements, and all personal morals. Church government, the history of creeds and dogmas, and other fundamental problems of organization offer a golden opportunity to open new vistas of regional history.

The church as an institution goes deeper into southern life than religious dogma and spirituality. It plays a vital role in everyday social matters which relate to a special press, education programs, race issues, politics, organized labor, and intellectual life generally. As a specific example, the church-related school has been basic in many communities in both secondary and higher education. Educational policies and philosophies of church schools have gone a long way in shaping the policies of state institutions; but, of more importance, public opinion itself has often taken its cue from the general trend of church-directed education.

Missionary activities, both North and South, have often stirred troubled waters. At other times these efforts have been rewarded with definite constructive response. But whatever the response there has been sufficient missionary activity to warrant serious consideration by the historian, and before an entirely satisfactory social picture of the South can be reconstructed much spadework remains to be done in this area. Periodically, premillennial sects have appeared on the scene, and often their appearance marks a changing phase in both religious and social structure. It has not been unusual for the growth of one of these sects to indicate an important shift of population or to emphasize that a new social attitude has arisen.

Possibly no phase of southern development has been more influential than that of the region's press. Newspaper publication has stood out as one of the South's most favored arts. Whether a daily or weekly, the southern newspaper has been important in the whole structure of opinion. That the newspaper press has succeeded is shown by the fact that many contemporary journals are approaching century marks. . . . Histories of papers themselves will be rewarding to the historian, but the scope for research in this area is much broader than newspaper biography. There is the important question of public opinion in the South. Although there is a considerable element of intangibility in the measurement of the effects of organs of public opinion, there is a safe margin on which to base the assumption that the southern press has been a powerful factor in this field.

It is doubtful that anywhere else in the nation has personal journalism flourished more than in the South. Country papers have nearly always reflected the personality of their editors, while city papers have been largely personalized by their chief editors. At least a dozen southern editors cry out from their graves for biographers, and well-executed studies of the influence of these men will go far to enlarge the explored domain of southern history. Aside from personalities are the various services which have supplied newspapers with materials of an opinion-forming or recreative nature. These services performed the more important function of bringing the South into touch with the outside world. This has been especially true in the field of advertising, where pressure has been exerted subtly on the reader and, with threat of economic boycott, upon the publisher.

Like every other aspect of the region's history, the race question has raised its head in southern newspapers. Negro newspapers, both daily and weekly, have been published with varying degrees of success. Of more than economic importance, these racial papers have assumed certain attitudes toward their southern backgrounds. In some instances the feeling has been bitter and caustic while in others it has been insipid. No study has yet been made of this press to ascertain its contributions and failures in the field of race relations. Almost in the same category is the subject of Republican journalism in the South. Many Republican papers have succeeded in exerting a telling influence in solidifying public opinion; certainly in some communities they have threatened Democratic solidarity on more than one occasion.

Southern magazines, published in profusion since 1825, offer another largely unexplored area for research. Many of these periodicals have flourished, while more of them have withered and died on the vine of literary hope. They have covered a wide range of interests, including religion, agriculture, literature, commerce, medicine, law, education, reform, history, science, patriotism, and labor relations. Fortunately, files of magazines can in the main be found in public repositories, and the research student is spared considerable anxiety in hunting for his materials.

Southern publishers have produced a considerable number of books, even as measured against the national output. Unfortunately, much book publishing has been local and restricted in character, but nonetheless it is revealing in its general intellectual pattern. Newspaper publishers and job printers have often taken up this enterprise to pick up extra revenue for their businesses. Politicians, religious leaders, educators, and scores of others have contributed materially to pamphleteering, which has no doubt yielded much personal satisfaction in a region where disputation has always been a well-developed art. No facility has better enabled the disputants to air their views than the pamphlet. But not all southern pamphlet writing has come from the field of controversy. Propaganda has shared honors in this area, as have many branches of legitimate instruction. There is a need for sound bibliographical inventories in assessing the quality and quantity of the southern pamphlet output. A study of southern opinion as expressed in pamphlets will enrich the field of historical literature, and any light thrown in this dim area will be highly useful.

Cultivation of the fine arts—music, painting, sculpture, architecture, and drama—dates from the beginning of history in the South, yet too little mature work has been done in the appraisal of artistic contributions to southern life. The fine arts constitute a chapter in social and intellectual history which, if well considered, will improve vastly the present understanding of many aspects of regional failures and developments.

Closely associated with the creative aspects of the fine arts are the many associations which have flourished in the region. Many of these have had for their purpose encouragement of the arts, while others have been associations of a purely social nature. Among these are the mechanics' institutes, the nationalistic societies such as the St. Andrew's and German Friendly, and others. Library societies, lyceums, and chautauquas have been instrumental in exposing people of many areas of the South to culture. The impact of these organizations is largely unknown, despite the fact there have been many studies of one kind or another relating to libraries especially.

More in the entertainment than in the cultural field are the numerous types of fairs which have enlivened southern society since the days when the first Southerners began to take pride in their livestock and field crops. Closely akin to the fairs are the varied types of patriotic and public-interest meetings represented in Confederate reunions, community picnics, celebrations of national holidays, Christmas, and other occasions for festive associations. Historically there has always persisted this lighter vein in the matter of human relationship, and it can be assumed that much of the southern turn of mind has been affected by its varied types of relaxation.

In contrast to the entertainment aspects of southern culture are the more serious pursuits of science, history, and literature.

Many organized efforts have from time to time guided group thinking and endeavor into more unified channels. Any study of such undertakings would be rewarded with available records and perhaps a key to southern efforts to fan a spark of learning into a flame of general information. Individuals have contributed almost as much as organizations in these areas of learning, and possibilities for valid biographical studies are great.

Much has been written about the rural South, but there is to date too little tangible evidence that the southern scholar has thought much about the urban South. Yet there is almost no limit to the scope or possibility for revealing research in this field. Urban life and development offer many suggestive topics for exploitation. Among these are towns as trade centers, as cultural centers, and as county seats. The southern town has an important enough history behind it to justify study. It is interesting to contemplate results of studies which approach southern urban development as it complements agrarian life on the one hand and as it competes with a staple-crop agrarian system on the other. Southern political history is intimately tied up with the towns. Courthouse rings, city rings, ward bosses, newspapers, and other urban phenomena have left their deep marks on the southern political face.

Problems of intensified racial relations, problems of public health, city planning and lack of planning, the introduction of the industrial village, utilization of natural and mineral resources, and the advent of modern technological progress have been associated with urban growth. Added to these are problems of crime on the one hand and the variegated country-club movement on the other. Many old southern cities have evolved from quiet communities slowly wasting away from inertia into thriving industrial centers. Other cities have been bustling places of trade almost from the opening decades of their existence. Where the latter is true there is insufficient understanding of their influence in the long-range economic affairs of the South.

Closely related to urbanization in the South is the history of industrial labor. Southern labor history involves a rather complex variety of subjects. In this area, as in almost all others, is the problem of race relations. Agrarian legislators have not always hastened into the field of government regulation. As a result of this failure the history of female and child labor is long and often sordid. To date a remarkably small amount of sound research has been published in this area.

The bulk of legislation in the South dealing with labor and public regulation of work conditions bears the stamp of agricultural misunderstanding and indifference. State statute books stand as mute witnesses to the failure of legislative bodies to make proper advances into what they have often considered an alien field. On the side of acts of commission by state governments is the long and tedious story of convict-lease labor. Although the post-Civil War press was much concerned with this issue and special groups within the states were agitated by this social failure, a large part of the story of contract labor is yet to be told. Almost in this same category is the history of contract labor which was imported from Europe in the form of immigrants. In fact, the whole southern labor picture is either colored by immigration into the South or, perhaps more, by a lack of immigration.

Except for indentured servants and Negro slaves, almost nothing is known of agricultural labor. The history and background of tenancy have often obscured understanding of agrarian labor in its broader aspects. This field of study involves questions of migratory workers who have moved from one side of the South to the other, creating an imbalance of the labor supply in many of the older areas. Labor has migrated from farm to mill village and from the South to the industrial North, leaving behind a crazy-quilt labor picture.

Seasonal laborers in many areas have helped to make a fluid situation of labor conditions and demands. As the South has become more important as a truck-growing section, migratory and seasonal labor has become more a part of its labor history.

In the field of purely social history there are almost no areas which have been exploited adequately enough to explain them. To begin with there are numerous antisocial manifestations in the South's history. Ku Klux Klansmen, old and new, have reflected a lack of respect for organized government. Night riders, tollgate raiders, and white-cappers have taken law enforcement into their own hands in efforts to remedy unsatisfactory situations in the economic system. Selfrighteous local groups have often struck at more convivial elements in the community by passing curfews laws, regulating private observance of "decent" hours and greater moral turpitude. Overshadowing many of these phases of southern social history is the dark one of lynching. This unhappy chapter of human relationships has perhaps been written about and discussed more than any other. Yet there is room for an intelligent and dispassionate major study. Despite the existence of a considerable volume of published material, this social failure has been little analyzed and explained.

Less stringent in the region's history are the organizations which have had for their purpose the relaxation of the southern population. These include the jockey clubs, trotting associations, and horse shows which have been popular almost from the beginning of the South's history. Much has been said about these in an incidental way, and many things have been written about them, but there is much ground yet to be broken. Practically no synthesis of this area of human relations has been undertaken. The horse has ever been a popular animal, but the scholar has for the most part remained indifferent to its role in southern social life.

Closely allied with the activities of the sporting horsemen are those of professional and semiprofessional athletic organizations. Organized baseball has profited at the turnstile in the South, and from southern diamonds have come players who helped make the great national game one of phenomenal interest. Every community in the South has at one time or another had its team, and it has been a lame and crotchety Southerner indeed who has not envisioned himself a baseball player of national fame.

In the same vein, college athletics have grown from raw, bumptious playground games for exercise and relaxation to semiprofessionalism. The more charitable historian may see in the rapid expansion of southern college sports a growing tendency for Southerners to fight out their inflammatory issues on the athletic fields, while the less charitable, but more realistic, will perhaps be curious enough to see if there is not some connection between the astounding records of southern college football and basketball teams in competitive play and the phenomenal lack of facilities for encouraging adequate, mature scholarship in colleges and universities. There seems, in some cases, to have been an inverse ratio between the standing of a school's athletic team and the level of its intellectual capacity. Too, there is some surface evidence, at least, of the South trying in a subtle way to lick the Yankees by playing them off against each other on southern athletic teams. The time is ripe for mature studies of academic standards in relation to institutional desires for flamboyant athletic reputations. We not only need histories of sports and biographies of sportsmen, but also studies should be made to determine the impact of sports on southern life itself.

Early southern sports were often unorganized and reflected the temper of a raw frontier country. There was a spontaneity about them that revealed the true spirit of the region. Often these sports not only involved a desire for relaxation, but likewise courting and marriage customs. In the same vein much southern hardship and labor was reduced to a pleasant experience in the common workings, community gatherings, and celebrations. Possibly this broad aspect of southern life comes nearer to demonstrating the true genuineness of vaunted southern hospitality than any other. Certainly this aspect of southern social history reflected a light and friendly attitude on the part of large groups of people.

Social development and southern isolation have been closely bound together. In the field of transportation are many opportunities for major studies. Southern railroads in all their general historical developments lack adequate investigation. Histories of individual roads promise rich returns in understanding of specific problems and regional reactions to the development of adequate transportation facilities. Paralleling the building of railroads is that of stream utilization by steamboat lines and the building and using of southern highways. For the most part the latter chapter in southern economic history is an unexplored one. Beginning with the old system of trails, down through the toll road era, the system of local "warnings" in which ablebodied men were forced to maintain the roads, to the present era of "good roads," the historian has an exciting story of growth and improvement.

Many activities contributed to sweeping away the southern barriers of isolation. Since distances in the region are relatively great, all of these developments are more or less important. Among them are the telegraph and telephone systems, rural free delivery of mail, the star routes, air lines, radio, transportation of school children, and the organization of long-distance truck lines and regularly scheduled interstate bus systems. In fact, the whole field of southern transportation is one of open sesame to the economic historian who would explain the region's growth.

Finally, among the areas of southern history which deserve careful study, there is the problem of understanding the region's political and social behavior. There is still the challenge to especially well-qualified scholars to set down in black and white some of the region's concepts of its own internal political behavior as well as its broader relationships with the rest of the country. Recurring social upheavals at the polls and in Congress make it almost imperative that some analysis of major southern problems show how far the South may be expected to go in both defining the limits of its issues and in meeting them. Inevitably much study of this particular aspect of regional history will involve the historian in intellectual and philosophical interpretations of regional psychology. But such a study might be rewarding in the establishment of a certain sense of political direction or lack of direction.

(from *The Journal of Southern History*)

TRAVEL LITERATURE Many writings in American history would lack color and interest if it were not for the use of travel accounts as sources. These contemporary views contain important personal glimpses of our past.

For Europeans the settlement and development of the North American continent was high adventure. Not only did exploration and settlement of this part of the world open an escape valve for European peoples caught in social and economic lags at home; they also brought about in America a transfer and adaptation of old world institutions. A new world of trade was developed, and international rivalries grew on every hand. For the first time imperial powers were brought into serious rivalries and then into conflict in distant places, with a demand upon all of a nation's resources to protect its interests.

For the individual, settlement in North America meant the beginning of a new life. A great abundance of virgin land offered Europeans opportunities to change their economic and social status almost within a single generation. They could now cross the Atlantic and begin life over in an environment beyond the old restrictions which had bound them in countries not yet fully released from feudalism, from religious bondage, and from political interference with individual choice.

In another field, that of science, the opening of North America to settlement by Europeans had special meaning. Botanists, naturalists, geographers, geologists, chemists, and mineralogists had to expand their classifications in the natural world. Knowledge of new plants and plant adaptations to environmental conditions on this continent helped men to revise contemporary scientific ideas in this field.

Naturalists who concerned themselves with animals, birds, and fish likewise had to rework their material upon visiting this continent. Some of the best travel accounts are those written by scientists in search of fresh information about new world fauna; and their accounts give excellent ideas of the contrasts between European and American natural conditions. For the modern American these accounts not infrequently answer important questions about the prevalence of various kinds of natural life in the early years of settlement here.

Geographers and geologists, too, were faced with strong challenges, and were among the first to sense a sharp impact of distance in considering the surface of North America. Imagine the amazement of explorers and scientists when they first encountered the American river system! Englishmen, especially, were improperly oriented to comprehend the great lengths of American streams. All Europeans were impressed mightily by the force with which the water of streams pushed down to the sea. Spaniard and Frenchman alike, whether soldier, priest, or explorer, discovered how intricate was the network of rivers and lakes. Their contemporary accounts tingle with the high adventure involved in these early explorations. The staggering volume of notes kept by Jesuit missionaries and published in the voluminous *Jesuit Relations* provide rich documentation for a major European approach to the continent.

Hardly had settlements been planted along the Atlantic Coast and in the St. Lawrence Valley before travelers made their appearance. In fact, John Smith himself might be considered one of the first English visitors to publish his experiences in a series of books, thus setting a pattern for the travelogues of his fellow Englishmen. From 1607 to the present the volume of English travel material has grown to huge proportions. Once institutional beginnings were made, visitors came to America on almost every ship arriving from England—merchants, government officials, clergymen, and land scouts for prospective settlers. All of these people came on special missions and their views of the new world were likely to be narrowed by their objectives. Merchants, for instance, were alert to prospects for trade, the exploitation of land for agriculture and the development of mineral resources, the formation of towns, and the location of roads and harbors. Beyond the settlement line, both merchant-trader and missionary saw the Indian and his way of life from tribe to tribe, and many of these travelers gathered information which even yet is significant in the study of Indian life. Government officials came to see at first hand certain problems in the administration of public policies and laws, and compiled a fairly trustworthy account of the deviations from old-world political patterns.

Whatever the mission or business of the traveler, or whatever his national origin, the new world seemed strange to him. Geography was often baffling and the force of nature was all but overwhelming. Already second generation Europeans on this continent were modifying their national characteristics. The powerful new influences of environment in an expanding western world were unlike anything the foreigner had known before. To comprehend the simple fact of distance was difficult for him, and he never really fathomed the emotional and spiritual change which became a continuous factor in American life. In this process of change, Europeans becoming Americans thought of progress simply as the improvement of the conditions of life with each succeeding year and with each new generation. Progress seemed measurable on the highly visible gauge of growing towns, expanding farming communities, increasing roads, newly built mills, churches, and courthouses, along with conquest of Indians and the forces of nature. When a native talked with a traveler, he spoke in terms of great expectations, seldom discussing the realities of the moment since the latter spoke for themselves.

In a more positive way the whole process of colonization, including the larger aspect of human progress and pioneering, found ready chroniclers in those travelers who made continuous efforts to analyze the processes of change. A genuine travel account obviously had to be written by someone who had traveled somewhere to view the scenes he described, though there were, of course, armchair travelogues of pure fabrication. Too often the foreign traveler came poorly conditioned to accomplish what he promised. He seldom understood what he saw, and in many instances emotionally and intellectually never left home.

One of the greatest shocks suffered by early visitors, especially by the British, was the fact that people only, not environments, were transferred across the Atlantic. This inability to see a rising new civilization in the new American environment marred scores of travel accounts down to 1860. The immigrant came under the influence of American environment the moment he strolled down a gangplank to set foot ashore. On the other hand, the traveler could either accept or reject conditions as he found them. The fact was that many of the English visitors closed their books with the refrain that they were glad to have visited North America, but were really overjoyed to slip back into the civilized atmosphere of their island. At the end of his visit, one traveler wrote: "And now for a detestable voyage (for how can a winter voyage across the North Atlantic be otherwise than detestable?). Sea sickness, storms, and horrors of all kinds: With prospects, however, of speedily enjoying the happiest moment (to a British traveller) of every tour—that on which he touches British soil again."

Before 1787, travel accounts tended to lack the well-centered interest or purpose which they acquired once a unified nation came into existence. A larger number of accounts were written by officials who had business dealings in only a single colony—or in only two or three colonies. Consequently their travels and human associations were limited in scope. People who came as missionaries or traveling preachers saw little of life on a broader scale; for example, the Quakers had eyes for little else than the affairs of their own faith. They traveled long distances apparently without seeing much of the country, or failed to leave descriptions if they did see much of it. Yet there were some travelers who braved the rigors of bad roads, nerve-racking stage journeys, and sea travels to get a good view of the colonial system.

Before 1776 few travelers looked upon colonial America as anything other than an adventure in colonialism in which British influence early became a predominant factor. While the view of colonial people emerging from these early books is often badly fragmented, there are occasionally penetrating observations. Occasionally an official or crown view comes into focus. Strange to say this material lacks any appreciable sense of the rising friction between the colonies and the crown. Occasionally a Tory spoke his piece about the agitations which led to the Revolution; but generally the scholar will search a large volume of books to locate a few nuggets of fact on this phase of American history. In the Revolution itself a few travelers were able to give a view of the transitions which were taking place in politics, in the process of the war, and in the general framework of society itself.

After 1787 the travel literature about America became more exciting. Now there was a new focal point of interest in the great experiment in federalism. The propaganda for independence had emphasized freedom and democracy so much that travelers came to examine the applications of the doctrine expressed in the Declaration of Independence and the new state constitutions. Some, of course, came to see the federal system fail in its application of the idealism of Jefferson and Franklin. One thing, however, stands out in this period and in the years to follow: George Washington made enormous personal appeal to Englishmen and Europeans who came near Philadelphia or Mount Vernon. He was more than a military leader who had defeated the British. He was the physical embodiment of eighteenth-century democratic idealism.

The states in the Confederation stood in a new economic relationship not only to each other, but to the old world. On a smaller scale the individual states represented a pattern of functioning federalism which was to characterize the formation of the nation. They were the seedbed of the new American system of government. For visitors from abroad few or no previous experiments in government involved so many innovations or local adaptations. This was the first time that a potentially major nation had begun its existence wedded to the idea of applied democracy. This in itself was enough to draw visitors interested in political ideas to observe the young nation in its formative years. They came both to see firsthand what was happening and to suggest ideas which they believed worthy of trial. Travelers have never been timid in making suggestions, and in the late eighteenth century any number of people had dreams about how a free people could best govern themselves. Philadelphia in time swarmed with politically inspired visitors, and at times the broad porch at Mount Vernon must have been a veritable political forum.

Democracy in action, however, had a far greater field of action than Philadelphia and Washington. It was reflected in the habits, customs, and social maturity of the people; after 1776 the people were in the process of becoming Americans. Some of the population apparently had matured in a manner that accorded with the best European and British standards. The great mass, however, were regarded as crude, uncultured, brash, and repulsive. Washington had set a good personal example of dignity and decorum, but some of his immediate successors in the presidency hardly gave their ages a comparable tone, despite the highly cultivated nature of Jefferson himself. In the travelers' eyes, the federal period was a time of repulsive personal habits, of raw pioneering, and social confusion. Large numbers of travelers were unable to penetrate the surface to comphrehend the dynamics of the new nation and its society. Something approaching panic characterized the efforts of travelers to fathom American life. Even presidents of the United States were drawn from their labors by inquisitive travelers who came to discuss political theories, philosophical ideas, books, practical politics, federalism, commerce, and farming.

Between 1800 and 1860 travelers circulated constantly on the "grand tour," which was from New York to Boston and back, to Philadelphia, Baltimore, and Washington, then south to Richmond, Charleston, Mobile, New Orleans, and up the Mississippi to Louisville, Cincinnati, and Pittsburgh. Often this tour went to the Ohio and Mississippi valleys on the first leg. Because of this general routing much of the travel literature during the first half of the nineteenth century followed a set geographical pattern.

Following the organization of the Federal Government, three subjects became basic themes: government and politics, slavery, and the rise of towns and cities as trade centers. A great majority of the travelers, whether or not they were able to understand the complexities of slavery as an institution, came with already fixed opinions about it. Because of rising criticism at home, British visitors especially were vigorous in their writings about the institution. A considerable number of travelers made comparisons between conditions in the free and the slave states. To all foreign travelers, the existence of slavery in a country so heavily committed to a democratic political philosophy was the great contradiction of life.

American methods of farming were as interesting to foreign travelers as was slavery. They saw here a traditional mode of farm life adapted to a large landed area. The isolated life of the American farmer, separated by considerable distance from his neighbors, was in sharp contrast to farm organization in Europe and England. Land usage, methods of cultivation, types of field crops, and management of farm animals also offered material for much comment. Wastefulness of resources often caught the eyes of frugal Europeans who came from areas where farming was carried on in a very conservative manner.

Travelers' descriptions of American farming are to be trusted only so far as elements of truth become discernible by comparison with modern farm life in America. The average traveler was too inexperienced in this aspect of American life to make trustworthy comments. In one respect the traveler's view was trustworthy in discussing farming. He was able to make some astute observations on the differences between farm life in the South, on the spreading frontier, and in the middle states and the East. The frontier farm taxed his imagination. He was quick to see the slovenliness of the southern cotton farm, and the thriftiness and good order of the Yankee farm strongly appealed to him.

For the most part travelers were city or townspeople who scarcely knew what they were seeing, to say nothing of understanding precisely the life of country people. The crudeness of manner and dress, the dirt of the country taverns, the constant chewing of tobacco, the rancid smells, the coarse language, and the whining accents of rural Americans caused many foreigners to look upon the natives they saw along the way as little more than savages. Again, travelers perceived a sharp contrast between the people of the eastern part of the United States and those of the South and West.

American institutions attracted hundreds of visitors. Prisons were major attractions, and literally scores of visitors knocked on the gate of the Philadelphia Prison asking to be allowed to inspect it. Jailhouses and state prisons elsewhere were also visited eagerly by foreigners. Schools, colleges and universities, insane asylums, and hospitals attracted travelers to their doors. As many travelers were reformers at heart, they wished to compare the management of corrective institutions in America with those at home.

Every traveler visited some cities and towns. Here the great horde of observers felt more at home, and their detailed descriptions of urban life are to be accepted as being more worthwhile than those of the countryside. The American city, however, was often puzzling to foreigners. It lacked the neat order and careful planning of many cities abroad. The influence of architects and artists was lacking. Buildings were constructed in highly individualistic and often tasteless designs. Few massive memorials and monuments stood in the streets, and few memorial parks and circles gave use and beauty to public thoroughfares. Private houses were constructed in small single-family units, and people lived away from their businesses. The most striking feature of the American city, however, was that the aspect of permanence was lacking. Everywhere streets were being dug up or rerouted, and buildings were being pulled down to give way to larger and more efficient structure. In the post-Civil War years visitors were frequently startled by seeing houses being moved down the streets from one site to another. Nothing stayed in place. No monument was sacred, no public building was safe from the wrecker. Even church houses had to give way to change and progress.

Four years of civil war brought a crop of travelers to the United States. American democracy was on trial. Political observers, diplomats, newspaper men, authors, and opportunists all recorded their impressions of the country in travail. Once the country was actually involved in armed conflict, military men from many countries visited the headquarters of commanding generals, the battle lines, and the war departments of the two sides to view what was happening. Both

Grant and Lee knew what it meant to have foreign observers as guests in their military councils. Because of the tense drama of war, and the specialized preparation of many of the travelers, the Civil War descriptions are among the best of the travel books about the United States.

Once smoke cleared from the battlefields, visitors came to see the country in a process of reconstruction, and to gain impressions of the great age of both geographical and industrial expansion. The postwar visitors could move more rapidly about the country than did their predecessors. The route of the grand tour was for the most part relocated. There were, of course, many who visited the South to see what had happened to the region during four years of war, and to find meaning in the end of slavery and the rise of the free Negro. After the slaves were freed, the emancipated Negro in American society became a favorite topic, and traveler comment on this subject becomes important—not because the visitors brought with him experience enough to render wise judgment on the subject, but because in his naive way he gave some insight into race relations.

More travelers, however, followed the feverish trek westward. They wanted to visit the Great Plains, Utah and the Mormons, California and the Pacific Coast. The West had become a pulsating new land with all the thrills of the frontier plus many of the travel conveniences of the modern age. Railroads hauled most of the foreign visitors over the grand tour to California and back. Many travelers strayed as far south as Texas and as far north as Seattle. The great objectives, however, were the new cities. Chicago, raw, bustling, growing, fighting its way upward to become an American commercial nerve center, characterized the new materialistic America. . . .

The earliest travelers to visit Anglo-America commented on education, or lack of it. Hundreds of visitors concerned themselves with the process of American education. They visited schools and colleges, inspected libraries, museums, and scientific laboratories. They sometimes examined textbooks, visited professors, quizzed students, and discussed the purposes for which private schools were established. In the great body of travel accounts there is developed a reasonably good profile of American education. Almost no foreigners understood precisely the objectives of the American educators and schools; few understood the public school movement. As universal education became a more prominent fact in American cultural life, it proved more confusing to foreign visitors. Even in the twentieth century foreigners still find our academic procedures puzzling. This has been especially true of those literary lights who invaded this country from 1890 to 1945, and who went from a one-night lecture stand to the next, confronted by eager American undergraduates who seemed both immature and blasé as compared with the serious young men of Oxford and Cambridge, or of Berlin, Vienna, and the Sorbonne. The American female in search of learning hardly had a counterpart anywhere else in the world.

As America grew more prosperous and anxious to acquire culture, the railway cars were crowded with British literary men, government officials, and titled aristocrats hastening from one lecture engagement to another. En route they became experts on American culture, materialism, and restlessness. Everywhere there were commercial traveling men peddling goods and stories. Hotel lobbies were crowded with people attending conventions. These Americans away from home got drunk, gorged themselves on food, cut juvenile capers, and even did a good amount of philandering. Sophisticated visitors looked upon this restless horde as leading a new form of animalistic existence in which the almighty dollar became a main objective of human life.

Generally it may be said that the postwar accounts lack some of the rich human interest materials of those written in the earlier years of the nineteenth century; yet they are more numerous, cover a wider geographical scope, and often are more precise in their descriptions. On the other hand, the rising metropolitan press recorded its raw and uninhibited story of this late nineteenth century growth and social chaos. What the traveler did not actually see at first hand, he extracted from the news columns. The postwar newspaperman struck the travelers as being a blood descendant of the brash frontiersman who had stood about steamboat landings making prophecies and bragging about his accomplishments. Too few travelers saw Americans in their homes and about the routine of daily affairs to paint an extensive picture of domestic life, though travelers like Frederika Bremer and Fanny Kemble lingered long enough to take a second look into home life.

Though the family and the home as institutions received little comment, American food was a favorite topic. Most travelers appreciated the fact that Americans had an abundance of food. For many it was strange food, and the mode of its preparation was even stranger. The eighteenth-century Englishman was no better equipped to appreciate American food and methods of cooking than are twentieth-century Englishmen. For many of them, eating in hotels, restaurants, and roadside taverns, the food was greasy, poorly cooked, badly served, and made unappetizing by its very abundance. Eating habits were in keeping with the poor preparation of food. The American was in a hurry so he gulped down his meals, using his hands instead of knives and forks, and drinking cold water in such amounts as to frighten Englishmen who had fixed notions about the functions of the digestive tract. The toothpick was nearly always in evidence. Conversation was lacking during meals, and there were no leisurely meals where eating was made an art instead of a physical necessity. Yet as the cities grew, as hotels developed dining rooms, and as quality restaurants came into existence, travelers' attitudes softened toward American foods and dining habits.

If the American at home was slighted in the travel accounts, certainly the traveling American was brought into full focus. Whether native sons and daughters were viewed above swaying stage coaches, on steamboats, or on railway cars, they attracted attention. They appeared as crowds milling in streets, as smaller groups riding stage coaches, or strolling about steamboat decks; but wherever they appeared, they presented a collective national face. Out of the generous descriptions of the people in crowds, certain national characteristics can be fairly well classified. The American on the move was restless, he was garrulous, inquisitive, and often a braggart. In casual conversation with foreigners he was quick to express confidence in his expanding country. This American aboard a Pullman car presented the same general appearance as his forefathers aboard steamboats, but with the major difference that he was smug about his accomplishments. Speculators, traders, peddlers, preachers, adventurers, family men, dandies, rascals, gamblers, greenhorns, pompous stuffed shirts, political hacks, pious missionaries, innocent maidens, Yankees, Irishmen, Frenchmen, German immigrants, rugged laboring men, rowdies, Negroes, and actors, all of these were described by travelers. They left a grand composite picture of the people.

For the modern historian travel accounts are peep-holes to the past. No other historical source supplies precisely the type of intimate firsthand information that is to be found in this body of literature. Not even newspapers supply the same kind of contemporary information, nor write with the same perspective and wide scope of coverage. Diarists may present intimate personal views of life in a given age, but their information is highly circumscribed and for the most part static in nature. Seldom does this personal material have the grand sweep of a major travelogue or the freshness and detachment characteristic of a foreign observer. . . .

At the outset several questions must be asked of travel

accounts. What was the nationality of the traveler? Where did he come from? What reasons did he give for traveling? What were his special economic, social, or political interests? If he were a Quaker visiting Quaker communities it is likely that he saw or thought little about anything but Quakers. Both George Fox and John Woolman traveled through interesting country, but they recorded almost none of their nonreligious experiences. Preachers and religious workers often made miserable observers. They were so preoccupied with congregations, sermons, and theological arguments that they had no time for anything else, and where they did record their views and experiences they marred them by overemphasizing their special interests.

The same thing can be said about many commercial and political travelers. The commercial visitors have left good accounts of economic life, but often they expended their energies in making comparisons with old-world economic conditions. Politicians, especially the British, spent much time in Washington sitting in the Congressional galleries trying to make sense out of American political procedures. Many of them viewed Washington as both the political and social hub of the nation. They went to official receptions and parties, tramped the streets viewing the city's architecture, and gained an impression of American character from the conduct or misconduct of members of Congress.

Perhaps no other people attach quite the same importance to travel accounts as do the Americans. Almost from the beginning of foreign visitation to the earliest settlements in the new world, Americans were self-conscious and anxious to make impressions upon visitors. Never have we been hesitant about revealing to travelers the most intimate parts of the great American dream. Our aspiration and our national pride have all been stripped naked before our visitors.

In a broader sense the foreign visitor has fired our ego, has taunted us into refining our habits, has revealed weaknesses in our political and social institutions, has criticised our arts, and our letters and press, our cities, and our public manners. Alexis de Tocqueville and Lord James Bryce analyzed our institutions in two of the ablest critical appraisals we have. These semi-travel accounts are quoted wherever estimates of American social and political history are discussed. Only within the past decade have historians discovered the highly prophetic passage in de Tocqueville regarding the rising American and Russian powers. . . .

As for ourselves, visitors long ago became a fixed part of our national life. So long as they keep coming, we can tell ourselves that we are an exciting and alert people. In later years we have even subsidized visitors to come to the United States. We have used the freedom with which they are able to travel here as an effective weapon in the great struggle between the democratic and communist worlds.

From John Smith to Nikita Khrushchev visitors from abroad have viewed the American scene. Mr. Khrushchev, to be sure, has published no account of his recent visit, but this was done for him by the world's newsmen, photographers, radio commentators, and editorial writers. These detailed public reports on important state visitors comprise a new and rather important type of travel literature which reflects the political interrelationships of nations. . . .

Travel literature is, of course, well known to scholars in many fields, and it is used in the preparation of hundreds of books and articles. There is lacking, however, sufficient bibliographical assistance in both locating and appraising this great mass of materials. The important project of listing travel books and articles in a great national bibliography under the patronage of the American Historical Association failed of fruition. One or two national group bibliographies, and one regional bibliography cover a considerable body of materials.

Before scholars can be made fully aware of travel accounts

as historic sources it will be necessary to ferret out the hundreds of other brief travelogues which were published in periodicals and newspapers. This will be an enormous undertaking, but it will be richly rewarding. This is also true of unpublished letters which lie untouched in foreign and American household trunks and libraries. So long as new and unexploited travel materials exist, scholars must regard the writing of much American social and cultural history as largely an open-end undertaking.

Specifically, travel accounts offer unlimited opportunities for scholarly research and writing in the field of social history. Historians have yet to present a broad study of the structure of American society. Before this can be done acceptably, more research is necessary in the mountainous volume of travel literature and description. This material adds the third dimension of outside observation. In turn no full judgment can be made of this material without understanding something of the structure of American society itself. Research in social history of necessity involves a resort to contemporary and personal sources.

Elements of our history such as population movement, location of immigrant groups, and the orientation of foreigners to American conditions are vividly reflected in visitors' observations. Public health and the occurrence of violence, of economic failures, and of social frustrations are discussed in travel books and articles. Few sources reveal so clearly the elementary impulses which led to entries of claims for large blocks of public lands and town sites; they drilled prospective settlers in the ways of reaching and acquiring them. In this day of soaring book prices, and the growing scarcity of this type of original material for sale, the scholarly hand could be set to far less productive tasks than editing and reproducing series of carefully selected travel accounts.

(from *Research Opportunities in American Cultural History*)

THE COMMON-MAN TRADITION IN THE LITERATURE OF THE FRONTIER Pioneering in the American backwoods was one of America's most exciting experiences. Its frontiersmen penetrating the dense forest lands began the process of planting the white man's civilization in the rich western river valleys. They transported beyond the mountains few of the world's material goods, but they came bountifully endowed with a sense of personal and national destiny. Their task was boldly outlined. They were to clear away the woods, drive the Indians back, open fields and pastures, build cabins and houses, blaze new roads, establish towns, and begin the development of necessary human institutions.

There was never any limit of uncertainty on the part of the pioneers that they could subdue both Indians and geography, but they had misgivings for the future so far as historical credit for their acts was involved. In much of the contemporary writings there was a lamentation of the shortage of historians and paper to record adequately the achievements of the early settlers.

Hard-handed old pioneers would now lie happy in their forgotten graves if they could only know that the historian did not fail them. Today rows of foxed and fading books tell their story, and these volumes enjoy the guardianship of librarians in luxurious modern rare-book quarters. They would be even more pleased if they could realize the economics of the current Americana market. In a sense it is tragic that the vast horde of pioneers who yearned for recognition cannot be brought back in a grand jubilee to view the past from the vantage point of this moment. The humble annalists, local historians, and memorialists would be flattered to know how much their simple little books are appreciated. But the shock of current prices might be too great for them to endure. Some of their yellowing chronicles have come to be worth more than the established government price for a good quarter of a section of land on which a steady God-fearing sire could raise, in the first quarter of the nineteenth century, a numerous brood for the glory of the land.

There was, in fact, no lack of historians of the frontier then or now. It would be difficult to guess the number of contemporary books, personal memoirs, essays, gazetteers, and travelogues which give portions of the pioneering story. Almost every year since 1784 at least one new title dealing with this subject has come from the press. Currently some of the old classics are being republished for the second and even third and fourth times.

Every American library which lays claim to any respectability owns a collection of these books. Since the 1920's there has been a diligent searching of the record to discover the influences and impulses which helped to create the American. In special essays ranging all the way from those which appear periodically in local historical publications to the more erudite addresses delivered before the learned historical societies there has been appraisal of the country's human background. What manner of men transformed a wilderness into fields and towns, and transported American civilization into the backwoods and across the plains? Disciples and foes of viewpoints expressed by Frederick Jackson Turner have been equally industrious in re-examining the records of American pioneering.

Since 1918 the United States Government has spent millions of dollars in efforts to translate American history to people in all parts of the world. A simple Japanese scholar struggling with poverty and disease in a mountain fastness concerns himself with the broad question of what is the American national personality. A Hindu boy in a bankrupt fugitive college in Bengal raises the question of the secret of America's people in hope that he can find a solution for his own problems. The same question has invoked discussion among more sophisticated scholars in Europe and England. This question cannot be answered simply or in a concrete way. It exists in parts, and so do its answers. Early pioneers in the rushing tide of national expansion sensed that such questions might be asked in the future, and they hoped that their experiences might comprise a part of the answers.

There are no more desirable books in America today than those which might be classed as of general origin. Most of them record simple stories of plain people making deep-seated adjustments to primitive conditions in a raw new country. A young woman struggling overland atop an overloaded horse recorded her experiences as she migrated westward. Every fresh moment was one of expectancy, and every passing day demanded new compromises and adjustments which led her away from the past.

Hunters who tramped the woods in long hunts were inspired to record their solitary experiences. A buckskin warrior trailing red enemies across the vast woods, or dodging their rain of arrows beside river banks, told stories of fear, of personal heroism, and of triumph. Into all this body of original materials crept a golden thread of social history to give a lasting insight into the processes of adjustments and changes which became indelible parts of the American personality. In local backwoods vernacular many of these unlettered historians told more than they knew. They documented even the rise of new national speech forms.

A seminal book is Joseph Doddridge's *Notes on the Settlement and Indian Wars of the Western Parts of Virginia and Pennsylvania, from 1763 to 1783.* This history covers the chronological scope of twenty basic years in the beginning of the great westward movement. Its author was a self-trained minister whose sense of history was derived from reading the Bible and observing the stirring events of the world in which he lived. In an unusually compact preface he revealed emotions of the pioneer American with greater clarity than some modern historians have done in extensive volumes. Frontier life in Pennsylvania and Virginia varied little if any from that in other areas of frontier expansion across the continent.

While Joseph Doddridge was undergoing the seasoning necessary to produce his book, several members of the ill-fated Braddock Expedition into western Virginia and Pennsylvania recorded their impressions in published form. These military travelers viewed the humanity they encountered as strange "other world" people who had descended into a weird social condition that bore little kinship with English and European backgrounds. General John Forbes, for instance, considered the same people as living separate and apart from his concepts of civilization.

With more precision and sympathy, Thomas Jefferson presented a social and physical analysis of the same territory in his classic *Notes on Virginia, 1782,* a book which has gone through many editions; the latest is William Peden's in 1955. Two years after Jefferson's work came from the press in Paris, John Filson of Kentucky published his famous book, *The Discovery, Settlement and Present State of Kentucke* (Wilmington, Delaware, 1784). Frankly the author wished to do no more than publicize the western country in a most attractive light. His book can hardly be called interpretive history, and much of his factual material is of limited value. Its importance lies elsewhere. Filson glorified the process of American expansion as a thing of all but divine direction. There is expressed in its pages a keen sense of manifest American destiny, and an enthusiasm for pioneering.

For Filson, recorded history was fabricated from the acts of people. Thus it was that he treated the personality of the frontiersmen by using one of the backwoods' most dramatic characters. Daniel Boone, in the eyes of both John Filson and Lord Byron, was the counterpart of an ancient classical idol wandering through the virgin forest in the fulfillment of a mission of destiny. The simple language of Boone and his backwoods neighbors was too gross to use in the telling of so heroic a story. Boone's autobiography was cast by his amanuensis in the stilted language of the eighteenth century, and the essence of the story was that of a trans-Appalachian Ulysses wandering home from a lonely wilderness vigil, and of Boone's fighting to rescue this Ohio Valley Eden from the hand of the Indian. Long after the western academy master's stilted language was forgotten, and his *Kentucke* had become an exceedingly rare collector's item, Boone the folk hero enjoyed increasing fame. He was made a personal symbol of expansion, of rugged frontier individualism, and of the great conflict between red and white men in the West.

Filson, like Boone, was a pioneer. He was aware of the anxiety of his neighbors that history should not overlook their sacrifices and hardships. The most horrible fate which could befall the frontiersman was not to be tomahawked in the dead of night by a Shawnee brave, but to be ignored by the historian. It was a matter of deepest concern that Americans should know and appreciate the human foundations on which American society rests. . . .

It is doubtful that any other pioneering people anywhere else in world history were so anxious to please the historian as were the American frontiersmen. When Dr. John Monette of Washington, Mississippi, wrote his preface to his two-volume *History of the Discovery and Settlement of the Valley of the Mississippi* in 1846, he made an eloquent plea for his personal subjects, "The history of the West," he wrote, "is full of thrilling interest and incident connected with their [the pioneers'] struggles for the occupancy of this great and fertile region, which they have left as a rich inheritance to their posterity. The only requital they ask at our hands is the gratitude with which their names and their virtues are cherished by posterity, and the fidelity with which they are transmitted, as models of enterprise and perseverance, to future ages."

Pioneering was closely akin to religious crusading. In many

of the contemporary orations the people were looked upon as carrying on a holy war for the sake of the future. Attacks upon the Indians and the woods were campaigns against the inertia of the present to prepare for the onrushing future. Collectively the eyes of civilization were diverted to a distant time horizon when the conditions of American domestic society would equal the promise of the soil and its resources. Orators were consummate braggarts, and the prefaces to contemporary books were little short of boasts of what had been accomplished, and of prophecies of what was to come. The Indian fighter strode tall across the land and the page of written history as a confirmed hero. But it was that people's army which converted the country to Anglo-Saxonism and refined its domesticity that composed the stock hero of the frontier.

Taking the country away from the Indians was seldom if ever regarded as an act of exploitation of a weaker race, or of involving a moral question. Occasionally a contemporary historian sought an answer as to why the white man and Indian were engaged in mortal combat. . . .

The Indian received little commiseration in the white man's literature. Pushing the savage off the land was a commendable undertaking; it was an act which in time received the praise of no less an authority than President Andrew Jackson. He was to sanction in several of his official messages the then-prevailing sentiments of the frontier. If it took perseverance and blood to combat the Indians, it also took a tremendous amount of paper and printer's ink to record the history of border warfare. One of the most fascinating, though by no means earliest, chronicles of Indian wars is Alexander Scott Withers' *Chronicles of Border Warfare* (Clarksburg, Virginia, 1831).

In the original edition this little book, printed on a back-country newspaper press, has become a rare collector's item. Withers was an informal historian who presented the details of frontier warfare as a highly personalized thing. Without benefit of a depository of records, he was able to collect accounts from a wide territory and to organize them into a rather complete story. Indian warfare was of such an erratic nature that there was seldom anything resembling an established front of action. Areas of combat were as indefinite as the spreading line of settlement itself. Attacks were often made against the families of individual settlers who had pushed too far into the woods. Always these border raids involved families, and women and children fell bloody victims to the Indian code of war. There was no recognition of noncombatants, in fact there were actually no noncombatants. Constant surprise attacks produced incidents of individual action and heroism which became the basic materials of Indian warfare history and frontier legend. At no time in American history was the individual more likely to find himself confronted with the stern alternatives of losing his scalp lock, or climbing the hero's pedestal by an extraordinary display of courage. Acts of horror involving women and children added an unusually macabre note to pioneering in the path of danger. A great deal of the history recorded in the contemporary chronicles of border warfare was colored by this horror and grief which lonely people suffered at the hands of an implacable foe.

A wild shout at milking time, a twanging arrow flying through the air, a man cut off from safety in a corn field, or in the woods, or women and children besieged in cabins and blockhouses, were common stories of the border. There were, of course, militiamen on the frontier like those who followed Clark into the Illinois country, and who fought with Josiah Harmar, Arthur St. Clair, Anthony Wayne, and William Henry Harrison. But it is not the purpose of this paper to discuss warfare. In 1816 Robert B. McAfee published his *History of the Late War in the Western Country*. The War of 1812 had ended only the year before he got his volume into print, so of necessity it is largely a personal account of men and incidents which were known to the author. No American war produced so many heroes in proportion to the number of men engaged in battle as did this struggle. Frontiersmen had the combined pleasure of fighting Indians and British together, and historian McAfee gave free rein to this joy.

Sixteen years later, Timothy Flint, a minister with somewhat longer perspective, published his *Indian Wars of the West* at Cincinnati. He brought more maturity and humanity to his writing than did most of his contemporaries. He was able to relate border incidents of warfare to the greater frontier movement itself. . . .

The common man on the frontier had more at stake than mere momentary self-glorification. Social and domestic forces about him beckoned to the future. Vast stretches of unbroken forests were no more than fleeting bits of primeval beauty. Certainly the pioneer spent little or no time sighing over the great sweeps of virginal wonder and solitude. He dreamed of the future when vast piles of agricultural products would be on their way to downriver markets, when log cabins could be abandoned for bigger and finer log houses, and towns would spring up about county courthouses. Visions of the future veiled the stern realities of the present. The time would come quickly when an industrious and imaginative people would enjoy the fruits of their labors. In the common frontiersman's mind God meant for the trees to fall, the fires to flame up in towering walls which engulfed all nature before them. Indians and game alike were victimized by the spread of backwoods civilization.

Early frontier authors describing the spread of this civilization wrote in the vein of the ancient Hebrew fathers. Nearly every preface was an oration glorifying expansion, and progress became a sacred thing. Again Joseph Doddridge declared that, "This contrast will show him what mighty changes may be effected under the enlightened and free government in the course of a few years; while the worst states of society in other regions of the world have remained the same from time immemorial, owing to the influence of that despotism which regards any change of the manners of the condition of society as criminal, and therefore prevents them by the severest penalties, because *ignorance* and *poverty* are favorable to the perpetuity of that slavery, on the part of the common people, which is essential to its existence."

In a dedicatory eulogy to General Duncan M'Arthur, John Kilbourn wrote, in 1831, of both Ohio and the General that "Two small settlements only, to wit: those at Marietta, and at Cincinnati, had then just been commenced, within the limits of what is now the great state of Ohio; containing nearly 1,000,000 of inhabitants." The General was congratulated on his rise through the ranks to high office, and the state was praised for its achievements in the field of material wealth. In fact, Kilbourn's entire book was devoted to detailing the expansion of Ohio in such a remarkably short time.

A score of years after Kilbourn presented Ohio so favorably in his gazetteer, the Reverend W. D. Gallagher addressed the Ohio Historical and Philosophical Society for almost three hours on "Facts and conditions of Progress in the Northwest." This oration covered almost every subject from the dissolution of the human body to the wonders of the magnetic telegraph. But his emphasis was upon what he called the deeds of Anglo-Saxonism in the Northwest. God had prepared the great Ohio and Mississippi Valleys for this chosen race of people: "Scooped out by the hand of omnipotence with wonderful adaptation to the wants of man, and the purposes of his existence, lies the most stupendous and favored inland valley upon which the sun shines. Having for its eastern edge the Alleghany and Cumberland Mountains, and for its western the Rocky Mountains and the Black Hills, for its northern rim the summitlands between Lake Winnipeg and the headwaters of the Mississippi River, and for its southern the Guadeloupe Mountains and the Gulf of Mexico, it extends in one direction over twenty-four parallels of longitude, and in the other embraces eighteen degrees of latitude." In a long discourse on the changes which had come in the region, the preacher became lyrical in his praise of progress in the land. He exclaimed:

> By this time, over nearly the whole broad bosom of the region which I have mapped out, were scattered the habitations of men, and introduced the institutions of Christian civilized life. In the interiors of its different sections, the wigwams of the savage had given place to the cabins of the newcomers, and the farmhouses of the first settlers. On the small streams, which everywhere sent up their glad voices, giving the deep solitude a tongue that was eloquent, the hand of enterprise had taken the willing waters, and borne them to the clattering wheels of the manufactory, where they labored and yet sported, and like virtue, were overruled yet free. On the broad lakes, on the mighty rivers, the arm of steam—"That fleshless arm, whose pulses leap/With floods of living fire,"—was propelling the gigantic hull, freighted with hundreds of human beings, coming from afar to cultivate the land, to fabricate its crude products, to engage in trade and commerce, to "multiply and replenish the earth." On the great natural highways, populous cities had taken the place of primeval groves, and the elegant mansion, invited the oncoming multitudes to seek in and around them new and better homes. And the years of the fourth decade were told, and the population had swelled to 4,131,370 souls.

While native orators spoke in terms of rich lands stretching away in leagues between far-distant mountain ranges and vast bodies of waters, an army of American and foreign travelers came to view this pulsating society that was so sure of its possession of the land. Rows of yellowing books stand as testimonials to the opinions which they formed of the American hinterlands. Democracy spreading from one clearing to another often reflected little if any of the classic and philosophical ideals expressed in the writings of both European and Atlantic seaboard political theorists. Frontier democracy was an applied thing which was to be experienced in insatiable native curiosity, which proved so tedious to strangers. It was a smoke-grimed cabin with mud floor, an insect-ridden tavern serving greasy meals which were gulped down with animal-like ferocity, it was loud bragging of things to be, and a tolerance of the discomforts of the moment. New states, new counties, and new towns were organized with all but reckless political abandon. This was a standard measure of progress, and a verification of the efficiency of democracy.

The traveler held up a literary looking glass to the process of American expansion. Sometimes the images came true and in just proportion, but more often they were perverted and out of perspective. The foreign observer forgot to shift his mind and personal feelings from the expectations of maturity in a country where maturity could not exist. It was not what he said in his writings that gave validity to his books so much as it was what he innocently implied. Unfair though many of the travel accounts were, and as worthless as some of them are today, the great body of this literature constitutes a genuine compliment to the spread of civilization across the continent. The Children of Israel had only the Book of Exodus to glorify their struggles and hardships, but the American frontiersmen had almost all literary England and Europe to tell their story, aside from what the native sons had to say on the subject.

Following in the footsteps of John Filson a small army of local historians labored to record the rise of states and counties. The story of every frontier state has been told at least a half dozen times, and some of the early state histories are among the rare books on the West. An historian like Humphrey Marshall of Kentucky not only wrote of the rise of his state, but he attempted to set the political and personal record straight. In a time when there were so many cross-currents in national and international politics, there were plentiful opportunities for individuals to get caught in cross fires that might besmirch their reputations. Local historians had opportunities to speak of these border intrigues with both first-hand knowledge and prejudices of the affairs.

Out of the published literature of the frontier emerges an individual portrait which might be considered as characteristic of the common-man personality of western America. The vastness of the country gave rise to unlimited individual hopes for the future. Attention was focused not on what the country was, but what it was to become. There was geography enough to permit great expectation for tremendous growth. The soil was fertile, and national resources seemed unlimited. Economically, the frontiersman could aspire to unlimited well-being.

From the beginning the frontiersman's love of country was reflected in his institutional attachments. Whatever his economic promises might have been, it was in institutional growth that he placed his real confidence. Government, at the local, state, and national level, was a necessity for him. Local government touched his life most intimately, state government existed largely to give stability to local institutions, but the greater fabric of national authority was a matter of innermost pride and dignity. It represented the American to the world as an aggressive individual wedded to the proposition of protecting free men who could improve their economic, spiritual, and political lots as they progressed toward the future.

Neither the common man, nor much of the contemporary literature about his progress in backwoods America, dealt with the academics of democracy. . . . In the practical concepts of the American backwoodsmen democracy might be defined in terms of conquest of the land with a limited amount of governmental sanction, and a pliable enough local authority that could readily adapt itself to immediate individual needs without involving much sense of guilt or violating fundamental principles. It was called upon to protect settlers from Indians and criminals either by direct action at arms or by fairly expedient court decisions. Finally, it was the right of the common man to develop political heroes at all levels and to support them with robust enthusiasm. Democracy in the abstract was a thing of world importance. . . .

Isolation was never so great, or sectional feeling so intense, as to subdue a passionate spirit of nationalism. Both the common man and his provincial literature spoke of national solidarity with an intense reverence. Creeping into the early books dealing with expanding America are arguments against sectional division. Long before the Webster-Hayne debate and the Calhoun era, authors protested against the idea that the nation might become divided in the process of expansion. In the Union, the frontiersman saw the necessary strength to push back the borders even in the face of strong international resistance, to combat the Indian, and to stay the hands of the demagogues.

Most of the older books, of course, related to the Ohio and Mississippi valleys. As has been seen, authors grew eloquent in describing the geographical reaches of this vast heartland. Its soils, its stream resources, and vast space offered a freedom not found elsewhere in the world. There is either stated in bold phraseology or strongly implied in every piece of writing about this region a love of the agrarian way of life. In the latter quarter of the eighteenth century Joseph Doddridge viewed urban life in Europe with suspicion. The cities of the old world were static pools of society. The monotony of the scene, and the routine of people in the streets and in the slums led to the enslavement of people. Their imaginations were drugged, and their optimism suppressed. Life in the American backwoods was a changing thing. There are many accounts of the miraculous transformation of Europeans into thriving American farmers and husbandrymen. Progress became a virile force in the life of people from the raising of the first ax to level the forest to the building of steamboats. The imagination was sharpened by fresh air, wide expanses of land, the challenges of pioneering, and the wholesomeness of a simple society.

Fifty years after Doddridge had voiced faith in the American agrarian way of life, Timothy Flint became even more precise in his exposition on the same subject.

> Another pleasant circumstance appended to this view is [he wrote], that almost the entire population of the valley are cultivators of the soil. The inhabitants of crowded towns and villages, the numerous artisans and laborers in manufactories, can neither be, as a mass, so healthy, so virtuous, or happy, as free cultivators of the soil. The man, whose daily range of prospects is dusty streets, or smoky and dead brick walls, and whose views become limited by habit to the enclosure of those walls; who depends for his subsistence on the daily supplies of the market; and whose motives to action are elicited by constant and hourly struggle and competition with his fellows; will have the advantage in some points over the secluded tenant of a cabin or a farm house. But still, taking everything into the calculation, we would choose to be the owner of half a section of land, and daily contemplate nature, as we tilled the soil, aided in that primitive and noble employment by our own vigorous children.

This sentiment was the basis of an American myth. People believed that rural dwellers were physically stronger and more fit than were their town neighbors. The air of the town stunted human growth, the lack of hard labor softened the muscles of men and boys, and in time they fell into idleness and mischief because they had no proper outlet for their energies. The clean-living, well-nourished, and properly exercised country boy had a steady hand, a strong muscle, a clear eye, and a wholesome ambition to succeed. The cabin door and the furrow were spawning places of great and honest men. The lad who began here might hope to follow the furrow even to the door of the White House. Wholesomeness of country life found expression in another area. Militiamen who left the plow to fight the British and Indians in the western wood were indeed worthy soldiers. One good country boy was worth a half dozen redcoats, and could whip more than his weight in Indians. Later it was the boast that boys of the soil could whip equally as many Rebels or Yankees, depending upon their individual loyalties.

The most distinguished hero America ever produced, however, was not the man who cluttered Main Street with a monument to himself, or who became the subject of biographies, or had his name carved in halls of fame; he was the common man whose victories were won at the handles of the plow and the ax. He was the man who entered the virgin woods to build a home, to make a clearing, to build churches, courthouses, and jails. His story was reflected in the lives of hundreds of thousands of common men. The rare old leather-back books tell his story many times without mentioning specific names. He sat on his porch on a soft moonlight night in a thousand places and repeated many times the story of how he snatched his fields from the woods, the Indians, and nature; how he and his young wife slaved away to make a beginning. His numerous brood of children came on and he was able to help them get a start in life. Cleared fields rolling away from the house were his battle grounds. Flatboats and steamboats pushing down streams loaded to the gunwales with farm produce were his material offerings to a rich national economy. Churches, schools, banks, newspapers, and even courts were his proud tributes to civilization and culture. Atlases, annals, county and state histories, favorably disposed travelogues, and long obituary articles in country papers were the written records of his heroic part in building America. Democracy was to be translated only in part in the success of the national constitution and the various state charters. Fundamentally the success of American democracy lay with the attitudes of the common man who achieved settlement and economic success on the advancing frontier. . . .

(from *The Michigan Alumnus*)

PRESERVATION OF SOUTHERN HISTORICAL DOCUMENTS A few years ago I went to Louisville to meet a train and take Edward Weeks to Lexington, where he was to speak in the evening. On the way to Lexington, Mr. Weeks talked about the Southern Collection at the University of North Carolina. I was amazed to learn how much he knew about it, and I was pleased indeed to see his enthusiasm for the bold step that that institution had taken in developing it. Gathering materials for a university collection is a delicate undertaking, and the man who assumes such a job has to have the sense of humor of a clown, the patience of Job, and the integrity of Caesar's wife; and even then he will come home about half of the time branded a thief! I do not suppose there is any area of human relationships where well-meaning people can be more whimsical about a gentleman's agreement than in parting with family manuscripts.

Collecting historical records is possibly one of the most thrilling businesses a person can engage in, this side of swallowing fire, handling snakes at a Holy Roller meeting, or tracking down international spies. He can, within a short time, find himself in almost as many unanticipated situations as an imaginative who-done-it author could place him in. On one occasion in southern Kentucky I was on the hot trail of a set of records, and in the search I was told I would have to see an old gentleman who was lying ill in a nearby house. When I approached the door I was greeted in the most hushed manner and was ushered into the bedroom of a poor old emaciated gentleman who could hardly speak above a whisper and whose memory was even more faltering. I did get from him his consent for me to have the records. Actually, I was talking to a man lying literally on his death bed and already at the very threshold of eternity.

On another occasion I called at a very fine old southern mansion, surrounded with much of the moonlight and roses background. After I had virtually knocked the facing off of the front door, a slickly-shined black boy came out, dressed in a white coat drawn over work clothes, and asked me abruptly what I wanted. I told him I wished to see his mistress, and he replied, "Does you really want to see her?" When I said I really did, he took me around back of the house and up an outside set of stairs and into a bedroom where I found the good lady in somewhat more than partial state of undress. This was the first day the boy in the white coat had served as houseman and he was terribly ignorant of the subject of white folks' social amenities.

Not all of the incidents of manuscript collecting, however, are associated with the cold hand of death or the embarrassment of standing in the bedroom of a partially dressed lady. Much of manuscript collection consists of tedious diplomacy and downright physical drudgery. But whatever it is, it requires a strong nerve and infinite patience.

The horror stories of southern manuscripts are not too good for either a collector's blood pressure or his peace of mind. I could write an eloquent story, I think, on the subject of the statement, "I burned that two years ago." Perhaps one story will suffice on this point. Some years ago when I was searching for records in Mississippi, a dear friend and college-mate of mine told me about an unusually fine collection of papers, which he was sure I could have. His description was so exciting that I persuaded him to get in the car with me and go that night to interview the owner. After driving over 20 miles of Mississippi gravel roads, we arrived at the gentleman's house and found him extremely hospitable. He confirmed my friend's statement that he had a great pile of letters and papers in a store attic, but it was so dark and the doorway to the attic was so treacherously located that he did not want to undertake climbing up there until daylight. He asked me to come back the next day and promised that I could have the papers. The next morning, as soon as it was daylight, I was on my way. We procured a ladder, opened the door in the gable end of the store, and climbed up. He went up first and just as he stuck his head in the opening he shouted, "I'll be damned." I knew it was useless for me to go farther; the tone of his voice reeked with bad news. Someone, unknown to him, had cleaned out the attic, and upon inquiry it was found that the old papers had been hauled off and burned.

Literally millions of pounds of papers have been destroyed either by fire or by being dumped into gullies to prevent erosion caused by the wasteful system of southern land usage. On one or two occasions I have fished badly deteriorated papers out of waterlogged heaps in fields. But fire, rats, mice, and leaky roofs are minor enemies compared to maiden ladies and efficient housekeepers. A rat or a mouse can nibble away only enough paper to make a bed or cut a passage, but the good housekeeper's actions are almost invariably positive and final. Everything she cannot dust away with a mop, she burns. A few years ago I discovered that an intimate friend of mine, an excellent housekeeper but also the wife of a husband who had suddenly arrived at the doorway of literary fame, was burning his letters and papers. Fortunately she had, at the time of this discovery, burned only the first dribble of letters and practically none of his other papers; and I persuaded her to clutter up her house enough to keep the papers.

A new bride in an old house can play havoc with old wall-paper, woodwork, and furniture arrangement, and can cheerfully destroy the contents of old chests, trunks, and attics in general. When I read the society page on Sunday, I wonder how many manuscript burners there are in the weekly round-up! The new bride, who is out to display her housekeeping before her husband and her in-laws, is a cold, calculating creature with no sentiment about the "old things." All she wants to know is whether the stuff will burn.

But the maiden lady is an altogether different problem. She is most often the keeper of the sacred name and honor of the family, and her sense of these precious responsibilities becomes intensified with each succeeding year of single blessedness. People get the notion that their private letters will always carry the intimate connotations that they were meant to convey at the time they were written. There are few statements that will chill the manuscript collector like the one, "I just can't let you have Grandpa's and Grandma's old papers. They said such intimate things to each other." Or, the maiden ladies say, "There just might be something in them that we don't see that would disgrace us." This kind of egomania has prevented many a valuable paper from reaching the proper depository.

Family quarrels can result in some astounding decisions pertaining to papers, too. An impulsive brother or a hotheaded sister, fed up with the squabbling, throws the papers away or has them burned to settle the row. Nearly as bad, they may divide the records page by page until the documents are so badly jumbled and scattered that only a patient sleuth can ever track them down or restore their original order. Sometimes, however, a family quarrel will play into the hands of a collector—if he arrives at the right moment.

I do want to pay tribute to the maiden lady to whom, perhaps, I have been unreasonably harsh. She is perhaps, after all, the biggest asset in preserving manuscripts. It is she who has clung to the old family papers. She has often preserved them as the living embodiments of her family, and many are the family collections which have been disposed of sensibly by the surviving female. It is she who knows where the papers are and what the family relations are, and who can recall many of the incidents that resulted in their creation.

It is an irony of fate that papers have a habit of getting into the hands of queer people. I have at least half a dozen notes in my desk at the moment telling me of the location of papers and bearing the trite admonition, "Be most tactful, because the owners are downright peculiar." Personally, I like them peculiar—because that means I will eventually get the papers! Everybody is in a certain sense peculiar; but I have found the owners of manuscripts are frequently just peculiar in the eyes of their neighbors, or merely peculiar on one subject, such as Presidential policies, local option, the income tax, or the right-of-way for a new road.

I recall once going to call about the second-most significant collection of papers I ever acquired. I was told by a brother of the man on which I was to call that he himself would give me the papers but that he didn't know about his brother. In customary language he warned me, "That brother of mine is as curious as hell, and he may order you out of the house." I knocked timidly on the "curious" man's door, and a fog-horn bellow invited me to come in; the "prospect" was in bed. I went down a long hall to a bedroom door, and there lay the man in bed, with an evil-looking Colt forty-five strapped to a bedpost. I sat down and talked to the bed-ridden man for a few minutes. By accident I discovered that he had been a bank clerk in the little town where I went to high school, and in a few minutes we were talking about everybody and their bird dogs in the village. My getting the records became only incidental. My new-found friend told me that not only could I have the papers in the old storehouse, but also I might have his attic-full of papers if I could persuade his sister to help me get them.

Here I learned a little more fully a lesson that every manuscript collector should repeat to himself every day: Don't talk too much; and don't ask for everything in the first interview. When I went to see the sister she immediately raised that fateful question, "Do we want to let Papa's papers get into the hands of a stranger?" I went away for a few weeks to let the case cool off, and then I came back to reopen it. This time I did my best at softening up the lady, and finally she consented to my taking the first set of records her brother had given me, but on what I considered a hard condition. The bulk of the records was large and my supply of pasteboard boxes limited. She said a corpse was to arrive on the train at 4 o'clock and if I could pack the records and get away before it arrived, I could have them. That was the first time I was entered in a dead heat with a corpse, but the fact that the corpse had no choice and was traveling on the Southern Railway was a most fortunate break for me. Just as the belated train came into sight I was getting into my car, with the bills of lading in my pocket.

Frequently a man with a local reputation for being "curious" is only cantankerous. I once went to see an old gentleman whose father had been most active in the affairs of his community in middle Tennessee. His son had preserved his records in barrels and boxes stored in an outhouse. They were, nevertheless, in good condition; and, more important, they were complete so far as I could tell. He let me have the papers without much tedious discussion, but before I could get back to the University of Kentucky, he wrote the comptroller a letter that seemed to indicate that if I were not a thief I was in at least an advanced embryo stage of becoming one. When we were able to satisfy him that I was able to walk about Lexington in the daylight and that his records had arrived safely, he seemed to be satisfied. Later, after the papers were cataloged and filed, he wrote us to return them. We shipped the papers back immediately, and I again called on the old gentleman. He said that I could have the papers —that he had only wanted to see if we would return them. I overloaded my car with these papers and drove over most of middle Tennessee during an express company strike before

I could get an office to ship them. But—woe unto us—the old gentleman asked for his papers a second time, and so far as I know they are now back in the outhouse!

There are many depositories of private papers. Sometimes these depositories may be the least suspected ones. The average courthouse is often a catch-all for community records. People bring papers in for clerks and local politicians to see, or they leave their private papers in the vaults and forget them. Sometimes papers are brought in for trials but are not filed with the official records. Sifting through a set of county records in a courthouse that has not had a fire is often rewarding. We have found in these depositories papers that no one knew existed. It is often true that one of the clerks, especially the clerk of the circuit court, becomes interested in local history; he gathers in masses of materials and goes out of office and forgets them. In almost every aspect of the handling of official records, the southern counties have been exceedingly careless. They have stuffed them away in attics, crammed them into wet and cluttered basements, and—even worse—stored them away in jails infested with disease and vermin.

State records in many instances have been little better handled. Several of the States have hauled out and dumped papers that should have been cared for in fireproof depositories. As a specific instance, no one will know how many valuable papers were destroyed when the Kentucky State government moved from one side of the Kentucky River to the other. To hear the old timers tell it, the river ran full with books and papers that were dumped into it. Years later the departmental records of Kentucky were being sold for scrap paper. Two truck loads had already been hauled to Louisville to a waste-paper dealer's warehouse when the governor ordered them returned and deposited in the University of Kentucky Library. Some of the States have avoided such travesty by providing adequate buildings for archives. Many public agencies, however, produce records that are deposited far from the main centers of State activity and that, because of this fact, are often destroyed or forgotten.

The great volume of church and religious records frequently receives most careless handling. Possibly some of the most interesting volumes of manuscripts are the early records of church membership and the minutes of the meetings of the deacons, stewards, or vestrymen. These are scattered in the homes of the clerks and secretaries. I believe that the few complete sets of intact church records are the exception rather than the rule. An interesting set of papers pertaining to one religious group are the Shaker papers. The known papers are scattered all the way from New York to Lewisburg, Kentucky. One day, while buying stamps in the village post office at Lewisburg, I explained to the postmistress that I was in search of manuscript material, and she told me that her family had a small leather box of Shaker records. Her husband had attended a sale at the abandoned South Union settlement and had bought for a mere pittance the papers that incoming converts deposited with the Shaker elders. They were valuable economic papers, pertaining largely to the trade southward down the river. Another set of Shaker papers was found in a bank vault at Harrodsburg, where they had come to rest after the dissolution of the order at Mount Pleasant.

Just as the scattered religious records involve a long and tedious job of reassembling, so do southern economic records. When businesses cease operation their old records are left to gather dust and worms in the old buildings or are packed away in warehouses. Mercantile businesses are suspended, and their account books and papers are left in the old stores. Trunks buried under household and business debris contain rich finds of letters and other manuscript materials. Businesses, like county courthouses, have had a way of collecting many records which have little or no direct association with their specific interests. I have found large numbers of invaluable personal and community papers mixed in with store records. Some of them got there because of the merchants' interests in local affairs, and others got there by some accident of community life.

The papers of southern literary men have not been too well collected. We in Kentucky have had difficulty in bringing together the papers of James Lane Allen and John Fox, Jr. Although we shall perhaps never be able to complete the task, we have gone a long way toward this completion. I should like also to suggest that publishers—at least those who have not had fires—possess enormous amounts of correspondence and manuscript materials from authors, and it is my impression that they have not yet made up their minds what they should do with these papers. A careful listing and canvassing of these depositories, in my opinion, would have pleasant results. The South Atlantic Modern Language Association is at present engaged in the undertaking of cataloging the literary papers of the South. It cannot get far, however, until it has searched publishers' files.

It is interesting to note that so ardent a group of manuscript collectors and preservers as the southern historians do not yet have in a single file their semiofficial papers. In years to come, when a scholar sets out to track down the most important collections of records pertaining to the publication activities of the Southern Historical Association, he will have to call on the widows Stephenson, Cole, Binkley, England, and Clark to find out what has gone on. There is no collected file of these papers.

In the last 3 decades there have developed in the South several university presses of genuine importance. They have carried on extensive correspondence of major importance in the field of scholarship. Although it is true that they have done little so-called "creative" publishing, they have published a solid backlog of the more serious materials pertaining to the South. So far as I am able to determine, nothing has been done to collect their files, and I suspect that in a few cases these have been destroyed.

The same thing is true of newspaper records. I do not know of a single manuscript collection in the South pertaining to a major newspaper. If there is such a thing, it is probably unique. Magazines fall into the same category, and with one or two exceptions so do the records of book publishers. Between the hours of 3 and 6 o'clock on one cold Sunday morning in 1947, I rode, seated between two drowsy but burly colored brothers, to Louisville in a Kentucky University truck to rescue the papers of the famous old publishing house of John P. Morton and Sons. Fortunately we did rescue most of the records of this house, but the manner in which we did it was harrowing. We had to fight off waste-paper dealers while we crammed papers into boxes and sacks, without having a minute's time to canvass the whole collection to make sure we were doing a thorough job. I worked almost 15 hours getting these papers together; and the University of Kentucky Library is the wealthier for these records, which represent a significant chapter of book publishing and sales for the South from about 1840 to 1920.

The whole field of southern business records lies almost untouched. Who can write intelligently of southern agricultural progress, or the lack of it, without first examining the records of the Lynchburg Plow Co., the Chattanooga Plow Co., and Benjamin Franklin Avery and Sons of Louisville? The important textile records, I am sure, lie scattered in the junk-rooms of the mills, or have been destroyed altogether. On one or two occasions, the Baker Library at Harvard has called our attention to valuable textile records in Tennessee. It is true that the whole field of business manuscripts is broad and diverse, but it is time that at least one southern university should give serious attention to the collection of these records and to their housing in a building large enough, with a staff adequate enough to do the necessary collecting and arranging.

This will be a somewhat expensive undertaking, and the bulk of the records will indeed be great, but who can say that they are not important? Perhaps it is not too dreamy-eyed to hope that southern business executives may contribute both money and records to the creation of a centralized industrial archives. With the rise of industrialism in the region, business records will soon become of major importance in the field of southern economics and history. Their collection is a "must" on some university's list of things to do to place it in a favored position as a research center of the future. These records are, fortunately, not too hard to collect. At least the companies are easily located, and in my opinion business men would be no more difficult to convince of the importance of preserving their records than maiden ladies and "curious" men.

The South has come a long way in 50 years in the preservation of its records. It would take too much time to belabor the facts of what to you must be the obvious places where these advances have been made. Most States have archival departments that are aggressive in varying degrees. Most universities are becoming somewhat aware of the great rewards that await them in the field of manuscript materials within their communities, and even private historical societies are much more active than before. The efforts and encouragement of older scholars and collectors are now bearing fruit in the fine crop of young scholars in many fields of interest, who are industriously digging into the South's records of the past for answers to many questions of significant meaning for the present. No one doubts at the moment that southern scholarship is a going thing, but it cannot mature as it must without strong library and archival support.

Possibly there has never been a time in southern history when it was more important to be about the business of collecting records than now. As I have said, there is a growing scholarly demand for the materials, and the South itself is rushing headlong into a major industrial era. Old homes are being cut up into efficiency apartments or destroyed to make room for industrial developments. Towns and country villages are growing faster than ever before, and there is less and less space in private depositories for the retention of family papers. The older generation, which had a close secondary tie-up with the Old South, is rapidly passing from the scene; and the papers that have been preserved are falling into younger hands. Many of these young people are indifferent to these source materials—either because they are no longer masters of their own fate, owing to calls to the armed services, or because they are forced to move to the crowded communities of defense industries.

On the other hand, we are in an age of the silliest kind of commercialization of our history. Every tourist camp, soft-drink stand, roadside park, and antique shop has to collect its stock of local historical materials to offer the omnivorous peanut-crunching, drink-gulping tourist a bait to stop by to see the snakes, buy plaster of Paris horrors, and read Grandpappy's letters. Even *Life* and *Look* magazines have given what, in my opinion, is most unfortunate publicity to manuscript finds. These articles serve no good purpose; they erect serious barriers to the intelligent collection and preservation of vital historical materials. During these flush times of inflation private collectors have multiplied by the hundred, and they go about the land gathering up everything from buttons to letters. They have successfully combed many collections, sometimes taking selected letters or, much worse, sometimes snipping off autographs. A few of these collectors will be intelligent enough to leave their treasure troves to their old schools or to dignify their own names by establishing collections in some institution which suggests their making such gifts.

It seems to me of major importance that universities which hope to become important centers of scholarship should make great efforts to collect everything of pertinency around them. For 20 years I have carried on a continuous argument with two university presidents on the subject of employing a full-time collector to gather up the manuscript materials of Kentucky that are going to the wastepaper mill every year. The two presidents I have dealt with have been fine gentlemen and generous-minded administrators, but my pleas have not made enough impression to date for us to have any considerable volume of manuscripts. Neither president has had to be "sold" on the idea; but both of them have felt, I am sure, that such a proposal was unorthodox and should wait for the future and for greater financial resources. I wish to praise the University of North Carolina without reservation for its intelligent approach to this problem. That university has built a permanent asset which will endure as long as southern civilization holds together, and students yet unborn will bless the decision of the administration that dared to be unorthodox and encourage the collecting of so rich a storehouse of materials.

At this point I wish to pay tribute to three southerners because I feel a close kinship with them. One whom I never saw, Stephen B. Weeks of Trinity College, seems to have known something of the importance of historical records and to have begun a modest collection. I am sure he was an historian who was "on fire." The other two men have been my good friends, I have held both of them in warmest affection, and they have set an ideal for me. The first was William K. "Tubby" Boyd, who had both a genuine sense of the value of the original records and the energy and imagination to collect them. The other is Professor J. G. deRoulhac Hamilton. From my days as a graduate student I have greatly admired Dr. Hamilton. He has distinguished himself as one of the South's most ardent and valuable sons. Seldom has it been the fortune of a man to be both so able an historian and so magnificent a collector. In my humble opinion Dr. Hamilton has reached invaluable goals in the South. The extraordinarily fine Southern Collection at the University of North Carolina will stand as a monument long after that charming gentleman has had at least three flings at trying to beg away from Saint

Peter all the records pertaining to his admission of southerners from 1606 to 1890. But it will not be the Southern Collection alone, fine as it is, that will get him into a position to annoy Saint Peter. It will be the activities of that multitude of once lackadaisical southern defeatists, who sat by and allowed their records to go to the gullies, the rats, the brides, and Chicago. When Dr. Hamilton came along and gathered up enough of their papers to make them infernally mad, they got busy and are now doing something on their home grounds. No one can estimate the money that he cost the States of Alabama, South Carolina, Georgia, and Virginia alone by forcing them to wake up and collect and service their records.

There are still those whining, petulant people who cry in a weary refrain, "He robbed us." He did not rob anybody but the rats and the flames; he saved from destruction many of their choicest historical records. It is the same dull and tiresome chorus that has sung a dirge for Lyman Draper all these years. The South's historical records are more secure tonight than ever before in the region's history largely because Dr. Hamilton had the energy, plus the personal magnetism, to go out and persuade the owners of records to dispose of them intelligently. He has been a noble pioneer indeed, who opened vast spaces in the wilderness of southern manuscript collecting and preservation. But there are still smokehouses, attics, and abandoned buggy-sheds where he did not disturb the dust; and it is imperative that many institutions work vigorously at building his monument higher by gathering within their depositories as complete a record of southern civilization as it is possible to assemble.

(from *The American Archivist*)

AMERICANA IN A STATE UNIVERSITY LIBRARY The University of Kentucky Library is entering another phase of its growth and significance. In making this advance into the future it is placing itself alongside the good state universities of the South and the Ohio Valley, and it may even aspire to higher things. Its responsibilities to its constituency, however, are defined largely by the needs of this region. Like the American state university in general, the University of Kentucky is an institution of many localized and regional interests even though it strives to serve all scholarly demands of an academic community. Its library collection of necessity must represent in good part the literary and documentary collections of materials which have more localized origins. Too, the state university library, more than any other major educational accumulation of literary materials, has to be more liberal in the choice of its areas of selectivity. . . .

It was not until the middle of the nineteenth century that Lyman Draper gave a somewhat dramatic emphasis to collecting and preserving regional Americana. Draper's collection was less significant because of its completeness, or its selectivity, than for the fact that maybe for the first time in American history a regional and local collector sensed the significance of adequate documentation of grass-roots American history. He promoted the concept that, though American expansion was accomplished in local parts, it was fundamentally national in scope. In a less articulate way it was Draper rather than Frederick Jackson Turner who conceived the deep-flowing historical current of the westward movement. He had more than a glimmer of the great folk-migration in which few people made or kept records. The gaps had to be spanned by skillful searching and even more skillful interviewing. Enough personal stories had to draw from contemporary participants to give a comparative body to the whole. This, plus the fact that every piece of paper or whisper of oral information was grist to the Draper collecting mill, served to publicize in many quarters the fact that the folk record contained historical substance.

It took Frederick Jackson Turner to dramatize the Draper

Collection to the scholarly world. In his landmark essay on the significance of the frontier, and his subsequent essays on the subject, the collecting of local and regional materials took on a new intellectual dimension. Later, the decision to combine the library collections of the Historical Society of Wisconsin with the University Library gave further emphasis to the meaning of a regional historical collection to a state university and its instructional and research programs. . . .

Over the years state university libraries and archival agencies have assembled phenomenal storehouses of family manuscripts, local business records, personal diaries, memoirs, and official papers of presidents, senators, congressmen, governors, soldiers, farmers, gamblers, prostitutes, and plain people. Locked in the closets of these depositories are some fine collections of social, political, and business skeletons. There are revealed many personal intimacies which reflect the moral and emotional natures of a national people. Fortunately Americans of all social strata have recorded their frustrations and their victories. An example of this fact is a slender little shred of stained and aged paper in the University of Kentucky collection which verifies the truth of the disaster which befell a party of eighteenth century long hunters who found their fur and skin cache in the Cumberland Valley robbed by Indians and animals. A hunter named Bledsoe carved on a nearby tree: "1300 deerskins lost—ruination! By God!" There are also letters from foot-sore and frost-bitten militiamen which reflect more colorfully and precisely than most historians have done the foolish jingoism of the young Warhawks and the indecisiveness of the national administration which failed to ask the costs of battle in the War of 1812.

The state university library is strategically located in our organized society to collect these sources for the preservation of a fuller and more graphic regional and local history. First, the state university, and particularly the land-grant institution, is fundamentally focused in interest and emphasis upon a prescribed locality. Second, its modern staff is so organized as to make imperative the collecting of all available records in a region. Sources which have a highly relevant and current value for political scientists, sociologists, medical scientists, economists, and agriculturalists, tomorrow are of historical value. Thus the Americana base in a well-stocked state university grows in both breadth and depth with the passage of time. It ranges from a handful of dull public reports prepared by politically motivated state officials to the all-revealing studies by competent specialists who deal with most areas of our society. . . .

Rarity of an Americana collection in a state university library must by necessity be of secondary importance. Where a private or specialized institutional collector can engage in the assembly of highly selected manuscripts, pamphlets, and books, the state university library can neither be, nor should be so selective or specialized. There will always be the demanding fact of association. Beyond this, the philosophy governing the establishment and support of the American public university is deeply embedded in demands for the broadest possible service to the society in which it flourishes. That catholicity of choice was shared at the founding of the institutions. This does not mean, however, that a state university library should become either as ponderous or pedestrian as a dog-eared legislative document, or as weighty and dust-ladened as the last decade's crop of doctoral dissertations. It can be something of all things.

A collection of rare Americana is a bigger asset to the University of Kentucky than a comparable collection might be in many other institutional libraries. First, it reflects the general quality of the entire library resource of the University. Second, it has stimulated greater efforts at collecting, especially of materials in the local and regional fields. Finally, a good collection of regional and local Americana is one of the best possible means for the University to make available its intellectual resources to its supporting constituency, and to scholars abroad.

Collecting a solid body of Americana in a state university has a certain liability in leading librarians and others on to the hunt for the sake of the chase. It is easy to blind librarians and scholars to the overall purposes of the library when they become enamored by scarcity and rarity. Rarity and choice become objectives rather than usability. No one is foolish enough to suggest the general use of a university's rare book collection or the unleashing of unsophisticated professors and students in a manuscript collection. Yet encouragingly large numbers of faithful state university library patrons are post-adolescent students entering upon the challenging, if not exciting, search for facts which only rare, and, sometimes, unique sources can yield.

Constantly the community of scholars in the American state university is either adding new and interpretive information to the body of collected fact about the American people, or they are using old concepts which have long been accepted as established fact by use of new finds of materials. With each chronological and technological advance into the future, America becomes a more intimate part of the greater world about it. In this area of universality of scholarship, demands for information are insatiable, and so are demands for support to collect new non-American sources of information or to strengthen basic collections. To build adequate collections of non-American materials, and to keep them abreast of annual production of new volumes would more than absorb the income from either public sources or a large endowment, yet regional and local Americana collections take on much broader meanings in association with such solid foundation materials.

Actually we are just now entering an age when state universities will experience their greatest growth in all phases of their organization. Greater emphasis is already being placed upon graduate education which means the writing of ten-fold more theses and doctoral dissertations. We will produce a large number of, and, it is to be hoped, more discerning scholars who will be bent on re-appraising, re-writing, and writing anew about the American scene. With fresh knowledge, techniques, and points of view, generated by the associated fields of modern university research, historians, sociologists, economists, literary scholars, political scientists, and others are reviewing even the most commonplace fact about the past, and from newer and more revealing perspectives. A generation of older present-day scholars was challenged to re-write much of the published knowledge of American life in the decades of time since World War I. Younger scholars are going much further by introducing broader scopes of foundation materials, and new ranges of ideas and philosophies into their articles and books.

Most state universities in this southern region were little concerned in the first decade after World War I with building good collections of Americana. There were a few men scattered about the South who engaged in serious study in the regional fields. A few more delved into local history more out of amusement and for self-satisfaction of an antiquarian interest than for engaging in serious scholarship. It made little or no difference with administrators of universities whether or not professors actively engaged in research so long as they met classes, and, perhaps, suggested to students that there were large and vague areas of unexplored space in all the intellectual fields. The noisy clamor for faculty production to establish and sustain the reputations of universities had not begun. At the present time more books of appreciable worth come from single departments in many southern universities than came from all the South in 1920. Whether or not the pressure to publish actually makes intellectual sense is another question. The central fact is that heavy demands for more extensive collections of local and regional materials are made by pressured faculties to sustain the universities' desires to become research centers.

The librarian of the University of Kentucky in 1918, at the

time this institution aspired to university status, could not possibly have conceived of either the institution's present collection of Americana, or of the scholarly use now made of it. In a region which still yielded a super-abundance of manuscripts and books of growing scarcity relating to westward expansion, the University could lay claim to little or no Americana worthy of a scholar's serious notice. Funds for the purchase of manuscripts and books were unavailable. No one was seriously interested in collecting materials because there were no demands for their use, and there were no facilities for either their processing or preservation. There were still people who mourned the loss of the Draper papers and the rich Durrett Collection. The University of Kentucky and the Commonwealth of Kentucky made no more than a token gesture at keeping the Durrett papers and books in the state. This story can be repeated many times across the nation. The state universities had not become aware of the importance of regional and local materials, nor had scholars on their staffs become active in preparing basic regional studies. Neither professor nor librarian had a full appreciation of the significance of Americana, and some shrugged off the idea of making important collections with the excuse that it was curiosa.

In another area of university development the importance of regional materials has been given emphasis. This is in the growth of the university press as an institutional publishing agency. Not until the advent of the press did scholars have assurance that many of their more localized studies would ever be placed in print. At the same time the presses have initiated major research projects which have resulted in extremely valuable regional publications. One of the main purposes of the state university press is to give outlet to scholarly studies of a regional nature. There is indeed a close correlation between libraries and presses.

To ignore the importance of regional materials in building public university collections would be to ignore the great idea of the land grant college that it would be of the broadest possible service to people in a given region. Unfortunately interpretation of this idea was narrowed largely to serve vocational demands. Crusaders for the land grant philosophy paid lip service to the full training of the sons and daughters of the people, but failed to give even a glimmer of the basic intellectual qualities which an institution would have to cultivate in order to achieve its broad objectives. Literature, history, the arts, political theory, pure economics were of secondary importance. The library in the minds of the organizers was to be a source for ready reference and supplementary reading of an elementary order.

Following the end of World War I, state universities became something more than "people's colleges." They came to take on the characteristics and intellectual aspirations of their private sister institutions; but beyond this, they sensed the needs of their patrons in much broader fields of learning, and on a broader geographical scope. A revolution occurred among state university faculties. No longer was it enough to have on staffs men who were adequate enough teachers in the traditional schoolmaster sense; there were increasing demands that they also be productive scholars. At this point more mature demands were made on libraries. Much of the scholarship in the state university had to depend upon resources in the region and locality. From such sources came John D. Hicks' *Populist Revolt,* Walter Prescott Webb's *Great Plains,* James Randall's Lincoln studies, Frederick L. Paxson's *History of the American Frontier,* Verner Crane's *Southern Frontier, 1670-1732,* Howard Beale's *Critical Year,* R. C. Buley's *Old Northwest,* Frederick Shannon's *Farmer's Last Frontier,* Charles S. Sydnor's *Slavery in Mississippi,* and Henry Nash Smith's *Virgin Land.* All of these books are landmark studies. These are but a few, and maybe not representative of even the more important works which have come from professorial studies in public universities.

As state universities have grown in academic maturity, their libraries have caught the attention of private collectors. Many a highly literate alumnus, who first experienced the joys of books and collecting in a classroom, has brought together a fine private library of books and papers, and has given it to his university. Private collectors who have had no direct educational association with an institution have given their treasures to a university because it had the necessary staff and facilities, and promise of perpetuity, not only to offer security, but even hope of enlightenment and growth. This has been an enormously important means by which state university collections have been enriched, if not actually made. The University of Kentucky with its magnificent Samuel M. Wilson library of regional and local materials documents this fact. Every state university worthy of its name has at least one collection which gives it foundation strength in the field of Americana.

As important as private collections are to the establishment of sound university libraries, the activities of the universities themselves in the collecting field have greater meaning. In no way is the significance of private collecting to be depreciated, but the university has the virtue of broader scope, of persistency, and of public access. The institutional perspective of necessity has to be more inclusive than that of the individual and private institutional collector. Because of this fact there are drawn into state university libraries thousands of pamphlets, books, handbills, and other materials which as single pieces have worth only because of a growing scarcity and anonymity, but which give substance to a larger collection. Some documents and papers are frequently available only to the public university library. Because of its numerous lines of communication the availability of materials may become readily known to university collectors.

In this way, much of the University of Kentucky collection of Americana has been assembled. In less than thirty-five years its holdings in this area have grown from a slender handful of rare books and pamphlets to an asset of respectability. With a yearning for a degree of universality, this institution, however, can never be allowed to forget that it has roots in a region and a locality. In these areas most of its scholarly production in the non-scientific fields brings the richest rewards. Its good basic collection of Americana insures it a place in the affections of scholars in an ever widening circle of patronage.

The functional responsibilities of the University of Kentucky Library are broad. It must offer intelligent guidance to the people of the region in the preservation of the records of their times and of the structure of their contemporary society. The Library has become at once an important teaching and research facility within the university, and a major depository of Kentucky's day by day record. Its collection of regional Americana is an ever solidifying foundation for achieving one of the basic aims of the peoples' state university as a central force in the ordering and re-ordering of the changing patterns of American culture. The great basic collections in the libraries across the land belie the cynical charge that the people are anti-intellectual in both achievement and attitude. Perhaps nowhere on the globe have so many public universities brought together such rich storehouses of source and published materials as have the American state universities. In the organization of these collections the American people have made their most enduring expressions of faith in the intellectual processes of civilization. The state university is obligated to bear a serious responsibility in making sure that no gap occurs in the collecting and utilization of the rich local and regional Americana resource.

(from University of Kentucky Library *Bulletin*)

INDEX OF MAIN TOPICS